Praise for
your own kind o

'The words that kept coming to me over and over again as I read this book were authenticity and decency. Clare Bowditch made me feel how wonderful and difficult and amazing it is to be a human.' **LEIGH SALES**

'Brutal at times but funny as f@#k. This book will change a lot of lives for the better.' **BERNARD FANNING**

'Reading this book felt as intimate as having a long, heart-breakingly vulnerable yet hilarious conversation with Clare by a fire with wine in hand. It is a celebration of the human struggle, how we can learn to befriend (and say "f@#k off" to) our demons, and ultimately write our own story. There is so much hope in this book.' **MISSY HIGGINS**

'Clare Bowditch opens her heart and history with staggering generosity—unpicking the birth of her creativity and the early scars that forged her. Much like the woman herself, *Your Own Kind of Girl* is unflinching, entertaining, inspiring and real. I inhaled this book.' **KAT STEWART**

'This book is like a life-buoy, tossed across a generation by a sick and frightened young woman, who grew up to be Clare Bowditch. An extraordinary tale faithfully remembered and generously told. What a woman. A transfixing and powerful memoir.' **ANNABEL CRABB**

'A brave and generous work. Never didactic or patronising, Bowditch nonetheless has much to share as she invites the reader inside the tender heart and evolving mind of a young woman determined to make sense of herself and her place in the world. Told with Bowditch's trademark warmth and openness, this book is an act of compassion as much as it is the product of diligent reflection and insight.' PEGGY FREW

'For parents, indeed anyone that would like to understand mental illness, and that recovery is possible. Clare writes with extraordinary self-awareness and insight. Her journey encourages anyone to keep going; to believe that there is something better, to take one step at a time toward it, and not to give up. A truly compelling story of resilience, survival and growth.' DR CHARLOTTE KEATING

'A deeply revealing insight into how a true artist is born. Brutally honest, compelling and affecting, Clare's luminous warmth shines through every page.' KATE MILLER-HEIDKE

'Finally, an author who has found the words to describe that excruciatingly complex relationship many women have with food.' JAMILA RIZVI

'Clare's story (so far) reveals how resilience is created from the suffering life inflicts. Clare's honesty and warmth shines strongly through the pages of this inspiring and moving memoir.' PROFESSOR PAT McGORRY

'Vibrant, touching, hilarious. Clare's heart-baring makes me want to live brighter, tell more truths, and laugh—in a sweet way—at my self-criticism and fears. This book is a healer.' **DANIELLE LAPORTE**, author of *The Desire Map*

'Clare takes us to the edge of the stuff we flee from—the late-night inner turmoil of an eating disorder, the loneliness of being the "fat kid" and death—so that, as her friend Leonard Cohen once said, the light might come in.' **SARAH WILSON**

'I fell in love with this book from the start—it's a brutally honest, witty, smart and courageous account of Clare Bowditch finding her path and her power.' **EDDIE PERFECT**

'What I love best about the glorious Clare Bowditch is how richly she embraces life and holds to what's most sustaining. Her beautiful book is so like her music: bold, original, earthy, funny, grateful, honest, truthful and tuneful—and fabulously female.' **STEPHANIE DOWRICK**, author of *Choosing Happiness*

'Clare Bowditch cements her status as one of Australia's most mesmerising storytellers with this debut. Her ability to lay bare the vulnerabilities, hurts and triumphs of a woman's life is second to none. She's my kind of girl, for sure.' **CLEMENTINE FORD**

Clare Bowditch is a storyteller who lives in Melbourne with her husband Marty, their three teenage children, a white groodle, and one lone surviving free-ranging guinea pig. In terms of 'the fancy stuff', Bowditch is a bestselling ARIA Award-winning musician (Best Female Artist), *Rolling Stone* Woman of the Year (Contribution to Culture), Logie-nominated actor (for her role as 'Rosanna' on hit TV show *Offspring*), and a former ABC broadcaster who still misses her talk-back callers very much, and hopes they're doing okay out there. In her spare time, Bowditch does a lot of public-speaking and event-running. She uses humour and the collective terror of 'public-singing' as tools to teach skills around courage and self-leadership. She is also the founder of Big Hearted Business, a love project designed to support creative people in their businesses, and businesses with their creative thinking. As a musician Clare has performed and toured with the likes of Leonard Cohen, Paul Kelly, Cat Power, John Butler, Snow Patrol and Gotye. The person she enjoys touring with the most is her drummer and husband, Marty Brown.

your
own kind
of girl

a memoir

CLARE
BOWDITCH

ALLEN&UNWIN
SYDNEY•MELBOURNE•AUCKLAND•LONDON

First published in 2019

All lyrics reproduced courtesy of Mushroom Music Publishing: p. 5 'Are You Ready
Yet?', written by C. Bowditch/M. Brown/W. De Backer; p. 17 'When I Was Five',
written by C. Bowditch; inside cover and p. 45 'Your Own Kind Of Girl', written by
C. Bowditch; p. 81 'Amazing Life', written by C. Bowditch; p. 106 'Thin Skin', written
by C. Bowditch; p. 147 'Your Other Hand', written by C. Bowditch; p. 170 'The Thing
About Grief', written by C. Bowditch; p. 192 'I Thought You Were God', written by .
C. Bowditch; p. 207 'Empty Pockets', written by C. Bowditch; p. 225 'One Little
River', written by C. Bowditch; p. 258 'On This Side', written by C. Bowditch;
p. 306 'Human Being', written by C. Bowditch.

Allen & Unwin
83 Alexander Street
Crows Nest NSW 2065
Australia
Phone: (61 2) 8425 0100
Email: info@allenandunwin.com
Web: www.allenandunwin.com

A catalogue record for this
book is available from the
National Library of Australia

ISBN 978 1 76052 895 9

Set in 12.9/18.9 pt Garamond by Bookhouse, Sydney
Printed and bound in Australia by Griffin Press, part of Ovato

10 9 8 7 6 5 4 3 2

For all the girls I've loved before

In celebration of the grand legacies of
Rowena Bowditch
Dr Claire Weekes
and
John Patrick Hedigan

Contents

A brief letter of introduction

Thank you very kindly for finding your way to the first page of what I suspect will be the most honest story I will ever have the mixed pleasure of writing.

To be clear, this is not a memoir that details my (let's be honest, *relatively modest*) success as a musician—most of the stories in this book come well before any of that. Meaning, sadly, there's not much in here by way of dirt on all the famous people I've (never actually) slept with, or even just . . . met (with one notable exception). As for any subtle bragging about fancy titles the world may or may not have given me? No. That's pretty much covered in my short bio at the start. The fanciest title you're gonna hear me called from here on in is probably my childhood nickname, Fatty-boom-bah (which I'm not sure really counts).

This is just the story I promised myself—aged twenty-one—that I would one day be brave enough, and well enough, and *alive* enough, to write.

At the time, that thought—that I might one day actually do something useful with my life—seemed outside of my reality, and yet, at the same time, it acted like a tiny flare of hope just in the moment I needed it most.

What were the chances of me coming good on that hope? Slim.

At age twenty-one, as you'll soon understand, I wasn't exactly renowned for my ability to follow through. Quite the contrary. My list of failures was already long and shameful, and if I knew how many more I would have to suffer before I 'made something of my life', I'm not sure I would have had the gumption to keep going.

And, still, I latched again and again to the memory of this hopeful feeling: that one day I would write a book, one that proved I was *more than this*.

That was twenty-one years ago. What took me so long?

Well, look, I've been a bit busy. That is true. But that's not the real reason.

Even on the day I promised I would write this book, I knew it would be a long time before I was ready to share it with anyone. I needed the hope of the promise, but what I didn't need was the pressure of rushing it. And so, as a work-around, I added one little caveat—I could start writing this book whenever I was ready, but I didn't have to actually finish it until I was really, really, really old. Say, forty? (How very rude.)

And so here I am, decades later, 'old lady Bowditch', now digging deep into my memory, my childhood diaries, and my song lyrics, to pull out stories from a time before I knew myself, and before there was any indication that anyone else would ever get to know me either.

A short word about the title of this book; it comes from a song I wrote in 2008 called 'Your Own Kind Of Girl'. It's the one I still get lots of letters about, and still find hardest to perform on stage. Despite best intentions and dogged preparation, I often choke up somewhere around the second verse. As confessed already (both in the song and earlier in this letter), for much of my early life I lived in the hope that someone, somewhere, would tell me that I was 'more than this'—that I was more than my failures, more than my grief, more than the terrible stories I told myself about myself. I suspect that's why I find this song so hard to finish; because that is exactly what my audience *does* tell me, every time I let them see who I am. They remind me that these stories are common—so very common. They remind me how beautiful life can be when we find ways to share them, and live through them, and change them. This, l suspect, is the loop that allowed me the courage to finally, *finally*, finish this book.

This is the story of the stories we tell ourselves, and what happens when we believe them.

It goes a little something like this . . .

CB xo

P.S. An additional note for those fellow travellers who, for whatever reason, find affinity with the term 'Sensitive Creative Type', it's for you I mention here that this memoir contains stories that were difficult for me to write, and may be difficult for you to read, depending on where you're at. Should you at any point feel yourself in need of comfort, reassurance or emotional support during our time together, just head to the back of the book. There you'll find a section called 'Additional resources' filled with helpful info.

1

Happiness

Are you ready yet
To be happy?

'ARE YOU READY YET?'
(*The Winter I Chose Happiness*, 2012)

I used to wonder if there was a name for whatever it was that was wrong with my brain.

My memory, for a start.

I could be quite good at remembering small things, like smells, and spelling, and sounds.

As a child, when I heard a song on the radio, I'd find my way back to its melody afterwards by the pictures it left in my mind. To me, songs were things with shapes and names and colours and temperatures. Easy to remember. Impossible to forget. They were as real, and alive, as pets.

So, yes, I could be quite good with small things.

It was the big things that sometimes stumped me—big things the world seems to value most, like facts.

Take, for example, the year I turned twenty-one, the year I could not for the life of me seem to remember the fact that despite what happened, perhaps even *because* of what happened, my childhood was often happy, and fortunate, and good.

Which is perhaps why, as an act of minor rebellion against the part of my brain that once forgot to remember its own happiness, I am going to lead with that story here.

✳

I was born the youngest of five, each of us one and a half years apart in age—perfectly spaced, like beads on a rosary. I guess you could call our family a rare triumph of the rhythm method. My parents deserve a medal, I think. A ribbon, at the very least.

My mother and father met by chance, at a party in Melbourne. Mum was from Amsterdam, just here for a visit. Dad was a local boy. He was studying law; she went on to study nursing. They started off as friends, then they began writing each other letters, and then, through the words, they fell in love, and eventually settled just a few kilometres from where Dad grew up, in a sleepy bayside suburb called Sandringham—'Sandy' to the locals.

First of the children was Johanna (Anna, the Leader), then Elisabeth (Lisa, Our Sparkle), James (the Boy Genius) and Rowena (Our Rowie, the One and Only). I am the baby, which explains a lot.

My first memory is of sitting propped on my mother's hip in church, singing along to the words of hymns I didn't know yet, thinking how much better this would all be if the priest would only hand me the mic. I must have only been two or three but I know this memory is my own, rather than one described to me, because when I think of it I can still smell what I will later recognise to be frankincense burning, still see the golden light streaming in through the stained-glass windows, still feel the warmth of my cheek on my mother's shoulder, feel the vibration from her chest to mine as she sang. She always had such a sweet voice. Pure and true. Quick to harmonise. I remember my father singing along with her, one octave down—his glorious, booming baritone. I loved, more than anything, to copy him—copy the way he lowered his chin as he piped out those churchy tunes. And I also remember the thrill of copying the priest, putting on my opera voice, mimicking the funny way he sang the words 'Holy Spirit', and how the people around us, including my parents, tried not to laugh. And this, I now see, is one of the moments in which my identity as a joker, as a seeker, as a singer, as a Bowditch, was fused.

I remember the first time I watched *The Sound of Music*, the first time I used my pretend opera voice to sing 'Edelweiss'. I remember telling my mother how much more fun it was to sing words instead of speaking them. I remember asking her why we even bothered with talking when we could all just sing, the way they did in musicals, and she said I was welcome to sing as much as I wanted. So I did, I sang all my thoughts, for what felt like a year; sang everything from 'Pass the salt' to 'Go away, you silly knob-knob'. My sister Lisa was the first to crack; the first to say, 'If you don't stop singing like that I am going

to be forced to thump you on the head.' And, oh, what pleasure
I took from singing even louder after that, knowing that she
would never really thump me, because, as I sang to her at the
time (perhaps in the tune of 'Morning Has Broken'):

I am the baby,
You know you love me,
Can't help adore me
For I am God's gift.

It is still in me, this memory of the thrill of being chased by
my sister, being scared at an age when fear felt like being on a
swing, like flying.

I remember my very first wish, one made on a sweltering
summer's day as I hopped from foot to foot, heat shimmering
up ahead on the concrete ramp, all the way from Sandy Beach
to busy Bluff Road. I picked a white dandelion, blew hard on it,
watched the white puff break, each seed parachuting away as I
made my first wish to Dear God and all the Fairies to please,
please, give me a daughter when I grow up. I have always wanted
to be a mother—a mother like my own mother, the middle of
eleven, children born healthy and at home in a narrow, three-
storey, multi-generational house next to a canal in the heart of
Amsterdam, in the middle of World War II, opposite the very
same church where, on the day of her birth, my mother's father
walked her across the road to have her baptised.

I remember swimming in an above-ground pool in someone's
backyard, running in circles with my friends to make a whirlpool,

8

being so small that the water was up to my neck, and in my stomach I still know that delight of the moment I broke into my first-ever dog paddle. I remember yelling out, 'I'm doing it! I'm doing it!' Back then, in the water, I felt so powerful, so magical.

I remember Dad's shed—full of tools, and electrical cords, and old pieces of car engine. On the wall, in the dust, hung his silver fencing costume and two rusty swords—his épée and foil. Strikes me as odd now, but for much of my childhood I thought being 'a fencer' had something to do with building actual fences. Not until much later did James explain to me very patiently that, no, fencing was a sport, and our dad was a champion fencer. An Olympic fencer. One day, hiding in his cupboard, looking for peanut brittle in his pockets (such an odd treat for a man with false teeth to eat, but anyway), I discovered his original green-and-gold Olympic tracksuit with the words, *Australia, Tokyo, 1964* embroidered on the back. I asked him if I could wear it. He said, 'No fear!', by which he meant no way. He had very few prized possessions. No luxury items to speak of. But this—his Olympic tracksuit—was his, and only his. Respect.

I remember being too short to reach the kitchen bench but feeling strong and fierce as I cracked the lid off a jam jar which, I now realise, Dad had most likely loosened for me, perhaps just to familiarise me with the feeling of victory. That was the kind of thing he would do.

I remember the feeling of beating James in an arm wrestle for the first time. I remember running up and down our street in bare feet, going from neighbour to neighbour, telling them jokes and asking them if they had seen my sisters or brother.

I remember wild dancing with a light green-and-gold-threaded Indian scarf, chasing my small friend Aaron around his kitchen table, pretending to be Kate Bush from 'Babushka', and how it made him scream, for some reason. This was before I understood that not all children liked Kate Bush as much as I liked Kate Bush, and that maybe my impersonation was a bit too real for him.

I remember my kind-hearted mother giving a bowl of milk to the stray dog she called Sam, the black labrador slash kelpie mutt who just wouldn't leave. I remember how he didn't like balloons, or vacuum cleaners, because they were loud. And Mum said maybe someone had been mean to him in the past, but he would be happy here, living with us, and he was. It was cancer that got him in the end. He was seventeen.

I remember the city, Melbourne; the flower clock in the Royal Botanic Gardens, how sometimes it would just be dirt with metal hands rotating around it and then, the next day, it would be full of flowers again, like a miracle. I remember running my hands along the water wall at the National Gallery of Victoria, flicking coins into its fountains and making wishes. Wishing for a baby girl. I remember lighting candles in St Francis' Church, the smell of the wax and the feeling of it dripping onto my wrist. I remember trying to hop up onto a stool at Pellegrini's cafe on Bourke Street—one of the first places in the city to have a coffee machine, back in the sixties, which was why my parents did their early courting right there. I remember watching the owner, Sisto, red bandana around his neck, ladling my icy cold pink grapefruit granita from a steel vat into a tall glass.

I remember the sweetness and the brain freeze as I sucked the drink up through my straw, and how my mother spoke so clearly whenever we were out, and that was the only time I ever noticed her Dutch accent: when she tried to speak clearly.

I remember standing on a stool at the sink next to my mother and singing songs and knowing the harmonies without trying and I remember how good that felt, to be able to do something well, to be able to delight her. I was a clever girl, she said. *What would I have done without you?*

I remember trying to make my mother laugh by pulling down my undies and kicking them off and then picking them up again with my toes and throwing them in the air and catching them. I remember how these silly little things cheered her up, and how I loved the sound of her laugh. How it settled my heart like nothing else.

I remember my father and his brothers singing Beatles songs like 'Let It Be' around a fire when we were camping, singing songs by The Seekers, Peter, Paul and Mary, Nana Mouskouri and Bob Dylan. A campfire, three chords and the truth: that's all it took to make a singalong.

I remember learning that my father had a real job because someone put a bronze plaque on our front fence that James told me read *Ian Bowditch. Solicitor.* I remember his legal papers stacked all over the house; yellow and blue and pink. I remember the time when he was out, and I wanted to please him, so I decided to organise all his papers for him; put all the pink ones in one pile, and the yellow ones in another pile. I remember thinking how happy this would make him, but instead, when he came home and saw what I had done, he made the loudest noise I'd ever heard him make, like a bear roaring, and I cried and hid under his desk. I remember my mum coming in, calming him down, and how eventually he crawled over to me under the desk to apologise for being so noisy. He said he didn't mean it. I was a good girl. He liked me very much, he said. He patted me on the head, like a puppy. I learned later that those papers were from one of the most complex cases he had ever taken on. They had taken him weeks to sort and me only minutes to unsort. And then only seconds, really, for him to forgive me, and me to forgive him.

I remember knowing that my parents were good people, and that I wanted to be a good person too, but I used to worry that maybe I was bad.

I remember starting kindergarten, my mother walking me in and my first teacher, Mrs Bibby, greeting me at the door and showing me where to hang my yellow raincoat.

And I remember wanting to be small, like the other children, and I remember how I never felt small, only big. Too big, even when I was very little. Big boned, big mouthed—these were things I remember people saying about me. These were some of the stories people told me about myself. For some reason, these are the ones I started to carry, and make real inside me. It didn't occur to me, not until much later, that maybe people were wrong. Maybe I wasn't too big after all.

I remember my mother steaming vegetables, the way the windows would fog up, the way she would use her finger on the window to draw love-hearts, and write our initials inside them, all together—A.B L.B J.B R.B C.B I.B M.B—and how we would stand next to her giggling, and I would copy my older sisters, drawing shapes that seemed to make people laugh, although I didn't know why: two big balls, and a banana sticking out the middle. And how Mum would try not to laugh, would say, 'Now, now, none of the yucky stuff. Just nice stuff, please.' Butterflies, rainbows, crosses.

I remember waking up on my birthday, and finding a special birthday chair waiting for me, all pretty and decorated with flowers from the garden, and streamers too. On the walls, Mum had hung paper honeycomb lanterns that she had had sent over especially from Holland. This was one of the traditions from her childhood—that on your birthday, you got your very own birthday chair, all decorated, just for you, and no one else was allowed to sit on it.

I remember how we would make tapes for our relatives in Holland, and how I loved to sing into the portable Sony tape recorder that my mother gave me: one where I could use my little fingers to press 'play' and 'record' at the same time. I remember making long dream-like soundscape tapes of singing and talking and telling stories and walking around the house with Sam the dog; how I carried the tape recorder with me from room to room; how I told the tape recorder all about the world I saw—made up songs about the vacuum cleaner and the hot-water bottle; and how I listened back to them afterwards, delighted. Anna and Lisa and James and Rowena also made tapes. I still have them. On them, Mum and Dad encourage us to sing together, mostly in English but sometimes in broken Dutch.

I remember knowing how much my mother missed her family in Holland. She had moved here when she was nineteen, not so much for a holiday, she says, but to find herself, to find out the meaning of life. She was a philosopher, you see, a rebel, a self-taught scholar, still furious about the Holocaust and how God could allow such a thing to happen. She looked like Audrey Hepburn, although more beautiful, or so said my father. Mum told him she was just 'putting it on'. Clearly, Dad bought it. He said he didn't know what he would have done if he hadn't met my mother at that party back in 1962. She wasn't even meant to be there. She had wanted to go to Paris but her father forbade it, said it was not right for single women to travel like that. Instead, he allowed her to visit her sister who had migrated to Clayton, in Melbourne, Australia. Back then, Clayton was just a suburb of paddocks and new houses. Mum found Australia confusing at first. She couldn't understand why nobody seemed to live in the centre of the city, for a start. Nor could she work out what it meant when you were asked to bring a plate to a picnic.

On the tapes, I can hear my mother's voice, speaking singsong Dutch, so gentle and sweet. Like I said, I don't usually hear her Dutch accent at all when she talks to me in real life, but on these tapes there it is, plain as day, as she tells us kids to go ahead and sing for Oma Annie, her mother, who would go on to live until she was a hundred. When I listen to those tapes now, I hear James and Rowena singing songs together about minnows and fleas, songs that make my chest go tight with feelings so precious that I don't know how to keep them safe, even today. Maybe that's why I have always had the urge to write things down: to keep a record, somehow, in case my mind forgets.

On the tapes I can hear Dad too, Mr Baritone, who surely had a voice for broadcasting, as he recites 'The Owl and the Pussycat' by heart, saying, 'Hey, now,' gently when we—Anna Lisa James Rowie Clare—argue over who gets to press the buttons on the tape recorder.

I remember Lisa skipping, and James reading, always reading. I remember Anna doing my hair and putting flowers in it and taking photographs of us all. I remember hiding with Rowena under a black-and-red-and-white doona cover in our bedroom, flapping it up and down and making wind. I remember the feeling of her elbows knocking into me, and the sound of her husky voice, and understanding she was the boss, and how good it felt to know my place. I remember following her, and being half dragged by her, and I remember her hair half up in a bun, although I can't be sure if that's my memory or a photograph I saw.

I remember planting red and blue pansies with Mum in the front yard of our family home in Heath Street. This was the house my parents built. It had heated tiling and a massive back-yard. This was supposed to be the time in their lives when, finally, everything came together.

I remember singing 'The Quartermaster's Store' in the back of the old Toyota HiAce stick-shift van—'There was Clare, Clare, sitting in a chair, in the store, in the store'—and how we'd go through every single person in the family, one by one, Mum,

Dad, Anna, Lisa, James, and then, when it came to Rowie, how we would sing for her too. I remember how hard my parents tried to keep the mood hopeful, how we all did, but how I always stumbled to find a word that rhymed with Rowena.

2

When I was five

You're fragile as a bee
And skinny as a steeple
And all these memories
Are they mine or other peoples?

'WHEN I WAS FIVE'
(*What Was Left*, 2005)

My sister Rowena had a crooked smile and a husky voice that made playful adults laugh.

In her prep photo, in her blue-and-white-checked uniform, she appears small and pale. Her hair, long and brown, hangs in looped plaits on either side of her head, blue ribbons in bows on the end. This photo used to sit on a sideboard in our TV room, near our family photo albums, which were lined up in chronological order. Mum has taken to each of their spines with a thin gold pen, her beautiful spindly handwriting documenting the year or years they cover. For the most part, the ratio is two years per album. Some bumper years—like 1993, when Anna gave birth to the first glorious grandchild, India—even warrant their own standalone album. There's 1989–1990 and 1991–1992. But if you look closely, you will see something telling in the chronology. There are only two albums covering 1974–1983. And it's in the second of those two albums that you will find photos of my sister Rowena on her hospital beanbag; a huge toothy grin shining out from inside her First Holy Communion dress, a gorgeous doll bride swallowed up in white.

One day, while looking through the albums, I noticed there weren't very many photos of me as a child. For fun, I ribbed Mum about it. I thought it would make her laugh.

'Mum,' I said. 'I thought you said you loved me. Why are there so few photos of me as a kid?'

Mum didn't laugh, she apologised. Said that she was sorry—there was just so much going on. Taking photos used to mean putting film in a camera, focusing the lens, developing the print. But Mum says the real reason she couldn't take photos is because it was just too hard, felt almost like a betrayal, taking photos without Rowena being home. The only ones that exist from this time are of special occasions, like her Holy Communion. There she is in the photos, Rowie, six years old, with two teeth missing, just like other children her age. Our parents stand beside her, Dad on the left with his hand on her shoulder, and Mum on the right, with me on her hip as usual, smiling. Big sisters Anna and Lisa in matching floral vests and white lacy high-necked shirts are on either side, and there's big brother James, posing like an angel, leaning over to rest his head on Rowie's white, sheet-covered beanbag. Although the photo is black and white, I think I remember now that her fingernails were painted bright red that day. Rowena could no longer see colours by then, only light and shade. But she still loved the idea of wearing red— such a grown-up colour. Mum never painted her own nails; it was just one of the little things she and the nurses could do to make Rowena feel special. They would paint her nails, and do her hair with clips, and put little butterfly rings and other sparkly trinkets on her fingers and wrists. I think she may even have been wearing red lipstick, although it's hard to tell. Maybe I've made that bit up.

My eyes return to Mum in the photo, hair tied back, a long dark fringe brushing her brow, crosses and holy medals on a chain around her neck, cheekbones protruding, skin sallow from grief, but still smiling, still a beauty. She must have been so scared. I can imagine it now that I am a mother myself. When I think about it too much, I want to throw up. At the time, I must confess, I did not notice at all. Not consciously, anyway. At three and four and five years of age, I was too busy learning to talk, learning to sing, learning to get what I wanted in ways that made people laugh. In this photo my dad smiles too from behind his original-hipster beard, his curiously broken glasses, his smart three-piece Sunday suit—the suit that served to hold us all together in moments like these. Surely that is the only reason people wear things as uncomfortable as suits and shoulder pads: because of what they symbolise, because symbols matter, because they make us feel strong. What we don't see in this photo, what is covered by Rowena's tulle dress, is the black tube travelling from her throat to the life-support machine that beeps next to her bed, the sound a code for: *She is alive. She is alive. She is alive.*

I think about us sometimes, how right everything had been. Two adults, five kids, one dog. I'm not exactly sure what 'normal' means, except we were pretty much it; just a normal family. And then, little by little, we just weren't, and we never would be again. To this day, the Sandy Bowditches are notoriously bad at saying goodbyes. At the end of every family gathering, we hug each other, say 'I love you' to everyone, and then, more often than not, we do it all over again, just for good luck. Mum is the worst. She doesn't let us or our kids leave without putting her right thumb to our foreheads in a sign of the cross; a blessing, just in case. What harm can it do, she says. Then, as we drive off in our cars, she stands out on the balcony waving. We roll down our windows and wave back, and we do that until the moment we lose sight of each other. I've got a sore neck just thinking about it.

My sister Rowie was five and in prep when she first began having trouble with her appetite. For some unknown reason she couldn't seem to keep food down. This left her fatigued, and severely dehydrated. The doctors couldn't seem to pinpoint exactly what the problem was. Soon she was so dehydrated that she was admitted to hospital. The doctors put her on a drip, did all the tests they could think of, found no obvious explanation for her sickness, and so—once she was feeling better—my parents took her home, and she returned to school.

Clearly, this was a deeply distressing time, although I don't remember my parents crying or complaining. What I remember is them praying, on their knees, for Rowena to come good again. Sometimes their prayers were answered. Sometimes Rowena would go to bed sick and then wake up the next morning feeling absolutely fine—her old self, once again.

Then, for no clear reason, the illness would return, and soon progressed into what could only be described as a rotating roster of random, baffling, increasingly debilitating symptoms. There was her lack of appetite, her fatigue, but also a problem with her sight. She developed a new habit of bumping into things when she walked. She told Mum and Dad she couldn't see properly, but then the symptoms would leave, and she would return to normal. We would return to normal. But never for long enough to relax.

My parents took Rowie to many doctors, both local GPs and specialists, who did test after test, yet no one could tell them what was wrong, or why. Rowie was missing more and more of prep. The children in her class sent cards saying, *Get well soon*. Mothers of Rowena's friends from school dropped meals on our doorstep and, in the supermarket, people stopped my mother and asked her if there was anything they could do to help. I remember pulling at her skirt impatiently, asking her if we could please go home now.

I get a prickly feeling at the back of my head when I think about this time. I remember the feelings—the seriousness, the panic—but I didn't yet have language to understand exactly what was happening. Most of what I tell you now is what my family told me, bit by bit, over three decades.

As the months rolled on, Rowena grew so sick, so weak, she could barely walk. Mostly she crawled. She no longer read her prep books, no longer even looked at the pictures. In the TV room, she sat closer and closer to the television, turned her head to the side, saying that she couldn't see the pictures properly. It was clear there was something wrong with her eyes, but none of the experts were able to diagnose what exactly. She was hospitalised three more times—either for dehydration or observation—but, still, nothing. There were no MRI machines back then; there was no way of seeing far enough into Rowena's body to know exactly what was going on. Mum and Dad took her from GP to GP, specialist to specialist, each appointment beginning with renewed hope that perhaps this time they might find a way to make her well again.

It came as a blow then, when an eminent paediatrician from a Melbourne hospital, a man my mother describes as 'kind and gentle', suggested that, with no medical explanation as to what was happening inside Rowena, perhaps it was time to refer her to a child psychiatrist.

This next part my mother can't talk about without crying, and I struggle too. My parents knew, in their hearts, that this was the wrong conclusion, and yet, with Rowena's body wasting away in front of their eyes, they were now beyond desperate, and this doctor was an expert, and by this stage they were willing to try absolutely anything.

The psychiatrist tried his very best—my mum has always made this clear. I can't explain why but, every time she says that, I feel a surge of rage with nowhere to put it. I want someone to blame. She says that there is no one to blame.

The psychiatrist—having been assured that nothing could be found medically wrong with Rowena—was shocked by her physical condition, but apparently impressed with her intelligence and courage. He appeared confident he could help. Although my parents had their doubts when he proposed to them the popular 1970s theory that perhaps Rowena was finding it hard to get attention—being the fourth child and all—they took it on for consideration. It might be an idea to try ignoring her, said the psychiatrist. Give her less attention. Maybe do activities with the rest of the children that she might want to take part in, so as to give her a chance to *will* herself into getting better. Perhaps when she saw the rest of us having a good time without her, she would come to her senses, get over herself, and join us.

Except she couldn't see us properly. That's what the doctors weren't able to pick up in their tests; when she told them she couldn't see, she meant it. Later it would make sense—her peripheral vision was still working; it was her central vision that was the problem. Perhaps this was why they thought she was making it up.

Yet, for those who knew Rowie, it was difficult to imagine she would ever make up something like that. She was as direct and true as they come, sometimes to a fault. Without meaning any offence at all, she once asked a woman with a long chin, 'Excuse me, are you a witch?'

23

Soon, there was no longer any question of whether Rowena's illness was mental or physical. It was finally acknowledged by all the doctors that Rowena's illness, although mysterious, was most definitely not psychological. By now, six months after her symptoms began, she no longer went to school. She required full-time care. My parents widened their search for answers, began making specialist appointments outside Melbourne, going with any lead they could find. By now her movement was severely limited, and then, one terrible day, it stopped altogether. Her whole body became stiff, like wood.

And this was the day she was finally admitted to the Intensive Care Unit of the Royal Children's Hospital in Melbourne, and that was where she stayed for the rest of her short, brilliant life.

I don't know if I was there that day. I don't know if I remember. What I do know is that, as I write this all down, I am aware of a cold feeling in my chest, and the sense of a voice in my head, a voice telling me to stop talking now, telling me that talking about these things is useless, and silly; that I should stop making such a fuss, that it was hard for everyone and by writing about it I'm only making it harder. And then I go numb. This seems to happen whenever I try to talk about this time in our life: I hear the voice, and then I feel this numb feeling, like I'm floating outside myself. Like I'm not quite here. Like I am making this up. I wish I was.

I am told that this reaction is quite normal. Trauma leaves you with holes in your memory. Everything that isn't urgent just goes. All these stories are stories that have been told to me. I try so hard to remember on my own, but I can't. I would have noticed when she stopped running and started crawling instead, wouldn't I? I was with her. Someone must have explained to me why we were no longer sharing a room—why Rowie was no longer there when I went to sleep or woke up. But I can't remember—not with pictures. It is my body that remembers these things for me. By the prickling in my head and the cold in my chest, the ache in my stomach and the wet on my cheeks, it's clear: I remember more than I can say.

I used to wish that someone could take me back there for a day, so I could fill in all the blanks. Then I wouldn't have to pain my family by asking them all the time. It's too hard to ask, and keep asking. I have asked too much already, I'm sure of it. But the compulsion remains: I must know more. And when I ask, when they fill in the blanks for me, I do feel different: more knitted together somehow. Less fractured. More whole.

So here is one of the things my mother told me: that when Rowena arrived at the hospital this time, was brought into the emergency department, the doctors now did a new test, one which revealed that Rowena had an extremely rare disease with an unusual name. A disease so rare that only a few thousand people in the world have ever had it. It affected her spinal cord and there was no known cause or cure. The reason she couldn't breathe is because of where it hit her on her spinal cord—right behind her neck. What they now knew was that the myelin around Rowena's spine and behind the optic nerve had disintegrated, rendering her without central vision. The simplest explanation was that she had a very rare form of multiple sclerosis. She was legally blind. She would never be able to walk again. Never be able to breathe again on her own; not without her machine. She could no longer feel anything from the neck down, although she could still feel touch on her face. She could feel kisses. She could give them too. If she had been diagnosed sooner, there is a chance the disease might possibly have been halted—although without MRIs, and with only rudimentary CAT scans, how could they have seen what was going on in her spinal cord? They could not have. At this late stage, my parents were told that unfortunately, there was nothing they could do to save her. Rowena did not have long to live.

For most of my childhood and well into my adulthood, I had no idea Rowena's disease even had a name. It was explained to me as some sort of childhood multiple sclerosis which, at three, was the biggest word I'd ever heard. I would repeat it in my head over and over, and whenever anyone from school or church asked us why Rowena was in hospital—which was many times a day: by now, everyone in the Sandringham parish and every family at Sacred Heart Primary School knew that Rowena was in the hospital, and she was dying—I would burst out with, 'She's got the multi-plus skleeosis.' I loved having a job to do, and saying those words was my job. Mum would pat my head and nod and say, 'That's right.' And then the adults would mumble some more, and I would try to work out what they were saying.

When the weeks stretched into months, and Rowie was still with us, Mum and Dad found a routine that worked: Mum visited the hospital during the day, often with me in tow, and Dad visited at night, after work, and on the weekend we all dressed up in our Sunday best for family time at the hospital.

During school holidays our family spent as much time together with Rowie at the hospital as we were allowed.

As the months stretched into a year and then two, Rowena kept going. Much later, one of her neurologists told me that she set a record for the longest time any child has ever lived in the intensive care ward at the Royal Children's Hospital. Mum says the nurses absolutely adored her. Because she was on a respirator, she was never on her own. She always had a nurse attending to her, either one on one, or one between two, to keep her company and make sure she could call out if she needed anything. From all accounts, she was cheeky, and funny, and often talked back. Mum says Rowena also had a photographic memory. She would often surprise Mum by recalling, in great detail, things that had happened years before. Despite her incredible limitations, from what I remember, and from what Mum tells me, Rowie remained generally rather upbeat. Mum says in a way she became a little mascot of hope for the nurses in the ward. Mum says it again and again—the love of those nurses was such a gift to families like ours. There is no way to thank them enough for the way they held us together. Knowing how much she was loved and cared for was the only thing that made it possible for Mum to say goodbye every night, to return to us, to her other children, who also needed her.

I remember Rowena's hospital room well. It was on the second floor, not far from the lifts. I remember the groaning of the metal trolleys, the squeak of the bed as it came up and down. There was a paper cut-out of a giraffe on the wall beside her, and pictures of Mary and Jesus and all the saints. There was a view of the sky from the window. She shared her section of ICU with five other children, whose faces and families were always changing.

As the year passed, our family routine evolved further. Mum still visited during the day and generally left in time to collect Anna, Lisa and James from school. Dad visited Rowena at night after work for a few hours, and then home to us for dinner. On Sundays we would all go in together. I only came in a couple of times a week now because I was spending more time at kindergarten. After kinder, I would usually go home with our family friends, the Andersons. I went to kinder with their daughter, Katherine. We would usually spend our afternoons chasing chickens in the backyard. Mum would come and collect me around 4 or 5 pm, or occasionally later, depending on how things went at the hospital, or how the traffic was faring.

I overheard my parents talking once about maybe moving to North Melbourne to be closer to the hospital, but we never did. They wanted to keep things as normal for us as they could, they explained later.

Although many people in our community would ask after Rowena, most of her visits were from family or very close friends, and this was due to my parents' wishes. The truth is that she had quite a busy schedule as it was. Several days a week, a teacher would come for an hour or so, then she had her occupational therapist appointments with specially designed games to keep her stimulated, such as making decisions on what to add to a cake that was being baked. Later in the day she would taste the cake and review her work. Then she had her time with Sister Teresa, the pastoral care worker who attended to the whole of the ICU and had a very soft spot for Rowena (as did everyone). Once, a nun popped in to say hello. Mum was holding me on her hip at the time and they were having a conversation. I wanted them to please stop talking about Rowena all the time. Mum said to wait a minute, she wouldn't be long, but I didn't want to wait a minute, I wanted to go home, so, to move things along, I just went ahead and very gently poked the nun's right boob with my finger. I remember being rather proud of doing that—how it got my mother's attention. How the nun laughed, and then my mother, explaining I shouldn't do that, and then how I laughed too. At the hospital, we laughed more than you'd imagine, considering how dire things were. This was still a childhood—my childhood—after all.

Once, when I kissed Rowena hello, apparently I got a bit too close and she whispered to Mum, like the boss she was, 'Can you please ask her not to spit on me when she says hello?'

Mum giggled. Rowena might have been small, but she still called the shots. I said, 'Sorry, Rowie, for spitting on you, I didn't mean to spit.' I wanted to be as close to her as I could, but I worried that I would accidentally knock the tube out of her throat, and the worrying made me even more awkward than I already was. Sometimes I would climb up on the bed and just put my head on her pillow and whisper into her ear. Sing. Ramble. I adored her. She was my little, big sister.

But at the same time—and it's difficult to admit this, although they say it's a classic sibling response—I resented her, too, and was jealous of her, of all the presents she got, all the visitors, the fact that every single conversation led to her, to her illness, to how she got it, to whether there was a cure, to the fact she was going to die, and it could be any day, so we'd best make the most of the time we had. It created a pressure, a storm in me: this thought that death was coming at any moment, and I should be able to stop it, but how?

Rowena was always thin. In the hospital, I watched her grow thinner still. I've always had a gift for worrying and, as a kid, one of my worries was that Rowena would disappear. I remember standing by her bed, comparing our limbs, noticing once how my arms were about the same width as her legs. I remember her stillness, how she lay propped up on those pillows to cushion the bones that poked out of her body. Every two hours the nurses had to turn and bag her—that is, clear her life-support machine and move her position to make sure she didn't get bed sores. The nurses were so careful with her, but sometimes when a new nurse was learning how to do it, Rowena would cry with pain in her neck—one of the only places she could still feel sensation. She never liked making a fuss. She would settle quickly, and then reassure the nurse that she was fine. I do not remember her tears, I think Mum made sure I was out of the room, but I feel them in my chest as though I know them and should have been able to do something to stop them.

Mum explained death to me early, using stories from the Bible and the metaphor of the cocoon and the butterfly. She said that

Rowena was actually meant for greater things, which was hard to understand, but I would have to trust her. She said all of us were meant for greater things: that this life was like a cocoon, and it was in the next life that we would come into the fullness of our possibility. I took all of this in, thought about it as I read *The Very Hungry Caterpillar* by Eric Carle, as I flipped through pages showing the cakes and gherkins and plums the caterpillar ate as he prepared for his transition, his transformation.

During the two years Rowie lived in the children's hospital, food became increasingly important to me, as did the routines and rituals of meals. This was one of the many frameworks around which my parents built stability in to our ruptured family life. Beyond religion, beyond faith, there was no reassurance available, not for my parents, not for Rowena, not for me, but food, and the dependable tastes and routines did help me to feel safer. It gave me something to anchor to.

There was fish and hot chips on Friday night, lemonade and crispy chips on Saturday night, which was 'movie night', and on Sunday roast lamb with peas and potatoes after mass (another of the dependable routines). Dad was a bit of a whiz in the kitchen. In addition to roasts, he also cooked meatloaf, a mean chop-suey and mile-high scones. Sometimes, he made his own pizza bases, and topped them with jam. Heaven on a plate.

Then, there was the hospital food: the softness of the jelly and custard and stewed apples Rowena ate, or didn't eat, depending on how she was feeling. There was the hospital cafeteria: the chocolate bars, the crunch of salt and vinegar Samboy chips; the sting on my tongue. Like Proust and his madeleine, the taste of these foods, even today, is like a portal back to Rowena; to a time and a place and a person who is no longer here.

Rowena rarely finished her food. I remember this one time, eyeing off her custard pudding in the plastic packet with the plastic spork on top. I stuck my finger into the custard, did it a few times, until Mum finally noticed and asked Rowie if she would mind me finishing it off for her. Sometimes Rowie spoke so quietly that you'd have to put your ear up close to her mouth to hear what she was saying. Mostly, she said, 'No, I don't mind,' but this time she said, 'Yes, I do mind.' I was terribly put out. How selfish, I thought. How mean. Why does she get all the good stuff? I didn't say it aloud, but I thought it, and I stomped around her bed a bit in a huff, sticking out my bottom lip. I remember wishing then that I could break a leg or an arm, so I too would get to spend the night in hospital, as though a night in hospital were some special treat, some special event, a thing a child might wish for.

My sister had to sleep on her own in the hospital every night. As an adult, when I say that, it gives me a terrible feeling in my throat, but those were the rules back then. To keep her company, we made cassette tapes that the nurses would play for her. As I did for the relatives in Holland, I would talk and sing into the tape for forty-five minutes, until it went 'pop', then turn it over to the other side and keep going. Later, when the tapes came home, I listened to them over and over. I sang the songs again, and changed them. This is how I came to think of myself as a songwriter; this is how it became a fact for me.

*

My sister was upset at me sometimes. Annoyed with me. Fair enough too. She was in hospital when we moved house in 1979. I was four and she was six and I realise now that of course she wanted to come home, and I got to go home every night, and I must have been a reminder to her, in a way, of the life she was not able to live. Some part of me knew that just by being there, I ran the risk of hurting her, of rubbing it in—how well I was; how I could do things that she couldn't do. I tried so often to settle down, tone it down, not rub it in. But there was also a competing impulse at play: one that said perhaps there was something I could do that would make it all right, that would inspire her to sit up on her own. That if I just kept trying, I would work it all out, and she would be okay. We would be okay.

My parents fantasised about hiring a full-time nurse and bringing Rowie home to live with us, but the hospital said this would not be possible—it just wasn't done back then, my parents were told. And, yet, who could blame them for hoping?

When I think back to this time as an adult, I still cry with gratitude for how kind, and how good, people were to our little family, and to our darling one, Rowena. For the two years Rowena was ill, our community carried us. Friends, neighbours, mothers from school, people from the parish, and strangers too. They dropped around with meals, they babysat, they held us up, they remembered us in their prayers. And a few of these people— only our very closest friends—were invited to come and hang out with Rowena. I remember how they told her jokes and read her stories by C.S. Lewis and Spike Milligan. Most of all I remember our neighbour Richard (Dick), and his lovely English accent, reading Rowie a story from Holland. Something to do with clogs. Once, only a few years ago, I introduced myself to a nun, a Carmelite sister, who was sitting behind me at the opera, and when I told her my surname, she asked me if I was Rowena's sister. That was the first time anyone had ever asked me that question. Yes, I said, and started crying, apologised, because I remembered still what their years of praying meant to our family. How much their letters and their faith comforted my parents. How it comforted them to know that Rowena, and all of us, were remembered, and not alone.

One Saturday morning in September, two years after Rowena had first moved into the hospital, there was an accident with her life-support machine, Rowena suffered a heart attack, and had what is perhaps best explained as a near-death experience. The nurses brought her back to life, thumping her chest 'in a special way'; that was how it was explained to me, by whom I can't remember. Dad, probably. But here is the remarkable part: before her 'little death', as my parents called it, she had been afraid to die; afterwards, she was not. Now, everything had changed. She said she had seen something beautiful that made perfect sense, a place she found impossible to explain, and that now she wanted to go back there.

'Go back where?' I asked.

'Heaven,' said Mum and Dad.

34

She was seven years old, and she said she wanted to go.

My parents must have cried, but I didn't see any of that. After almost two years of living on a respirator, Rowena was losing her voice. It took a great deal of energy for her to speak now. She chose her words carefully, spoke them quickly, so they'd fit in the short gaps left between her noisy machine and its next breath. Even still, it was sometimes difficult to understand what she was saying. I remember being right up near her face, putting my ear to her mouth. Mum did the same. Mum says that over the following days, she asked Rowie a couple of times about what she had seen, but Rowie must have grown tired of the questions because the final time she asked, Rowie answered quite firmly, in between the pumping of the respirator, saying, 'Mum, stop asking me questions. It's too beautiful to talk about.' Then she paused in between breaths and said, 'But I want to go there.' And that was that. Mum never asked about it again.

*

I remember one October afternoon, when I was five, Mum took me to the train station. It was sunny that day, but cold, and unusual, because instead of visiting Rowie in the morning as we normally would, Mum and I had been to the Moorabbin Arts Centre with my kinder class to see a live orchestral production of Prokofiev's *Peter and the Wolf*. In the theatre, after we found our red velvet seats right in the middle, near the front, the whole world went dark, and a man with a friendly voice appeared on stage to explain that each character in the story would be represented by a different instrument from the orchestra. The cat

35

was the clarinet. The flute was the bird. The oboe was the duck. The horn section was the wolf. Peter would be played by the string section of the orchestra, which was where it all began: with Peter in the big green meadow.

As the piece progressed, and I heard the sound of the wolf approaching, I grew scared and hid my head. It was the sound of the hunter's rifles—played by kettle drums, I think—that struck the terrible fear into my heart and I began to cry. I said I wanted to leave, so we did.

I don't know how we got from the theatre to Sandringham station. We were on public transport that day. Perhaps we caught a bus, or a taxi. What I remember is standing there on the platform, always a little further back from the safety line than everyone else. Mum didn't like taking chances with her precious baby (that's what she called me). She squatted down and held both my hands and my waist. The train sounded violent as it rattled in closer, and the suddenness of its *toot* made her jump a little. She saw me watching her and tried to make a joke out of her reaction by jumping again, higher this time, an exaggeration of the first, and making a funny sound of pretend fright.

She was so clever, my mother. She worked so hard to protect us, to maintain the innocence of our childhood, but it was impossible. Although she used games to mask her shattered nerves, and warded off my fear with farce and absurdity, it was still impossible. We all knew. But nobody ever lost hope, I don't think. I remember that she was always pointing out evidence of what she called the living presence of a loving God: the butterfly, the sand dune, the lavender. She did what mothers have always done since the beginning of time—she did her very best. And, still, things inside me often felt terrible.

Many times in my life, people have asked me about my mother and father during this time, and how they did it. 'I don't know how they survived,' they say.

No one has ever asked me how I did it, how I 'survived'— it's just not something people seem to ask children. Maybe we should. Maybe if someone had asked me how I 'survived', I would have twigged that the reason I felt that way was not because I'd done something bad and wrong. Rather it was because bad and wrong are what grief sometimes feels like.

So how did my parents survive? Because they had to. Even then, Mum was clear—us kids kept her alive. She says if she hadn't had me to care for, she would have died from sorrow. I was the youngest. I needed her the most. She says it was that need which got her up in the morning. She's said this for as long as I can remember. I loved that sense of having been useful, of having done my job. And, yet, it was a heavy feeling to carry. Guilt always is. I remember how bad I used to feel when I demanded her attention. I felt I was robbing Rowena. I tried, very hard, to ask for as little as possible, but I was not very successful. I couldn't seem to stop myself. I needed more, all the time. More attention. More reassurance. More food.

And somewhere in all of this, I made a little bargain with myself: that my mum would be okay as long as I made sure that nothing bad ever happened to me. I would need to be very careful, always. Later, much later, that was the thought that took up residence inside me: that I was not, under any circumstances, allowed to die. That even thinking about death was a sin.

On this particular afternoon, Mum helped me step up onto the train, one of the old Red Rattlers; grand and solid with tragically slashed leather seats and black linoleum floors tacked to the original wooden boards underneath with brass nails. Back then, you could open the train window and feel the wind on your face.

'Too loud!' I said as the train blew its whistle and rolled out of the station. I remember the feeling of slowly slowly and then quickly quickly as the train gathered speed, remember bright staccato strobes of sunlight and being blinded momentarily. I carry in me an image of my mother from this day, an image of her profile in bright silhouette, one of her hands clutching her necklace, her medals, her crucifix, the one she still wears to this day. I could not pick her expression. I watched so closely, trying to work it out. When she noticed me watching her, she cracked a smile and made a face, gave me a little wink.

But there was something wrong, and I knew it. I rested my head on her lap and, even though we were smiling, my stomach felt sick and I had no words for why.

We would have stopped at every station—Hampton, Brighton and then, later, South Yarra, Richmond and, finally, Flinders Street. And then we were there, at the hospital entrance once again. I don't remember how we got there; I think we must have caught a taxi. Mum can't say either. She can't remember. The shock, she says.

I have tried many, many times to piece it together, to work out what might have happened, which parts are real and which I have imagined. Sometimes, I see pictures in my head of things that I'm not sure actually happened. I see us stepping into the elevator, Mum pushing buttons, not laughing, and I know I need to be quiet, but I am scared so I talk. I see us entering Rowie's ward, then her room. She is not in her bed, which is impossible because she never left her bed, not even to go to the toilet. And then I have a memory of my mother, which I don't think is a true memory, but I feel horror when I think about it, because it's like I can hear my mum yelling in panic, saying, 'Where is she? Where is she?' and there is a sense then of a nurse walking towards her calmly with her arms open, trying to speak, and then my mother goes limp.

I also recall another scene, a different one, in which my mother never yells, 'Where is she?' In this scene, we are met at the elevator by two nurses, one of whom whisks me downstairs to the occupational therapy room and says, 'Don't worry,' when I ask where Mum is but she doesn't really answer the question. 'She'll be here soon. Can you see a doll over there? You go and get it. Let's play a game.' I think this might be what actually happened, although I cannot say for sure. I don't think I saw Rowie dying, but I just can't be sure.

All these decades later, all I really know for certain is that we were at the theatre, we were listening to Prokofiev, and then we were at the hospital, and after a bit of time my dad came, and then Anna and Lisa and James were there. Mum says they were brought to the hospital by their principal Sister Lois and the parish priest Father Coakley. Then Dad came into the waiting room and kneeled down in front of me and Anna and said very gently, 'She's gone.'

Even this bit is not quite clear, but when Anna reminds me of it, there it is: the feeling of truth, hot and cold like panic in my chest. Rowena was in heaven now, Dad told us. She was gone.

I heard a voice in my head that day. The voice was like my voice, but bigger, telling me that this was all a bit silly, and for some reason I became quite sure that she was not really dead at all, and would soon reappear. I would definitely see her again. It was not a big deal. This comforts me—the thought that I did have a kind voice inside me, a voice reassuring me that everything would be fine. I wish that feeling could have lasted.

I never knew my sister as I know people today. I can remember very few details of conversation or playing games or eating meals together. I see from the photos that we did all these things, but I can't remember them as vividly as I remember other things from my childhood. Sometimes I think I catch a memory, like that time hiding under a black-and-red-and-white doona cover with her, and hugging her, and being tickled, and being shoved in the face by her elbow—but I can't be sure that the memory is mine.

Most of what I know about my sister I know because other people have filled in my memory for me, and I know because I feel it in my chest all the time. I know it because I cry, still, over little things, like smells that remind me of the hospital, or the sight of children whose brown hair reminds me of her brown hair. I know my sister by the smell of the dried lavender in the little pillow that someone made for her when she first went to hospital, and the smell of the disinfectant they used to clean the floors. I know her by taste and texture: the crunch and sting of those salt and vinegar chips from the hospital cafeteria, the soft stewed apples and apricots and pears. I know her by the songs that were playing on the radio when she was alive, like Supertramp's 'Dreamer' and 'Let It Be' by The Beatles, songs by Bob Marley, Nana Mouskouri, Simon and Garfunkel, Stevie Wonder, Donna Summer, the *Play School* theme. I know her by colours: by the light satin blue of her Holy Communion ribbon, the speckled brown and cream tiles of the floors in the hospital, the lime green and gold of her dress-up scarf, the cream of a cabbage butterfly in summer, the yellow of the cafeteria custard, the red of her fingernails, the white of her Holy Communion dress, the one she was buried in.

I did not go to her funeral, as was the common wisdom of the day. They thought I was too young, that it would upset me. With hindsight, it's clear that I should have been there. I needed that funeral as much as everyone else. I needed to know for sure that she was gone, and not just hiding. Instead, Mum and Dad came to my kinder and we had a ceremony there: a tree-planting, to commemorate Rowena's life.

That was a brave thing for grieving parents to do—to come to the kindergarten and explain to the children that the tree was a symbol of my sister, who was now dead on earth but alive in heaven.

I wanted, so badly, for her to be alive, somewhere.

I have a photo from that day—one of the only pictures of me and Dad, just the two of us, from when I was small enough to fit on his lap and big enough to hug him back. It is on my phone as I write this chapter. It makes me feel brave, remembering what it was like to fit in his arms.

When I was a kid and someone asked, 'How many brothers and sisters do you have?' I never knew the right thing to say. Either I could say, 'Five, but one died,' but sometimes that just felt too hard. So then I'd say, 'I'm one of four,' and have to live with this sick guilty feeling, as though I'd left her out on purpose. But there was something in the guilt that made her feel as though she were close, still. There was something so familiar, about feeling bad.

Grief makes vessels of all of us, but most especially, of children.

I remember the day she died, the drive home, and there we all were, in the white Toyota HiAce, and as weird as it sounds, it felt like our car was floating. The sky was light lavender, still sunny, but it had been raining. It was late in the afternoon now and as we crossed a bridge down near where they later built a casino I saw a big rainbow. I can still see it in my mind, Rowie's rainbow. And then I saw an old man planting a tree by the side of the road, so I said, 'Mum? I just saw God planting a tree,' because I thought it was true and, also, because I thought it would cheer her up. She was in the front passenger seat, and I think she turned around and I think she did hear me. She hadn't been able to speak yet, and Dad wasn't saying much either, and I don't think the radio was on, which was unusual. Dad always had the ABC on. And I had the strangest feeling in my chest, almost like it was about to burst. It was similar to the feeling you get when you're a kid and it's your birthday or something— almost like excitement, except, a terrible excitement. Something really, really bad had happened—so bad, I kept forgetting what, exactly. I kept forgetting that she had died. Shock, I suppose. *Or maybe*, said a voice in my head, *the reason you keep forgetting is because you're just a bad, bad person.*

When we pulled into our driveway at Sandy, the feeling was so big in my chest I jumped up and out of the car and said, 'Can I tell the neighbours?' and Mum still wasn't talking but Dad must have said okay, because I ran across the road then to my friend's house. I had big news, and I knew it. I let myself in and when I saw my friend's mum I said in a very loud voice, 'Rowie's dead!'

Again, I don't know whether to trust my memory here but, in my mind, I see my friend's mum holding a vase, and then I see her dropping the vase, and I watch as it smashes on the floor, glass everywhere. Whether it was the look on her face, or the dropping of an actual vase, I can't say for sure, but that was the moment I got it: that this was not just terrible, it was so very terrible, it could not be undone. It could never be made right: not ever.

And it's here, in the middle of what psychologist Jean Piaget called the Age of Magical Thinking that I first experienced the thought I could not seem to un-think, no matter how hard I tried. It's the same thought, the same story that so many grieving children, and adults, tell themselves after someone they love has died—it was all my fault. For reasons that I didn't then understand, there was a very bad feeling inside me. I didn't know it was just a feeling. I thought it was who I was. Again and again, when that feeling returned, so did the story—the voice in my head telling me I was a *bad, bad person*, telling me there was something I could have said or done or even just *thought* that would have saved her life, but I had missed my chance, and now she was gone. She was dead. I was alive, and I was going to need to make up for that, somehow.

3

Your own kind of girl

Chocolate, you've got chocolate on your mouth.
Oh, you long to be like the other girls
But you weren't born to be 'some other girl'.

'YOUR OWN KIND OF GIRL'
(*Modern Day Addiction*, 2009)

If I were a better liar, if I could lie without a 'tell'—without a twitch of the eye or a sniff of the nose—I think I'd still quite like to lie about this chapter.

The truth is so messy.

My lie, on the other hand, would be very neat. It would be entitled: *An Inspiring Tale of Body Love*, by Clare Bowditch.

And it would just read as one little sentence, something like:

Despite my body's propensity to wax and wane like the bellow of a well-played piano accordion, it's never occurred to me to want to change, not even once.

But that is not my story. Not even close.

Naturally, I blame my mother. My whole life she's been in my ear, yakety-yak, with that classic line about how it's not your outsides that count, it's your insides.

Meanwhile, the world tells me different. Its terms are very clear: first as a girl, then as a woman, my best chance for success is to be thin or to get thin, and then for fuck's sake to stay thin.

Both these stories feel true to me. And it's on the shore of this paradox that I often find myself beached, unsure of whether I'm allowed to tell the true, unresolved story of my body, or whether I have to wait until I'm 'fixed'.

Like my life in general, I just wish it were all a bit simpler.

I thought by the time I wrote this I'd be ready.

Apparently not.

Apparently, just like prancing around in my bathers in front of strangers at the local pool after Christmas, I have to show up scared.

So here I am with the true story of my body; a story my body has already been telling, without my permission, for years.

I was always a big girl, right from the start. My mother called me 'a little peach'. My sisters called me 'Little Baby Poonta'. They said it was an affectionate nickname, and it was easy enough to believe them because back then, back at the start, back before I knew anything of the world and what it would ask of me as a girl, or a woman, I liked my jiggly body. I liked the way it felt when I danced, and swam, and woke up in my own bed, all warm and soft. Inside my body felt like a good place to live.

Then I turned three, and everything changed.

Up until then, although I knew I was big—bigger and taller than the other kids—I only understood it in the same way I knew that my hair was long, and my eyes were green, and my dog was called Sam. I didn't think of my size as some problem to be solved. I didn't think of my size at all. At kinder, I was too busy singing, finger-painting and chasing Jimmy—the first boy I ever loved.

Oh, Jimmy. Dear sweet little Jimmy.

Yes, he was shorter than me, but just like Miss Piggy and Kermit the Frog, I knew we were right for each other. I saw past his size. What I saw were his lovely blue eyes and his white hair, the way his face looked just like a Cabbage Patch Doll, only he was alive! I loved Jimmy so much that I told him so every day, all day, mostly by standing very close to him and singing him my original love songs like: 'Jimmy, Jimmy, I love you, Jimmy. I love you so, so much. I LOVE YOU, JIMMY! Hooooo!' (jazz hands).

Mum said my songs were *just wonderful!*

Jimmy—not so much. Sometimes, when he saw me coming, he'd put his hands over his ears and run away.

Despite this, I was still pretty bloody confident that he loved me as much as I loved him.

'How could he not?' said Mum. 'You're a peach. I'm going to eat you! *Run!*'

And I would. I'd run. Fast as the wind. Look at me go!

But one afternoon at kinder, when I approached Jimmy to sing him a new song, he said, 'Oh, no. Go away!'

'What?' I said. 'Why? I'm singing for you.'

'No,' he said. 'You're too big. Girls aren't supposed to be so big. Go away.'

Too *what*? Too big?

I looked at him, I looked at me, then I looked at him again, and realised, perhaps for the first time, I was not just big, I was *too* big. In that moment I noticed that my painting smock was tight against my stomach. In that moment it fused inside me: there was something wrong with me. The words circled in my head like guilt. *You're too big. That's why Jimmy doesn't love you.*

Mum was not having it. 'No way,' she said. She got down on her knees, down to my level, looked me in the eyes and called me *schuttie*, the Dutch word for sweetheart. She said, 'Schuttie, listen to me. There is nothing wrong with you. You are not too big. You are a peach. You are an Amazon. You are my little saviour. You are the reason I'm still standing—do you understand?'

I stopped crying then, because, yes, I did understand; much more than I knew how to explain with words.

Mum had known this day was coming but, even when it did, she still had no idea how to make it right. She had been warned already, she said, by a child psychologist at kinder, a woman who checked in on us from time to time; Mum had been told that even though I was bright and strong and clever, I was also rather tall. Top percentile. I looked a lot older than I was. In her opinion, there would be a gap, a discrepancy, between the age

I looked, and the age I was. I would be judged for that, she said. It might make things a little tricky.

That year—the year I started kinder and first had the feeling there was something wrong with me—was the same year my older sister Rowena got sick, and moved to the hospital. Things were not easy at home, although, really, I had nothing to compare it with. To me, this was all quite normal. I just kept doing what I'd always done—I skipped, I danced, I demanded the world join me in the musical of life.

I was a kid. I was three and four and five. Every day was a new adventure. Yet the membrane separating me from other people, their feelings from my feelings, was very thin indeed. I had no words for the complex emotions swirling around inside me. Often, I'd think I'd done something wrong, but I couldn't remember what, or how to make it better.

I wanted to believe Mum when she told me there was nothing wrong with me, that I wasn't too big, but I already suspected she was just saying that to be nice. I started hearing a voice in my head around this time—one that was full of accusation, and anxiety, and worries. It told me I was too big, too much. I was making too much of a fuss. I was too demanding. Even then I was well aware that nothing I was experiencing could possibly compare with what Rowena was going through as she battled her mysterious illness. As loud and frightening as these thoughts sometimes became, they were preferable to trying to fathom what was going to become of my sister, and whether what was happening to her was going to happen to me too.

These accusations ran through my mind like dark mantras I couldn't get rid of. The harder I tried to ignore them, the stickier they grew. There was something wrong with me. I took up too much space. I was too big. Too much.

*

They say the best way to survive a career in stand-up comedy is to begin your training in childhood, as a fat kid. That makes perfect sense to me.

Not long after Rowena died, I started my school life at Sacred Heart Primary School, Sandringham. I was cheerful and fat, and fortunately had very good friends, most especially Elly and Lynette. I liked using my size as a place behind which the smaller kids could hide. One of the legacies of Rowena's death was that I always wanted to make things right, so protecting the little kids from the bullies was as useful for me as it was for them. But although I was excellent at standing up for others, I was shithouse at standing up for myself.

My size, and the world's insistence that girls be smaller than boys, made me an easy target for teasing at school, and a gang of older boys made sure I knew it. When they saw me coming, they'd yell out, 'Here comes Big Bird.' When I ran anywhere, even just down the corridor, they'd say, 'Look out! Fatty-boom-bah on the loose.'

They found it funny. I found it brutal.

I didn't like it when they told me I was different. This feeling of not belonging sat big and heavy in my chest. My shame about my size was compounded when, at the age of six, I started to

50

notice that there were no fat Barbie dolls, no fat Miss Worlds, no fat ballerinas, no fat newsreaders, no fat female pop singers, no fat girl role models on TV—in fact, no starring roles for fat kids at all, not unless you were a cartoon character called Fat Albert, which, clearly, I was not.

I soon came to realise that the best option for a fat kid like me was to put myself down before they did and get myself a little laugh.

So when the boys teased me, I played into the stereotype of fat as grotesque and limped towards them like a hungry monster, making munching sounds and yelling, 'NOM NOM NOM! I'm hungry!'

It worked.

Now, when the other kids laughed, it wasn't just at me, it was also with me—at least to some degree. I was hooked.

Soon I had a whole coterie of impersonations in my back pocket: I was Fat Albert, Miss Piggy, Chunk from *The Goonies*, the Stay Puft Marshmallow Man from *Ghostbusters*. I'd make fart sounds, swear, wiggle my bum, squish up my face with my hands and recite nonsense. They were cheap laughs, but they worked.

My life at school took a turn for the better.

My career as an entertainer had begun.

My parents were a little concerned.

They saw how the world treated fat kids. They knew how hard it was for me to find role models, or even just clothes that fit, and they worried. If it was difficult now, how would this play itself out in my teen years? They never ever spoke about my weight to me, and I heard them defend me against the insensitivity of other adults—mainly one male relative who felt compelled to express his opinion of my body at family gatherings.

My parents wanted me to have every opportunity to participate in life to the fullest, and they encouraged me to take up basketball, a sport in which my height and weight could be a positive attribute. I absolutely loved it. To this day, there is nothing that gets my blood pumping faster than the smell of a freshly bounced basketball in summer. Basketball is one of the only places in the world where being my natural size put me at an advantage. I hardly had to run at all because I was so big and strong that I could lob that kid-size basketball halfway down a court with a simple flick of the wrist. Sure, I wasn't super quick, but my height did afford me status as a defender. I can still hear the voice of an opposing coach yelling out to his team at a finals match, 'Get on the big girl! Stay on the big girl!' I didn't care what he called me, because on that court I was trying, and winning. On that court I mattered.

My will to win wasn't limited to basketball.

Although I never saw my Dad pick up the rusty épée and foil that hung in the shed—by the time I came along, he was retired from sport, and just your everyday family-law solicitor with a beard who spent his weekends perusing the *Trading Post*—I was still well aware that I was, technically, the daughter of A Champion. The sight of his green-and-gold tracksuit in the cupboard next to his suits always filled me with a kind of pride, and one day a happy thought occurred to me: what if I too possessed inside me a kind of . . . Olympic potential?

But which sport to choose? There were no fencing lessons on offer in my neighbourhood in the 1980s, but the local Rotary Club did run Little Athletics at a nearby oval, so I went along. When they tested all the kids' various strengths and weaknesses, it became clear that what I was really good at was chucking things, most notably the blue spaceship-shaped object one of the men called a 'discus'.

I loved the feeling of that little blue spaceship in my hand. I loved knowing there was something I could do that other kids my age could not. The feeling lit me up from the inside and, week after week, I showed up and practised.

In time, I invented my own special pre-throw move: I'd breathe out, nod my head as I dragged my left foot like a bull preparing to charge, then I'd spin my fat little body in three huge circles, yelling, 'One, two, threeeeeeeeeeeee!'

At night, in bed, I'd imagine myself doing my special move, practising it in my mind and watching that discus fly through the air again and again until I fell asleep, a champion, like my father.

I still practise important things in my head over and over before I fall asleep—piano lines, speeches, dance moves. It's a habit that has stood me in good stead through all the stages of my career. But I no longer practise The Discus.

By the end of year I'd proven myself worthy and was chosen to throw the discus for our Little Athletics team in the local championships. I remember how proud I felt that day, how I threw just like I'd been practising in my head at night: once, twice and then (whistle) *look at her fly!* Even before the discus had landed, I knew that I'd won a place.

And I was right.

When my name was called over the loudspeaker and I walked to the podium to collect my ribbon, I thought of my father. It felt so wonderful to be the one who was going to carry on his grand sporting tradition. Everything seemed golden that afternoon.

After the ribbon was pinned to my chest, I turned to walk back to the bleachers, but was stopped by a volunteer who kindly invited me to 'really enjoy this moment' and to go and stand with the other champions on the dais.

Listen, when you're a big kid you get a feeling for maths and volume. It's a matter of self-preservation. The last thing any fat kid wants to do is draw attention to their size by accidentally breaking someone or something. I looked at the dais and had a very bad feeling. It was made of chipboard, for a start. My dad had taught me that chipboard was no good. So I politely declined.

But the volunteer mistook my hesitation for shyness. Taking me by the hand, she said, 'Come on, Clare Bowditch, you deserve this! That was a beautiful release. You get up there with the others.'

She was right, I thought. I did deserve this.

So I stepped onto the dais. Looking out at the cheering crowd, noticing the blue sky, the light sunshine, feeling the cool wind on my face and neck, I experienced three of the happiest seconds of my entire childhood.

Four seconds in, I heard the sound of something cracking, only to realise it was the dais beneath me. I should have known it was all just too good to last. I felt my feet hit the grass and, with them, my dignity.

Although I tried to ham it up—to make the crowd laugh by jumping up and out of that hole like a pogo stick and making crazy faces as I ran in little circles of adrenaline on the grass— deep inside I felt weak with shame. I already knew what the older boys at school would say when they found out. They'd say, 'Fatty-boom-bah. Fatty-boom-bah. Fatty-boom-bah.'

✳

By the time I was ten years old I no longer fitted into clothes in the children's department. Mum now had to take me shopping in the ladies' section.

I don't know how I got the idea of going on a diet, but one day in Year Four I came home from school and told my mother that I had had enough.

'Enough what?' she asked.

My bottom lip quivered. 'Enough of being fat,' I said.

She tried her usual tricks, telling me I was a peach and an Amazon, but I was done. I didn't want to feel different anymore. I wanted to feel normal.

Mum got it then. She didn't argue, she just grabbed me and hugged my face to her chest, then dragged me up onto her lap (which was no small feat for a woman as slight as my mother, but she gave it a good crack).

'No more worrying,' she said. 'We will sort it out.'

The next week, Mum picked me up from school early to take me to my first appointment with a famous diet doctor in

St Kilda. As we sat in the waiting room at the clinic, just before the receptionist loudly called out my surname for the whole world to hear (*Shhh!*), Mum told me, 'Remember, regardless of your weight on the scales, you are loved by God beyond all measure.' (In case I haven't mentioned it, my mum is a *little bit* Catholic. She once told me that if she ever did get a tattoo, it would probably be a mural of the Sacred Heart of Jesus, right across her chest. She's pretty dedicated, shall we say.)

Dr Von Thinburger (not his actual name, but neither was it *terribly* far off) was tall and slim with dark hair that seemed to sit slightly above his head. He was also wearing a white lab coat. Clearly, we were dealing with a professional.

He welcomed Mum and me into his office with a smile and asked me why I was there (*Ah, hello? Are you blind?*). Mum explained that I was tired of being teased about my weight. Just like Mum, he told me not to worry, we would soon have this little problem sorted. I found his confidence reassuring.

The doc asked me to stand, took out a measuring tape, jotted down the inches of my waist, arms, bust, hips and thighs, and then invited me to hop up on an old-fashioned silver scale. ('Remember, regardless of your weight on the scales, you are loved by God beyond all measure.') After that, he picked up a camera, asked me to stand against the door, and then he took a couple of photos—first front, then side. These were to be my very first 'before' photos.

In them I am smiling. We must have popped home in between school and the appointment because I am in my smart-casual clothes from the ladies' section of Target: a floral yellow and blue t-shirt, blue slacks and cream slip-on shoes. I looked just like a little Italian nonna, only I was ten. All this attention was embarrassing but, at the same time, I had a hopeful feeling in my heart that day. Imagine if he was right and my problem really could be solved? Imagine if I could wear crop tops and bubble skirts like my friends? Imagine if I could know what it felt like to be . . . normal?

Dr Von Thinburger asked me to sit down, then produced what he called a BMI chart. He pointed to each of the four sections: underweight, normal weight, overweight and obese. I was in the obese section, he told me.

I didn't know what the word 'obese' meant, but I could tell from the way he said it that being obese was not a good thing.

The doctor handed my mother a piece of paper, saying, 'From now on, please have Clare follow these instructions very carefully.'

I don't know how much you know about diets but, as far as they go, this one was very strict: low fat, low carb, no dairy, no sugar, and definitely no peanut brittle. I was to eat only three small meals a day of measured protein with a cooked vegetable or salad, a splash of apple cider vinegar or lemon juice, two thin crackers and one piece of fruit.

Once he had talked me though the meal plan, the doctor eyeballed me and said, 'Clare, you have to do exactly as you are told. If you do, you will see very quick results. You might feel tired for a few days but, after that, it will be easy. Maybe even fun. Look, here are some little recipes you can try!' He handed me a photocopied booklet.

Flicking through it, I saw black-and-white pictures of what I can only describe as things inside things: cottage cheese inside a tomato, a tomato inside an orange, an egg inside a tomato, an egg inside another egg. Fascinating.

'What's that on top of everything?' I asked.

'Parsley,' he said. 'As a garnish. You can eat it, but not too much, okay?'

I nodded.

He told us to come back in a week.

I'd walked in feeling ashamed, but I left feeling hopeful. Having a plan felt so much better than not having a plan.

On the way home, Mum and I did some shopping from the food list, bought a food scale, and that night I ate exactly what the doctor had ordered.

The next morning, for the first time in my life, I made my own lunch: weighed and measured onion-and-chive cottage cheese inside a scooped tomato with apple cider vinegar and a small garnish of parsley.

I was not yet ready to share my diet news, so when my friends asked me at lunch what I was eating, I replied, 'Nothing! Mind your own beeswax.' It came out louder than I intended—so loud that Mrs Wool, our Friday substitute teacher, asked me to please come over to her desk. I stood before her, red-faced, holding my lunchbox.

She looked at it curiously. 'What are you eating?' she asked.

I replied quietly, 'It's onion-and-chive cottage cheese inside a scooped tomato with apple cider vinegar and a small garnish of parsley.'

'Oh,' she said, 'that's an unusual lunch for a little girl to be eating.'

'I'm on a diet,' I whispered.

Her eyebrows went up. 'A diet? Well, good for you, Clare Bowditch. How does it work?'

So I told her, blow by blow, gram by gram.

As I spoke, she started jotting notes on a pad of paper, saying, 'Go on.'

When I had told her everything I could remember, she said, 'You don't, by any chance, have a photocopy of your diet, do you?'

'No, sorry,' I replied.

She asked me if I could maybe remember to bring the original in on the following Friday, so she could have a proper look. 'I'm just curious,' she added.

And that was the day I learned that some grown-ups are very interested in diets. Her interest felt like a warm glow in my chest. Approval, I think they call it.

I felt approved of.

I liked that feeling—a lot.

Over the summer, I followed my new diet to the letter. I learned to cook all the recipes in the book. I weighed and measured my food to the gram, using the scale. I cut the fat off my meat and then weighed it, and then my brother James taught me how to smash it with a mallet so it went thin and was easy to cook. (Although I learned the hard way that this technique shouldn't be used with white fish. What a mess!) I even steamed my own cauliflower, and then mushed it with a musher, and sprinkled it with curry powder, just like the recipe said.

And every week, when Mum and I showed up at Dr Von Thinburger's office so I could be weighed and measured, I was filled with glee when I saw him marking down my decreasing weight.

He kept saying I was doing extremely well. And whenever he said it, I felt that warm feeling again. Thrilling.

As the summer rolled on, my clothes started getting looser, and my running started getting faster. I did feel tired sometimes, though. I was growing taller and much thinner at the same time, and I sometimes felt a recurrence of my old childhood fear that I had done something very wrong, except I couldn't remember what.

One time, when I looked down at my legs, I noticed my knee bones for what felt like the first time ever. Automatically, I thought of Rowena, of her thin legs, her thin arms. She was skinny. So skinny. These same thoughts came to me at night when I felt my ribs resting on my bed. They felt like hauntings, these thoughts. They made me wonder, and keep wondering, if getting thin was a good thing or a dangerous thing. Sometimes, my new body felt so small it scared me. I told myself I shouldn't think such things. These are not normal thoughts, I said. And I kept them to myself.

I didn't want to worry my parents.

As the summer rolled on, and I began to adjust to my new body size, my feeling of fear was slowly replaced with more of that proud feeling, the one I had when Mrs Wool or Dr Von

Thinburger complimented me. Now everyone was complimenting me—neighbours, people at church, ladies at the shops. Everyone told me I was doing a great job. Everyone seemed very happy I was losing weight.

On my final visit to Dr Von Thinburger before school started, he told me once again how pleased he was with my progress. On my weight-loss chart, my achievement was marked now as a long descending line on a piece of graph paper. He said I was no longer obese, or even overweight. I was normal. I was the normal weight for my age for the first time in my entire life. And now, he said, I could begin reintroducing old foods back into my diet again.

'Peanut brittle?' I asked.

'No peanut brittle,' he said. 'Not yet. But you can have an extra orange if you want, and you can even have some hard cheese instead of cottage cheese. Would you like that?'

I nodded, even though he and I both knew that what I really wanted was peanut brittle.

✳

When I walked through the school gates on my first day of Year Five, I was wearing a brand-new school uniform. The old one no longer fitted me.

The first person I saw was Mrs Smith, the usually friendly librarian, who walked straight past me.

That was strange, so I yelled out after her, 'Mrs Smith, how was your summer?'

She turned and, smiling curiously, said, 'Lovely! Sorry, dear, I don't have my glasses with me. Who is that?'

'It's me, Mrs Smith—Clare Bowditch!' I replied.

I watched then as her mouth opened and closed like a puffer fish gasping for air. She came right up close to my face, stood back, looked me up and down, and said, 'Clare Bowditch? Is that really you? Where did you go? My goodness! You are so tall! And so thin!'

So thin. For as long as I could remember I'd longed to hear those words. I was so excited, I jumped up and down, laughing.

That day, it was as if my whole life changed.

Before assembly, my friend's mother, Mrs C, came over to me and said, 'I had no idea how beautiful you were!' My face flushed pink. Really? I was shocked and I didn't know how to respond, so I stayed silent. But I felt her words curl up inside my heart like a small warm animal.

At the assembly, a teacher made a joke, asking, 'Who is the new girl?', pointing at me. Everyone laughed.

After the assembly, Renee, the most popular girl in Year Six, came and looped her arm through mine. We had never spoken before, but she said that she was proud of me.

Weirdest of all was when a friend came over at lunch and said that Jimmy—the guy I'd loved since kindergarten—wanted to ask me out, although he was too scared. Again, I turned pink and went mute. Jimmy took this as a sign that I wasn't interested in him, and we never spoke of it again.

At the end of the day, as I collected my bag in the corridor, I learned that Mrs Wool was not the only woman who wanted a photocopy of my diet. So did two of my friends' mums. The lady in the office was happy to oblige.

At first, I liked this feeling of helping the mums. I've always liked, and still like, being useful. But in these conversations about my diet, I heard some of the mothers talk about food in ways that weren't familiar to me. They used words like 'good' and 'bad'—words I was already very sensitive to. They also talked about calories, and counting calories—things I'd never had any real exposure to. My own mother had always been very careful in her use of language around food and weight. Although she claimed to be 'as vain as they come', her approach to beauty was very low key in comparison to most. She didn't shave, didn't wax, didn't dye her hair, paint her nails or wear foundation. She occasionally wore mascara and lipstick. She washed her face with water. She put on Nivea cream or Oil of Ulan in the morning, but that was about as far as she went. She was naturally slim, and got slimmer during times of stress. So beyond a copy of the book *Fit For Life*, and occasional phases when she would suddenly start eating lots of Pritikin bread and make her own kombucha out of a big blobby scoby that was growing in a glass jar in a shadowy corner of the living room, she never really talked about diets. Even though this was the opposite of her intention, her lack of interest in these things left me a little defenceless against the strong opinions of some of the other mums—grown women who mustn't have known any better. Must not have realised how closely I was listening, and wanted to copy.

The praise about my slimness kept coming, and after a little while it began to dawn on me that my feeling about it had changed. There was something uncomfortable stirring in me now: something I couldn't quite put my finger on. Until I got thin, I'd had no idea what a big deal this whole 'fat' thing was for people. Most people in our community treated me so differently now it was almost as though they saw me as an entirely new person.

I understood it—I think I understood it—but I began to feel overwhelmed. I felt a little bit angry, even, that people didn't seem to understand I was exactly the same Clare I'd always been, just thinner.

My mind was having trouble catching up. Sometimes I still forgot I was no longer fat. When I look back on photos of myself at this time, I am shocked at how thin I really was. I still felt most myself when I wore baggy clothes and my body was covered.

When I was fat, I tried never to swim in public. Being in my bathers in front of other people always seemed to lead to someone saying something about my body that hurt my feelings. Now that I was thin, I decided I would allow myself to swim, but the ghost of all that teasing does not easily disappear. Because I was still scared of what people might say about my body, I took to wearing a big t-shirt over my bathers—one that covered my bum and the top of my thighs. I hoped no one would notice.

But my friend's mum did notice. When I showed up at the beach in my long t-shirt, she said playfully, 'Darling, you can take off the t-shirt. You're not fat anymore, you know!'

I pretended not to hear her and ran to the water, sinking my body low, where nobody could see it and comment.

That was the last time I swam in public for a decade.

✳

My life as a thin kid was certainly much easier than my life as a fat kid.

I still remember how lovely and easy it suddenly felt to run. Before losing weight, I'd never known it was possible to move that quickly around a basketball court. I was not only tall and fast, I'd become a decent shooter as well and, when the opposing coaches yelled out to their players to keep on me, I was not the 'big girl', rather I was the 'tall girl'.

This change in my status came with an increasing amount of confusion. After basketball one day, I heard my friend Jane's dad ask, 'Who's the new player? She's good.' I'd known Jane and her father since kindergarten.

'It's Clare Bowditch,' Jane replied, unaware that I was listening. 'She used to be the fat one, remember?'

'It is not Clare Bowditch!' bellowed her father. He actually thought she was joking.

He turned to look for me, then walked over and said, 'Are you Clare Bowditch?'

'Yep,' I replied.

'My God! You used to be so fat! Look at you now!' He looked me up and down, then he made a face that, for some reason, I just didn't like.

That year, I won a trophy for being the runner-up best and fairest in the team. It was the first time I'd won a prize since The Dais Incident in Year Four. It felt good, and yet, curiously, not quite good enough.

*

Although I no longer worried about my big stomach, because I didn't have one, I had lots of other worries; ones that were difficult to make sense of.

As intoxicating as the attention was after I became thin, it came at a cost. When I was fat, even though I was sometimes teased, I was still quite sure of my world and my place in it. I knew my value. I knew where I belonged. But now, as a thin kid, I saw a crack in my universe that just hadn't existed before. I saw that when you were thin, people seemed to like you more. And that just wasn't right.

I ached sometimes for the old me—the one who didn't know that it wasn't just the mean kids who had an opinion on my body. I used to believe my mother when she said it was our insides that counted, not our outsides. But now that I was thin, and people treated me differently, I didn't know what to believe. I often felt like an imposter.

I did love the attention. I did love the approval. I loved when people took pleasure in my hero's narrative—my journey from fat to thin. But, in a way, I think I got a little hooked on all that. In the past, I had looked to my mum and dad to reassure me that I was okay. Now, I looked to the world—to the other kids, their mothers, to the magazines.

Inside me, there was a quiet anger bubbling. I was angry, I think, on behalf of my old self. Although I looked different on the outside, on the inside I was just the same person I'd always been. I was Clare Bowditch, daughter of Ian and Maria, sister of Anna and Lisa and James and Rowena. Why, now that I was thin, did people act as though I was suddenly more worthy of their attention? There was something wrong with that, and I knew it. My ten- and then eleven- and then twelve-year-old brain had trouble making sense of these things. Mum and I talked about this quite a lot.

In the end, although I didn't necessarily agree with the way people treated me, or why, being thin was much easier than being fat. Although I missed the comfort of my fat little body, and the feeling of knowing where it belonged in the world, I didn't miss the teasing, or the fact that normal kids' clothes didn't fit me. I didn't want things to go back to the way they'd been before.

I knew I must never ever let myself get fat again.

＊

I read an article recently about girls and puberty, and I learned something that I wish I'd known when I was a kid: just before puberty, it's important and natural for girls to put on weight, because this weight gain is the trigger for the cascade of hormones that tells their reproductive system to release its first eggs. If I had known that, if someone had explained that to me, I wonder how different my life might have been?

One morning in Year Six, I jumped on the scales and saw that I had gained weight. How could that be? I had noticed I was feeling hungry all the time, but I had been doing my best not to overeat. I would need to be more vigilant.

From then on, every morning before school I locked myself in the bathroom and recorded my weight, which, to my dismay, seemed to be climbing. Not by much, but by some. That was enough to release the old spectre of anxiety that started circling once again with its message of 'too big' and 'too much'.

I knew what I had to do—I just had to follow the old Dr Von Thinburger diet, and everything would be fine. But, as hard as I tried, I couldn't seem to do it anymore without overeating. I took this as a sign of moral weakness. The voice in my head told me I needed to buckle down, try harder.

Calories. Until this point, I didn't really know what a calorie was, but from the conversations with my friends' mothers, I had learned that one of the ways ladies lose weight is to count their calories.

At the local newsagency, with my saved pocket money, I bought my first calorie book. I discovered that when I planned my meals in advance, when I knew exactly how many calories I was supposed to eat, and ate accordingly, it made my life feel more contained. In a curious way, it brought me a sense of comfort. A sense of control. It gave me somewhere to hide when the sticky thoughts came visiting.

I didn't tell anyone about my new diet: not my parents, not my sisters, brother or friends. I hid my calorie book under my bed. I didn't want any fuss this time. I just wanted to lose the weight quietly, and have this all be over with, once and for all.

The story in my head—that I was getting fat again—felt both terrifying, and true. Photos of me around this time reveal the exact opposite: they show a very slim young girl who is smiling and waving at the camera. The smile is genuine. But, behind closed doors, my battle with my body was turning darker. I did not notice that I was growing taller. All I saw was that my weight on the scale was still rising. It was time for me to try something more drastic.

During first-aid class, I learned that there was a syrup you could drink that made you throw up. I had read about bulimia in *Dolly* magazine, but I didn't like the idea of putting my fingers down my throat, so this sounded like a good option to me. I saved up three weeks of pocket money, went to the chemist, got the syrup, and that night at home, aged twelve, I gave bulimia a red-hot crack.

Fortunately, things went badly. The liquid was disgusting, it made my stomach ache horribly and, when I did throw up, the smell reminded me so much of hospital, and Rowena, and her death, I never did it again. Out of ten, bulimia gets a zero.

But dieting? That was different. Everyone did that. That was normal.

You might wonder where my parents were during all of this. They were there, of course, but not only was I sneaky, they had a good reason to be distracted. This was the year my brother James, who was fifteen, had a stroke. Juvenile ischemic stroke. Like Rowena's illness, it was rare, with no known cause. Not again, I thought. As usual, Mum and Dad used Jesus as their role model. They walked under an umbrella of grace and love that, to this day, I still can't quite comprehend. Although it meant being plunged back into the hospital system, once again, our community held us, and somehow we pulled through. After a year of daily rehab, James made a full recovery. Legend.

But while it was all going on, my obsession with diets offered welcome relief to the thoughts running through my head—that James was going to die. And if not James, someone else. Possibly me. I didn't want to think about it, yet I couldn't seem to stop.

What began as a fairly standard, but quite secret diet of low-fat food and obsessive calorie counting soon morphed into something quite unique, and queer. A game, of sorts, to see how far I could push things and still not get caught. Some days I ate only four crackers, pickles, mustard and a small slice of cheese. Other days, when I made myself a sandwich for lunch, I would cut off the crusts, chop the sandwich into quarters, and throw three of those quarters away. These practices left me hungry— sometimes starving—and horrifically vulnerable to the kind of rebound overeating that inevitably leads to a binge. Whatever was in the house would do when I binged: white flour with butter and sugar, or oodles of toast. Given the circumstances, bingeing strikes me now as one of the smartest things my body could have done. I was growing, and I was trying to starve myself. Of course, my body was going to prompt me to eat whatever food was available.

At the time, however, I took my bingeing as a sign I was weak and bad, and I would need to try a whole lot harder if I was going to avoid getting fat again. The voice in my head kept me company during this time, and it also grew much harsher, now saying things like: *Pull up your socks, you fucking fat loser.* I thought that talking to myself like this made perfect sense and was the only thing that would keep me on track.

✻

My transition from the small pond of Sacred Heart Primary School to the much larger Star of the Sea Catholic Ladies College was, in short, not smooth.

I was nearly thirteen by then and, yep, I thought I knew what was what. I could swear and everything. I thought I understood the lay of the land. I started high school feeling bright and confident and quietly up myself, but I soon fell victim to the familiar pull of wanting to belong and longing to be accepted by the bitchy girls who seemed to hold the invisible keys to power.

At some point, someone who didn't like me very much, who wanted my best friend to be her best friend, discovered my Achilles heel—my worry about my weight—and she did not hesitate to put in the boot. In those days, schools used to weigh and measure their students, and write this information on cards to be filed. This girl somehow got access to the filing cupboard, found out my weight and yelled it across the schoolyard. I was mortified. *Too big. Too big. Too big,* said my head. From there, the teasing grew violent. My head was smashed against a heater, my wallet thrown away, yoghurt poured on my school dress, hate letters planted in my desk. I got told that if I looked at that girl one more time she was going to kick my face in.

As a result, I learned once again that the best way to fit in was to join in.

By Year Nine, I'd drunk all the drinks, smoked all the smokes, told all the lies and done things with boys on the sand at Half Moon Bay Surf Life Saving Club at night that I didn't like thinking about the next day. All up, I made quite a fucking job of my teenage years.

The one positive from this time is that I began the habit of writing in my diary—writing down my feelings, and my worries, and my drama. In there, I also wrote my diets. Writing down my meal plan in my diary each night was one of the things that made me feel safe, and sane. From these records, I can see that although my weight went up and down on the scales, I had not yet twigged that my sudden changes in weight reflected a problem with anything other than my size, and neither had anyone else. The same cycle of positive attention that I had gone through when I lost weight at ten repeated itself as I lost and gained weight at thirteen, fourteen and fifteen. When I was thin, I felt powerful, but exposed. Wrong. When I was fat, I felt belittled, but safer. Wrong, but also right, because I wasn't buying into the stories of the world, or so I told myself.

Regardless of where I stood on the scale, the one thing I refused to do was swim in public. It could be a thirty-nine-degree day, I could be at the beach with my friends, and I still would not take off my clothes. It's not that I didn't want to swim, it's that I didn't want to give anyone the chance to comment on my exposed body. Never again. No fucking way.

Looking back, it's clear that there were lots of things I wanted to do around this time, but didn't let myself. Surfing, for example. I worked in a surf shop and I wanted to surf, like my boyfriends.

But, back then, girls weren't encouraged to go surfing, and I was so desperate to fit in that I did not back myself. I told myself to shush, it was enough to be on the shore with a thermos full of Milo for when the boys came in. It was enough just to be there at all.

＊

One Saturday night I got drunk at the beach with my friends, then we went to Maccas. As I leaned in the doorway with a Big Mac in one hand and a cigarette in the other, I heard someone call my name. Someone with a Dutch accent. It was my mother, doing a drive-by. She had grown suspicious of my lies (I'd told her I was having a quiet night at a friend's house) and now she was on to me.

Mum was not impressed. The next day, when she called me into her room to talk it over, I saw in her face that my actions were breaking her heart. But when she asked me what was wrong, I didn't know what to say. All I could tell her was that I was sick and tired of being fat. I cried as I told her that all I really wanted was for someone to admit me to some hospital somewhere and put me to sleep for six months so I could just wake up thin, and this hell would be over.

The story I had been telling myself was the story I had been sold, the story I had read about in the girls' magazines, the story that I knew—if only momentarily—to have been true for me: that when I was thin, I was happy. But by the time I was fifteen, the misery of willing that story to come true and of failing again and again had all become too much for me to carry. I think, more than anything, I was just exhausted.

Mum looked in my face and told me it was going to be okay. We were going to get me some help.

That week, Mum stuck a postcard to the fridge—a black-and-white picture of an early-twentieth-century woman: a big-boned, flowing-haired, strong woman in a ball gown flexing her exposed biceps. She wanted me to know that even though they were hard to find, there were role models out there. I was an Amazon, she said. I was not born to be like other girls. I was going to be my own kind of girl.

My first psychologist was a woman called Annika. She'd been recommended to Mum by a hospital that treated children with eating disorders.

'She isn't Catholic,' Mum told me, 'but she is Dutch, so that's a start.'

When I walked into Annika's office by myself for the first time, I didn't really know why I was there, but I assumed the terms of this engagement were pretty clear. I was there because I was fat, and Annika was going to help me get thin again.

During that first consultation, however, Annika said she didn't want to put me on a diet, she just wanted to talk. I thought she was holding out on me, but I played along and answered all her questions.

She asked about my dieting, and I told her. She asked me when I first remembered overeating, and then she asked about Rowie, and the hospital, so I told her.

That took most of the session.

While I spoke, I did a thing I've always done. I pressed my fingers lightly above my top lip. There was a rhythm in my head that had always been there, like an invisible pattern under my skin calling me to play it. I don't think I would have even noticed I was doing it if Annika hadn't asked, 'What are you doing with your hands?'

I told her I wasn't doing anything, just making some patterns.

'Do you do that often?' she asked.

'Always,' I replied.

She asked if I had any other habits like that, habits that I repeated, and I thought about it and said, 'I don't think so.'

She smiled and encouraged me to keep an eye out for them. She wanted me to write them down.

This was an important moment. Annika was teaching me what it felt like to be open to enquiry, to ask questions from a gentle place. She was asking me to observe myself, without judgement. She was telling me I didn't need to have it all worked out: that we had time. That this was a process.

During the next week, as I observed myself, I was surprised to notice that, yes, I did have a few funny little habits. I'd been doing them for so long, they just seemed like second nature.

I wrote a list, which I read out to Annika at our next session.

FUNNY HABITS by Clare Bowditch

1. I do a pattern with my hands—1/3/5 and 2/4, then back again, and I sing a song to go with it.

2. I play games in my head like:

   A. 'Tap Tap', where I tap my feet every time I pass a telephone pole in the car.

   B. 'The Typewriter', where I type and retype words in my head, forwards and backwards.

   C. I imagine my hands playing songs again and again on the piano, until I get it absolutely perfect, which is rare.

3. I play number games to help me sleep at night—ones where I count backwards in various mathematical increments, like nines or sixes.

4. When I hear music, I see colours; each instrument is a differently coloured ribbon that streams out in front of me. I am not sure this technically qualifies as a habit, but it is, perhaps, a little odd.

5. I stand under the cold water in the shower for exactly six seconds at the end of every shower. No idea why, except six is my lucky number. That was my number in basketball.

6. I have not walked on a crack in almost a decade, to my knowledge.

7. When I see a crack, I always need to step over it with my left foot.

8. At night, I need to check at least twice that the back door is locked, otherwise I can't sleep. Sometimes I need to get up from bed to check again, just in case.

9. I like counting calories in my head before I go to sleep, adding them up, and I like converting pounds and kilos from one to the other as a game.

10. Even though I do track my calories, I never feel I am tracking them well enough. Sometimes I have to re-track them three or four times at the end of the day, just to be sure.

I stopped talking then, and asked, 'Why do you want to know?'

Annika took her time to answer, as if she was giving it some thought, then she said, 'Well, sometimes, when we feel confused, or we're struggling to process our feelings, or feeling like we don't have much control over our world, we do things that bring us comfort. These habits. Do you feel a sense of comfort when you do these things?'

'I don't know,' I said. 'I just do them. They're just things I do. Doesn't everyone?'

Annika replied, 'Yes, to some degree we all have funny habits, personal habits, but some of us have more than others. Sometimes it's useful to begin observing when you do them, and whether you do them more when you're anxious. And it's also helpful to learn to calm our minds in peaceful ways, like meditating, rather than feeling trapped all the time with the games we play to make ourselves feel safe.'

Speaking of which, this whole conversation was making me feel tight in the throat; I didn't like being called out like that. I told myself she was talking gobbledygook and wondered when she was going to give me a diet to follow. I noticed for the first time that as my mind raced, my hands seemed to automatically start playing their little 1/3/5 patterns. Weird, I thought.

That day, Annika guided me through my first-ever meditation, a slow one in which she asked me to imagine I was a rose, blooming. At first I was worried she was going to somehow brainwash me so I was determined to stay alert, but soon, through no effort, I felt peaceful. Relaxed. It was an unfamiliar feeling, but I liked it.

At the end of the session, though, when Annika asked if I would practise the meditation on my own as homework, I thought, hang on, I've been coming now for two weeks and I haven't lost a pound. Why hasn't she given me a diet yet? Why haven't we talked about food? Does she think I'm crazy? I don't want to be told I'm crazy. I just want to be thin.

Even though it had now been clearly explained to me, I still didn't realise at the time that what I was struggling with was not just a problem with diets and my weight, but a problem with my mind and my feelings and the stories I was telling myself. Like the sticky thoughts from my childhood and my guilt about Rowena's death, the thought of food also presented itself as an ongoing sticky thought—a point of obsession, more pleasant than the guilt, but nonetheless addictive. I had no way of understanding then that Annika was trying to draw my feelings to the surface, and she was succeeding. All I knew was that, despite the lovely feeling I gained from the meditation, outside her room I was feeling more scared than before. In the past week, my thoughts had been flooded with questions about Rowena, and what happened to her. Old images and feelings; things I had no way to explain, and nowhere to put. I felt out of control, and I didn't like it. Not one bit.

On the car trip home that day, Mum asked me what had happened in my appointment, but I didn't want to talk about it. I looked out the window and played Tap Tap.

When we arrived home, I headed straight to the kitchen and, through a mouthful of gherkin and cheese on toast, told Mum I didn't want to see Annika again. It was too far away, and too expensive for her and Dad, and just too weird.

She told me not to worry about the money: 'Don't be silly!' But I did worry as I didn't want to be a burden. I just kept telling her that I was fine now, until she believed me.

'Are you sure?' Mum asked.

'Yes,' I replied. If Annika wasn't going to make me thin, I thought, what was the point of going to see her?

Looking back now, I wish I had stuck with the process. But the truth is that I was just too scared. Seeing Annika was like taking the lid off a garbage can. I was so scared that, if I let her get to know me, she would discover the thing I was most scared of, the thing I already suspected to be true: that there was something very wrong with my brain.

I still believed my biggest problem was not with my head, but with my weight, and if only I could find the right diet, all would be well.

*

Over the next six years, I did go on to become a true world champion—in the art of failing diets. If you named a diet, I'd have tried it. I'm not just talking the one-pagers from the ladies' magazines, either—I'm talking the real deal: the Cabbage Soup Diet, the Egg Diet, the Grapefruit Diet, the Royal Jelly Diet, the Meal Replacement Shakes Diet, the Lean Cuisine Diet, the Cottage Cheese Diet, Gloria Marshall, Weight Watchers (four times), the Drink-Diet-Coke-And-Chew-Sugarless-Gum-And-Smoke-A-Lot-And-Don't-Sleep Diet, as well as several dozen rounds of Monday morning 'Just don't eat at all' attempts, and the Atkins Diet (turns out you *can* eat too much bacon). I am pleased to say I never tried Jenny Craig, but that's only because it cost money and I was a broke student.

It would be a long time before I understood why I ate, and dieted, the way I did. I had no concept back then that the way we eat, and the way we feel, are often entwined. I see it now, clear as day—my 'piano accordion' body was trying to do me a favour, was trying to tell me something.

It would take me some time yet to work out what that something was.

4

Amazing life

You want an amazing life
But you can't decide
You think you're supposed to be
Fully formed, already,
Don't you?

'AMAZING LIFE'
(*The Winter I Chose Happiness*, 2012)

'Good afternoon, Martin Dawes Telecommunications, my name is Clare, how may I help you?'

I never imagined I'd be the kind of person who wore a suit to work.

When I was nineteen, and a family friend offered me a job—customer service in a corporate call centre in the industrial suburbs of Melbourne—my first reaction was laughter. Me, in a suit? I had a nose-ring and long half-dreadlocked hair. I barely wore shoes! Sandals, if you insisted, but not a suit! I wore the only clothes that a girl my size could find in the shops in those days: flowing hippie dresses that went swish in the wind. Wearing a suit wasn't really my vibe.

Then again, neither was it my vibe to hang out in the dole office every week being told by some aggressive knob-jockey behind a glass partition that because I was not filling out my job-seeker diary correctly I would not get paid this week. Apparently, writing songs and stories were not jobs, they were hobbies. I needed to 'get a real job', and I tried, and kept trying, but Australia was still in the grip of *the recession we had to have* and a job was not an easy thing to come by, even for someone like me, who had been working in retail since I was fourteen years old.

I was nineteen now, and already worried that I'd left my dreams far too late as it was. Did I really want to work in a call centre?

Let's just say that things hadn't gone terribly smoothly since finishing school.

I did not end up staying at Star of the Sea Catholic Ladies College. Couldn't explain at the time exactly why I needed to leave; just that I did. Something about the uniform, the rules, the bitchiness, the lack of autonomy, the lack of boys—who can say? All I knew was that I was 'naughty', getting 'naughtier', and although I couldn't tell you exactly what I longed for (besides a ciggie), I knew I longed for more. Much, much more.

It's still a mystery to me exactly how my older sister Anna eventually convinced my parents to allow me to attend a school that, at the time, had a reputation for being one of the most progressive alternative liberal-thinking schools in the whole of Australia.

Preshil, it was called. Independent, secular, co-educational—
everything a girl like me could want. Established in the 1930s
by a progressive young lady called Margaret J.R. Little, Preshil
was a small but proud school, founded on the motto 'Courage'.
Nestled in between the more conservative private schools in
Melbourne's inner east, it would take me three hours a day on
public transport to go to and from Sandringham to Preshil,
but after a slightly bumpy start (turns out, contrary to what I'd
heard, there *were* rules at Preshil, and attending classes was one
of them), I truly did find my place there. My people too. This
is where I met my best friend Defah (pronounced Deeee-fah)
and my second family, the Lubitzes. It's also where I met my
first big love—Joffa. The experience of self-determination, the
creative support from the teachers, the music program, and the
small classes (some of which were held in trees) really did suit me.

Three years later, when I graduated, it was on a high. I'd
aced my exams, and I had a mark that would have allowed me
to do just about anything I wanted. And what I wanted was to
save the world. At the very least, I wanted to do something that
mattered, something significant, something that made me feel
I was living up to the promise I'd made myself as a child: that I
would use my life to make things *right*.

Given this, it remains a mystery both to me and to my family
exactly how I ended up studying . . . ahem . . . public relations.
I loved my years at Preshil, but let's just say, careers coun-
selling wasn't its strong suit, and I believe I may have thought
public relations had something to do with . . . social work? Oh
dear. In any case, I was the one who ticked the box, and I was

also—three months after beginning the course—the one who signed the papers to defer.

Now free, I decided what I wanted to do was travel, and a rather fabulous year of adventure followed. I spent most of it travelling up and down the east coast of Australia with my guitar (which I could barely play) and my kindergarten friend Zandy in her little Mazda 323, and then did it all again on Greyhound buses with my boyfriend Joffa. We volunteered on organic farms in exchange for board, picked bananas for cash, snorkelled on the Great Barrier Reef, jammed in Byron Bay, slept on the beach in Newcastle, had close encounters with crocodiles and snakes at Cape Tribulation, made pipi chowder on Fraser Island, whale-watched in Hervey Bay, gathered coconuts on Magnetic Island, ate oysters out of a can, drank cask wine out of plastic cups, read Kahlil Gibran's *The Prophet*, wrote the whole book out by hand for fun, learned how to play Cat Stevens songs . . . this was living. That year was my first taste of true freedom.

But my money soon ran out, and now here I was, broke, and being offered a job.

I already owed my parents much more money than I knew how to earn. They never asked me to repay it, but I was determined to. I wanted to start again. I wanted somewhere to anchor. I wanted my life to begin. And vibe or no vibe, the call centre was the best offer I'd had in quite a while. So after I stopped laughing, I said, 'Yes, I'll do it.'

The only catch was this whole 'You need to wear a suit' thing, because I wasn't even sure they made suits in my size. In 1994, in the era of the first true supermodels, off-the-rack clothing stopped at a size 12, or size 14 if you were lucky. After ten years of yo-yo-dieting I, on the other hand, was now a size 24. And it was no good looking online; the internet still took three days to load a single page.

There was also the fact that I was not a fan of clothes shopping at the best of times. Never had been. But later that week, at a plus-sized ladies' shop in Richmond, I had an encounter with a sales assistant that changed my feeling about both clothes and customer service. The assistant was so friendly, and she seemed to understand how it felt to know that most of the clothes in the world did not fit you. She said, 'I think I have exactly what you need. I'm gonna go and grab it for you. I am going to make sure you walk out of here feeling like a million dollars!' She was the first sales assistant ever to make me feel like I mattered, that I fit, that there was something here for people like me. It was a brilliant lesson in customer service. It was all I really needed to learn, in fact, to thrive in the call centre. There is but one golden rule: give a shit about the person you're serving. Show them you care. That's it. That's how you win the day.

Even though the suit she sold me was non-crush rayon with an elasticised waist and about a hundred sizes bigger than my head told me was 'right', when I walked out of that store, I felt fabulous. I felt ready to begin my new life, as a normal person, who did normal things, in a normal way.

✳

'Good afternoon, Martin Dawes Telecommunications, my name is Clare, how may I help you?'

I drank a lot of Nescafé Blend 43 that year. By 10 am I was usually on my fourth cup. *All free*, said my team leader, Hannah. *You help yourself.* So I did.

The real perk of this job was that, much to my surprise, I actually liked it.

I liked the routine of it. I liked knowing I had something to wake up for, somewhere I had to be, someone I could help. I liked being good at something. It kept my mind busy. At first, working in the call centre was like a balm. It served to quieten the voice in my head, the one that told me I would never fit in. Never be good at anything. That I would always feel less than, because I *was* less than.

But that was not how my friends at the call centre saw me.

Hannah was a kind boss. Early on, after listening in to my calls, she told me I had a gift, a special gift, for handling irate customers. 'You always listen right to the end,' she observed. 'They feel heard. You never hang up on them.'

You mean I was allowed to hang up on them? Well—that was news to me.

Training was, let's say, a little thin on the ground. Martin Dawes was a new telco in Australia, there were only about thirty of us in the office, and we were all working it out as we went along. I started taking my first customer-service calls the same day I learned how to plug in a headset. When the customers who called were irate (and they often were, because do you remember mobile phone contracts from the nineties? They *stank*!) I'd just let them blow off steam, and then, when they were done, I'd tell them I heard them, and we were gonna fix it. I was never sure how, exactly, we were gonna fix it, but I discovered that confidence and kindness can carry you quite far. I did for those customers what the lady in the shop did for me: I showed them I cared.

Hannah said that if I kept this up, one day I might even make it to team leader myself.

'A girl can dream, can't she?' I said to Hannah.

She laughed. I loved making her laugh.

The thing I loved most about this job were my friends. We grew tight, fast. All of us were newbies, clumped together in a single-floor office. It was a new company, and I guess it felt good to be part of something new. Exciting, even.

On paper, my colleagues and I had absolutely nothing in common. Not a thing. We came from different backgrounds, nationalities, religions, social groups, ages, abilities, health concerns, likes. My friend Lena's favourite song was OMC's 'How Bizarre'; she'd never even heard of my idol, Jeff Buckley. Michael Fizzy spent his weekends hotting up cars; I didn't even know what a mag wheel was. Tamara had a huge teased fringe and lived with her horse on three acres of land in a suburb I'd never even heard of, but she was so patient, and always took the time to explain the correct process (and I needed many reminders). Chris was small with a sharp wit and zoomed around the office in his electric wheelchair at lightning speed. And when Georgie laughed hard she snorted like a camel, which made her laugh even harder. All I had to do was make a face at her when she was on a call and she would laugh so hard she had to push the mute button and put the client on hold. Viola was my age but she was already married and a homeowner. She had her honeymoon in the Seychelles. I'd never even heard of the Seychelles. We were all so different, but sitting there in adjoining cubicles at all hours of the day and night brought us close. It made us a family.

And because of the amount of time we spent together, these people knew me and my dreams way before I was willing to declare them aloud.

Apparently, I was always singing. That's why they called me The Creative One. They were always egging me on, telling me to sing, go on, sing. I told them to shut up and leave me alone, but they were on to me. Yes, I had dreams. I just had no idea how anyone went about living dreams this big.

Once, when Lena asked me what I was doing here—why wasn't I doing music?—I told her what I'd been telling myself for years: that there just wasn't a place for music like mine in the world today. I was born in the wrong era. I should've been born in the sixties, I said. Now, the only way for a girl to make it in music was to take her clothes off in a video clip and do what the record companies told you. I told her I didn't want to take off my clothes in video clips. I didn't want my songs to be about how sexy I was. (Lena joked, in her mother's voice, 'Isn't that obvious enough, just by looking at you?')

But she kept calling me on it. She said I was being a chicken. She said, How long are you going to stay here, hiding in your little cubicle? She said I had bigger fish to fry. Why else would

I sing so much in between my calls? Did I? I asked. Yes, she said. Always. She told me I could be out there touring with Jeff Bentley, or whatever his name was, anytime I wanted. She said all he did was moan, like a cow or something. At least I could actually sing! I told her to shut up, I loved Jeff, and it was Buckley, not Bentley, by the way.

The first time I ever heard Jeff Buckley sing live was in Gaslight Music in 1994 with only fifty other people in the room. I'd bought his album, *Grace*, earlier that week, and by grace I was told that Jeff was coming to town. He was going to play an instore. I was given a ticket. I wasn't sure what to expect.

But seeing him play live that night changed my life. It made me realise how much modern music could mean—that it wasn't just disposable. How it had power. How when Jeff sang, so pure, and then so funny and cheeky between songs, it felt like someone had heard me. I felt known. I felt alive. I felt hope. Music really did matter. Something in his voice, in watching him perform live, unlocked something in me.

Jealousy, for a start. I wouldn't admit it at the time, but with hindsight it's clear to me that every time I feel jealous of someone, or something, it's because there's some fear hiding in there. In this case, my fear was with what I thought to be the immutable facts of the situation: I was fat, and no record company was ever going to sign a fat girl like me. And the truth is, I kind of had a point.

In the 1990s, there was only one way to have a sustainable music career—you had to win the attention of a mainstream audience. At the very least, you needed a massive fan base, and the only way to get that fan base was through signing to a record company; to people who had massive budgets, who could pay for your recording, your advertising, your touring, and—all going to plan—somehow get your song on the radio. Without them, it was hard for your fans to find you. And to go mainstream you needed to fit the bill. And the bill, as far as my mind was concerned, was: don't be fat.

Even though the voice in my head told me it was pointless to try, pointless to write songs at all, *no one wanted to hear songs like yours*, seeing Jeff Buckley, feeling what I felt that night, somehow gave my latent ambition new ammunition, and I once again started writing songs. At home, in my bedroom in my share house in North Melbourne, I found my old cassette recorder, pressed play and record, just like I had as a child, and—using only my three chords, and the truth of whatever I was feeling at that moment—sang my heart out. I did it again the next night, and the night after that. It was as though my heart had cracked open a little, and now I was beginning to think crazy things. What if, what if, what if 'songwriting' was what I got to do with my life?

I had been happy at the call centre that first year: happy to entertain the thought that maybe I would end up being a normal person after all. I would be someone who wore a suit, and had a job, and maybe a mortgage, and I'd get promoted, and maybe one day Joffa would ask me to marry him, and we would have kids, and things would finally settle for me. Inside me.

Joffa and I fell in love in high school, when we were just seventeen. On the night of our first kiss, it was raining. In the seconds just before his lips touched mine for the first time, I remember the feeling in my stomach, like flying. Like something was right, for once. He was wearing a denim jacket with a woollen lining. He smelled of washing powder and beer and cigarettes and musky deodorant and chewing gum and his skin was so soft. And when he put his arms around me and drew me in, I knew this was meant to happen.

Our love affair was instant and brilliant and stretched on for years to come. At first, we just fit: saucepan and lid, yin and yang. We were like an old married couple, always going out for coffee and cuddling up on the couch with a cup of tea and a movie, cooking meals, playing adults. Things grew very serious very quickly, and before long we were so in love we could hardly bear to be apart at all. When we weren't together, we were on the phone, or writing letters to each other. Handwritten letters, three times a week. I still have them. We folded ourselves into each other's lives, each other's families. His mother cooked vegetarian curries for me, my mother gave him the lamb shank from the Sunday roast. He lived closer to our school than me, and in Year Twelve, for reasons that I dared not question, my parents allowed me to stay overnight at his house during the week. Although we were supposed to sleep in different rooms, we didn't really. Nobody said anything. I still remember lying with my head on his bare chest, listening to his heart. He told me he wanted to spend his whole life with me; that he had never known a love like this and he probably never would again.

I wish we had been able to keep things sweet.

At the very least, when they changed, I wish one of us had called it, quickly and cleanly.

It was not to be.

Perhaps it was the stress of the exams, the expectation of our future weighing on us, but by the end of Year Twelve things had begun to feel strained between us. Even though I knew it was almost impossible for childhood relationships to survive the transition to independence, to adulthood, I had occasionally dared to imagine that we might be the exception. However, what started as bickering soon progressed into a style of fighting ugly enough to make me think: this is not right. I considered cutting the cord, but was tortured by the worry that to do so would be a betrayal. I just needed to try harder. To stick it out. And in silencing what I suspect was the truth, I returned, once more, to the comfort of food, to that habit of eating down my emotions, my unhappiness, and my ballooning weight yet again became a source of unspoken, dominating, shame.

Joffa had his own demons, most notably a soft spot for dope. I, on the other hand, hated it. It triggered a panic in me so all-encompassing that, by the time I was seventeen, it was already clear that I was not the kind of person who should take drugs. I knew that, and he knew that. At first, out of politeness, he kept his habit to himself, but as the pressure of Year Twelve set in, getting stoned soon became his favourite thing to do. The amount he smoked worried me, and I told him so. He said I should mind my own business; he wasn't hurting anyone. He was hurting himself, I said. What was I, his mother? It became

A Thing. The tenderness and respectfulness that had been such a feature of our relationship began to fray.

That summer, after our final exams, his family took me with them on holiday to Noosa. At the famous Eumundi Markets, I saw a lady with a beautiful wooden-bead necklace that was *so* beautiful I became obsessed with replicating it. I wasn't sure where to buy beads like hers so, as an experiment, I bought a bag of borlotti beans from the supermarket, borrowed Joffa's dad's power drill, drilled a hole through each one, lacquered them and strung them on fishing wire. This was the kind of thing I did for fun, when Joffa and his brothers and their girl-friends were at the beach. Having something to do—a job or a project—just always made me feel so much calmer. More settled.

Joffa couldn't understand it. Why didn't I come out to the beach? And why didn't I want to join him and his brothers at the nightclub, drinking cocktails? What was I gonna do—stay at home every day, drinking cups of Earl Grey tea by the fire with his parents?

Well, yes, actually! Couldn't think of anything better!

One day, feeling brave, I agreed to join Joffa and his brothers and their girlfriends for an evening at a nightclub in Noosa. In the back of the car with Joffa, Mother Love Bone on the stereo, window down, wind blowing in my hair, I remember feeling young, and wild, and free. But as we entered the highway, with the car now speeding around thirty kilometres above the speed limit, that old bad feeling began to swell in my stomach. I told myself to relax, we'd be fine, but it just didn't work. When I too casually asked the driver to please slow down, he thought it was funny, and then I just felt like a prude, and stopped talking at all. For fun, the driver decided to see if he could drive and pull a cone at the same time. I didn't think that was a good idea, and I said so, but my distress seemed to be taken on as some kind of challenge and, before long, the passenger in the front seat had pulled out a bong, packed a tight little cone, set it up between the driver's knees, and—after one two three—a lighter flickered and the pipe was lit. I watched in disembodied terror as the driver, still speeding, sucked back the cone, held his breath for what felt like an eternity, and then puckered his lips to blow the smoke out the window like a victorious dragon while Joffa and the other passenger hooted in celebration.

I did not hoot. I just sat there, frozen in silence, the feeling of badness gushing through me, my heart beating so loud and fast in my chest that I had to hold my body to the seat to stop it from leaping out of the still speeding vehicle.

I got drunk that night. Really, really drunk. And it was only with the alcohol in my system that I was able to finally admit to myself that Joffa and I were growing in completely different directions. I didn't feel safe with him anymore. I knew that I needed to say something, but for reasons I didn't understand at the time, the thought of breaking up with him filled me with guilt so sticky, so true feeling, I just couldn't seem to do it.

Curiously, a month later, when he did it, when he said the words, I was . . . crushed. Absolutely crushed. I cried and cried, and after months of on again, off again, on again, off again, we decided to give it one more shot. And then another. And then another. And soon, what had once felt like home, began to feel more like the horror of addiction gone bad. We were not right for each other, yet we could not seem to make the break.

✳

'Good afternoon, Martin Dawes Telecommunications, my name is Clare, how may I help you?'

That first year at the call centre, I learned what a KPI was, and I took great joy in watching Hannah tick mine off, month after month. I had proven to myself that, when I wanted to, I could fit in.

But did I really want to?

After seeing Jeff Buckley play, I understood for the first time the transformative power of live music. I felt something calling me, a growing restlessness. I began to wonder, is this really where I'm supposed to end up?

One quiet afternoon, trying to make Georgie laugh, I surprised myself by answering a call in my mother's voice.

'Good afternoon, velkom to Martin Dawes, my name is Frida. How may I help you?'

Georgie laughed so hard, I had to put my customer on hold and tell her to shut up. I kept up the Dutch accent for as long as I could, riding on the joke, but eventually my mouth grew tired and I told the customer I was going to connect her through to a colleague who could help. I put her on hold, caught my breath, and picked up the phone in my normal voice

'Good afternoon, my name is Clare. I understand you need some assistance with your mobile phone?'

We laughed so hard that day. The hours flew by. As long as I was still being of assistance to the customer, I didn't see the harm in having a little fun.

This trick of answering calls in different voices soon became my regular schtick. I did as many accents as I could. I began to build characters around each accent, then construct back-stories. It felt like I was writing a new page of a short story every time I answered the phone.

My favourite character of all, the one that got the most laughs from my colleagues, was Candy Pants. In my mind, Candy Pants was a close relative of Dolly Parton. She sounded just like her.

'Good afternoon, Martin Dawes Telecommunications, my name's Candy Pants. How may I help you sir or ma'am?'

One Friday, just before I clocked off for the week, Candy Pants came to town. I was having a wonderful time of it, right up until I heard an unusual sound on the line. *Click*. My heart sank.

You know how sometimes when you call customer service and you're on hold there's a message that says, 'Your call may be monitored for training and quality assurance. Please let the supervisor know if you don't want your call to be monitored'? On that Friday, towards the end of Candy Pants' call, I heard the sound of a second click, and that is when I got it: I'd just been monitored for quality assurance.

When the call ended, I took off my headset. I knew what was coming next. Hannah walked over, smiled, asked me if

I wouldn't mind coming with her for a moment. I joined her behind her partition. I was mortified.

'I am so sorry!' I said. 'I don't know what's wrong with me. I was just mucking around. I'm really sorry.'

Hannah replied, 'Clare, I've already told you you're good at your job. I see the leadership potential in you. If that's something you want to develop, you're in the right place. But—and I don't want you to take this the wrong way—it seems really obvious to me, and to everyone here . . . well, have you ever considered a career in the creative arts?'

I felt myself blush. Was it that obvious?

I told Hannah not to be silly. I was sorry and I'd cut it out. I needed this job. It felt like the only thing going right in my life.

In the end, it was Joffa who said the words.

He had terrible timing. Terrible.

We were twenty now. Nearly twenty-one. Joffa was living in a share house with his brothers. There were beer cans and bongs everywhere. I'd been advised never to eat the brownies in the fridge. This was at the height of Joffa's love for dope. He loved it like he loved his dog. He lived for it. He couldn't imagine a day without it. He was so used to it that he could quite easily pull three cones before breakfast, put drops in his eyes, and still sit up straight for a visit from his grandmother. I remember her once telling Joffa that I was marriage material, and how he laughed.

It's not like he wasn't showing me who he was. It's not like he was leading me on. But I just kept thinking—kept kidding myself—he still loved me. We were going to work this out. He needed me. It never occurred to me that, maybe, he'd be fine without me.

But there had been signs that this was coming. Just the week before, at a party at his house, some girl I barely knew came up to me and slurred, 'You need to fuck off! He doesn't love you anymore!'

I was so shocked, so ashamed of being shouted at in public, I turned bright pink, walked into the backyard and looked up at the sky, sniffing and blinking and trying not to cry. What am I doing here? I wondered. What is wrong with me? Why can't I let this go?

Joffa found me, told me the girl didn't know what she was talking about. Told me to come inside. So I did. I still wanted his approval. I mistook it for love. With his arm around me, I thought anything was possible. I still felt it, flashes of that first-night feeling, that 'This is right' feeling, long after the wrong had set in. I thought I needed to stay. That it was my responsibility to save him. I didn't see it then, but it's as clear as day to me now: I thought he was killing himself. I was not going to let him die on my watch. But there was another thought at play here—one I kept pushing to the back of mind. If I was being really honest, I had to admit that I thought there was no one else in the world who would ever love me the way Joffa once had. The voice in my head said it again and again: *Who else could possibly love a girl as fat and broken as you?*

This was how I spoke to myself, back then. I had no idea of the trouble I was already in. No idea of the stories I was telling myself.

No idea that he and I were separate people, even. I thought we owed each other something; something more than this.

Just before we broke up, I noticed that his kiss was different.

It had already been clear for over a year, ever since that holiday in Noosa, that things were not going to work out. I used to lecture him about his dope, until one day he looked at me and said, 'Look who's talking, Clare. You're a fucking mess. You can't stop eating. Don't come over here telling me I have to get my life together when you are no better yourself.'

He was right. One hundred per cent.

Still, I was furious. Devastated. Didn't speak to him for two weeks.

But then, somehow, we played on and on, until the night when he finally said the words that would close the door on this love affair. We were in bed when he said it. Said, 'Babe, stop. We need to talk.'

He never said things like that. My heart started thumping.

'What?' I said.

'I'm sorry, we have to stop.'

'What's wrong?'

And then out tumbled the truth.

He couldn't do it anymore. Said he cared for me, but he wasn't in love with me anymore. Said we needed to break up, for good. Said, 'I'm sorry.' And he was sorry. I could hear it in his voice. But what I also heard was that he was . . . done. All this time, I'd thought I was here protecting him, but now I saw it was in fact him who had been trying to protect me. Trying not to embarrass me. Trying to let me down gently. And he didn't want the job anymore. He was tired of it. He was done. And that, I suppose, is where the old shame set in.

I rolled over, sat up, heard myself—sharp breath—sucking in air. Holding the doona to my chest, I felt a shame so grand and tall and old that all I could say was, 'I beg your pardon?', and pretend, for one second longer, that I hadn't heard him.

He repeated himself, more gently this time, but I was already off, crawling on the floor in the dark looking for my keys, saying, 'Yep, got it. Yep. No worries. Yep.'

I was pulling on my clothes as he turned on the light. He was wearing one sock, and a t-shirt. He followed me around the room, trying to apologise. He told me not to take it personally. When he said things were just 'getting so unhealthy', I stopped him there, said, 'Unhealthy? For fuck's sake. Since when did you prioritise health? Is that why you're stoned all the time? For your health?'

He went quiet. The only sound in the room was me talking to myself as I hunted for my other sandal, telling myself *I am a fucking idiot. I can't believe I wasted all this time thinking this would work out. What a fucking idiot.*

Somewhere in my scrambling, I accidentally knocked over his bong. Stinky water all over the carpet. I said, 'Shit shit shit,' but he was calm as ever. He just grabbed a towel to clean it up, asked if I wanted a cup of tea.

I looked at him. 'No, thanks. Go fuck yourself!'

I walked out the door without saying goodbye, carrying a feeling in me so sharp, so bad, I doubted it was possible to live through it.

I did not look back, I just walked to my car, felt the cold night air slapping the top of my ears, slapping the tops of my toes where my sandals left my skin exposed, and that was how it ended. That was how I left the home and the heart of the man who once told me he would love me forever but had now changed his mind.

When I think back to this moment, I can still feel the heat of that shame in my chest. I remember how my hands shook as I inserted my keys into the ignition, how fast I drove off, how my head started racing, and how there was a wildness in me after that, a danger. In my head, the voice piped up, a loud story about how maybe, on a whim, I should crash my car into a tree. *That would show him.*

When I caught myself thinking that thought, imagined the horror of it actually playing out, I was filled with a flash of panic so hot and strong I pulled the car over on the side of the road to calm myself down.

And still, inside my head, the words kept racing.

Fuck him, said the voice in my head. *He will be sorry one day. FUCK HIM. You don't need him.*

That's when the idea came to me: one clear idea, to cut through, to lift me above the horror of the rejection. I am going to move to London, I decided, and I am not going to come home until I am thin.

Why thin? Why not . . . brilliant? *Because,* said the voice in my head, *that's not why he dumped you. He dumped you because you got fat. And the best way to shove it in his face is to go away, and come back thin.*

I felt better now that I had a plan. I didn't have to feel like such a loser, I could focus on something else: on a future in which things would work out for the best. On the way home, I pulled over at a servo, where I bought a Diet Coke, a pack of smokes, and a big fistful of Freddo Frogs. Every time I stopped at a red light, I either lit a cigarette, or cracked open a Freddo with my teeth. Last supper eating, I told myself. Tomorrow, my new life would begin.

The next day, I woke up angry, and on fire. I was going to get out of this shithole, out of this town, this job, this horrible feeling. I was going to grow the fuck up. I was leaving.

There was just one small problem with this plan; not enough money. So I took on a second job at a second call centre. I'd leave Martin Dawes at five o'clock and start at the second call centre at seven. I'd wake early in the morning and go to the gym. I tried not to eat, but always failed. I would start my diet as soon as I got on the plane, I said. I hardly slept. The loud voice in my head got louder, urging me ever onwards.

No more being pathetic, Clare. No more. Come on, you fat fuck: show the world what you're made of. Show him you don't need him. Don't look back. Forward only.

Joffa called, but I did not call him back.

Once, at the end of a long day, when I hadn't slept much or eaten much, the bad feeling came on so strong I was sure that something terrible had happened or was about to happen. My hands started shaking. I was sweating everywhere. My heart felt like it was going to fly out of my chest. I knew this feeling— it was the same one I had had on the day Rowena died. What if that feeling was a clue that something equally terrible had happened? What if it was Mum, or Dad? What if it was Joffa?

I didn't know the feeling had a name. I didn't know this was a panic attack.

I would call Mum, in tears, asking if she and Dad were okay.

They were fine, said Mum. Everything was fine.

Joffa. What if it was Joffa?

I rang him. He answered. As soon as I heard his voice, I hung up. I just needed to know he was alive, that was all.

Everyone was fine; absolutely fine.

But the feeling seemed to lodge itself in me then. I kept telling myself I would be in London soon and things would be better. I would feel all right once I lost the weight.

I gave notice at Martin Dawes. My friends threw me a going-away party, gave me an oversized novelty card and a stuffed bear with well wishes written in black texta on its body. I was going to miss them something terrible.

I had my plane ticket now. I was on my way. I was never going to feel this bad again, I said. I was never going to let anyone dismiss me the way Joffa had. I was going to do something that mattered. I was going to be someone. And, I reminded myself, I was not coming home until I was thin. Thin as a willow, thin as a pancake, thin as a rake. Thin.

I did have other dreams, you know, besides getting thin.

My diaries weren't just full of diets.

I also wrote about other things, like exercise. Lots and lots of exercise that I planned to do, but never really got around to.

And also, occasionally, I wrote about grander things. Like the dream I'd had since I was four, the dream that one day, when I grew up, just like Miss Piggy, I would be a famous sing— *Don't even say it!* scolded the voice in my head. *Don't! Fat girls don't get to be famous singers! Shut up, lose the weight,* then *we can talk about the singing.*

That was the story I had told myself for most of my life: that I was too big to be a famous singer. Don't even think about it.

But that night, the night before I left for London, I sat down and wrote a list, a long true list, about all the things I wanted to do with my life and who I wanted to be, and how I was not going to live a little life. I was going to a live a big life. An amazing life! That's what I called my list, in fact:

My Amazing Life.

In my neatest possible handwriting, I wrote down that one day, I would:

— write a novel
— make an album
— act in the theatre
— learn a language
— run fast
— do something that meant something, something that made people feel included, something that helped people
— travel *everywhere*
— make a million dollars (minimum)

– and if I was lucky, one day, I was going to love, and be loved. I was going to meet the man of my dreams, we were going to have a house in the hills with a garden and a fireplace, and we were going to make music and soup and drink wine and read each other poetry and it was going to be just like a Joni Mitchell song, only happy.

And then, if I was really, *really* lucky, I was going to:

– be a mother
– and then a grandmother too—one of those really cool ones, who still stood up and did the lambada at family parties, even when she was ninety.

Then I closed my diary, tucked it into my backpack, blew out my candle, and fell asleep in my childhood bed for the last time in . . . maybe ever.

I was going to do it all, as quickly as possible.

I was going to live an amazing life, starting right now.

5

Thin skin

Born into this skin, that feels just a little too thin
Skin I'm never sure if I belong in.

'THIN SKIN'
(*The Winter I Chose Happiness*, 2012)

For the plane trip to London, I brought a packed lunch—a large salad with a balsamic vinegar dressing. It felt like a good symbolic start to this new phase of my life. It was like I was saying: 'From now on in, I'm going to take care of myself.' By which I meant I was going to stick to my diet, no matter what.

Unfortunately, sometime between the departure gate and the announcement that *You may now take off your seatbelts and move around the cabin freely*, my packed lunch leaked all over my carry-on baggage and other people's too.

I first became aware of the spillage when I felt something cold drip on my face from above. I put my finger to it, looked at my finger: rusty red!

Blood?

No—just balsamic vinegar.

Oh, bugger.

I had planned to eat only once on the flight: just that one salad, perhaps with a Diet Coke, or sparkling water with lemon, and some black coffee.

I had to keep telling myself I wasn't hungry, even though I was.

Nerves, I thought. Just nerves. Hold steady, woman!

With steely determination, I declined the flight attendant's kind offer of peanuts. That felt good. New. Powerful. I liked it. *No, thank you.* I practised saying it in my head, using my best British accent. *No, but thank you. Oh, thank you, but not for me, I couldn't possibly.*

All around me, the rustle of wrappers, the crunch of peanut after peanut and my hunger so loud in my stomach that by the time we were flying over the Great Australian Bight, I was just about ready to eat my own fist.

I held tight for another hour, but somewhere over the Indian Ocean, when the flight attendant again offered snacks—not just peanuts this time but ice-cream too—I persuaded myself it would be rude to decline a second time.

I'd start my diet again, start properly, when I was in London.

It was soon night. The moon seemed to follow us the whole way. Mum had said to look out for angels ('Mum! Please!'), but I didn't see any. It took about forty hours to get to London, including stopovers, but eventually we landed at Gatwick Airport. I collected my luggage. A customs officer looked at my guitar and asked if I intended to work while I was in the UK. I did have a working visa, so I said yes, but not with the guitar. I didn't know how to play it yet, I told him. Unsmiling, he stamped my passport, said, 'Next.'

My friend Libby met me at the airport. We planned to stay together at her friend Phil's house, in Golders Green. When we arrived, I had a shower, got changed, told myself I wasn't going to sleep I was just resting my head for a moment, and woke up seven hours later. It was 3 am. I was very hungry, but a voice inside me said: *Too bad. We're in London now. You're on a diet.* So I had a coffee, and wrote in my diary.

The next day, Phil took us on the bus to Piccadilly Circus, and then to Harrods, where we bought tzatziki and tomato, cucumber, breadstick and oranges. I pulled out my penknife, sliced it all up, and as I ate I felt as though this might well be the most delicious meal I'd ever eaten in my life. On my portable cassette player, Libby and I interviewed each other to mark the start of our adventure. On the tape, our voices are full of confidence, and hope.

On the Tube back to Golders Green, I tried to learn the names of all the stations. I wanted to settle in as quickly as possible.

That night, Libby and I stayed up late drinking beers and watching the sun set over the rooftops of Golders Green. We made spaghetti, then drank some more—cheap red wine this time. Later, we pulled out the tape recorder again, took turns interviewing each other, and then spent the rest of the night singing and dancing to songs on the radio. I didn't realise how much we'd drunk until Libby asked if I could pass her a cigarette.

'But you don't smoke!' I said.

'Oh yeah!' she said.

I realised pretty quickly that I was going to need to get a job. I couldn't believe how expensive everything was, especially things like fruit and vegetables.

I was now a couple of weeks into my stay in London, and my diet . . . it wasn't going as well as planned. As far as I could tell, I still hadn't lost any weight. In my diary, I wrote that a part of me had hoped that when I got to London I would somehow, magically, be able to *stick to a fucking diet for once*. But I just couldn't seem to. It wasn't even 'being fat' that was getting to me—it was that I cared as much as I did about being fat. Back and forth I went between caring and defiance, dieting and bingeing, a ping-pong affair that kept me busy and distracted and failing, failing, always failing. I wanted it to stop and, I told myself, the easiest way to make it stop was just to do what I did when I was ten and lose all the fucking weight.

I repeated to myself again and again that I was not going home until I was fit and healthy, by which I meant thin. I didn't want to use the word 'thin', not even in my diary. I thought it made me sound shallow. I didn't want to be shallow. I wanted to mean something.

But what, exactly?

One night, Libby and I went to a concert at St Martin-in-the-Fields that was just glorious. Candles and incense. Vivaldi's *Four Seasons*, Handel's *Gloria* and 'The Arrival of the Queen of Sheba'. Queen of Sheba: that was how my dad always described people who were up themselves. I missed him so much those first few weeks in London. He always made me feel so safe, as if everything was going to be all right.

The orchestra was made up of musicians from the University of East London. Apparently, the conductor was retiring after forty years and this was his last concert. Everyone sang 'Hallelujah' at the end and I recorded it secretly on my Walkman, just like I used to do at Jeff Buckley concerts.

I'd been doing this for years now: just recording sounds—birds singing, or even the drone of air-conditioning units or a whistling kettle—and then listening back to them at night and writing songs over the top. I thought this made me a bit of a weirdo, so I kept it to myself. Tapes and tapes of sounds and half-songs, all stacked in a box under my bed at home. Would I ever write anything good enough to share?

I'd been fiddling, actually, with the list I wrote before I left for London, the one about the amazing life I wanted to live. I didn't really have a chorus yet, not anything I was happy with, but I did have a melody and a little bit of finger-picking that seemed to work quite nicely for the verses. It went:

You want to write a novel
Make beautiful music
Act in the theatre with inspiring humans

Learn a language
Run like the wind
Help people fit in
Travel to every country
Make a million dollars
Smile when your children have babies
Make the heart your home, inviting and warm.
You want an amazing life . . .

That was all I had so far.

Later that month, after I saw Patti Smith play live at Shepherd's Bush and was blown away by her rock, I tried to play my 'Amazing Life' song back to myself, but somehow became embarrassed at how *soft* I was.

Why was I so soft?

Why couldn't I be strong, like Patti Smith?

The voice in my head told me that it was probably best I just *put that awful song away and never think of it again. Imagine what Patti Smith would say if she heard it.* She'd think I was such a *fucking loser.*

It didn't really matter who I was comparing myself to, the voice in my head told me again and again in no uncertain terms that I would *never, ever match up. Why are you even trying?*

One morning at breakfast, I did some calculations and realised I was almost out of money already. I'd thought my savings would last much longer but the Aussie dollar was in a bad way. I felt it growing tight inside me, this thought, this worry, about what I was going to do about money. I hadn't really expected to be feeling like this so soon. After a coffee with Libby, I went out on my own and somehow ended up at McDonald's for a second breakfast, which was *not* on the diet plan.

It was a Sunday. I was missing my mum. I went out looking for a church and entered the first one I passed. I figured it was Greek Orthodox because the guy at the front was wearing a crown and people were kissing his hand. I didn't understand anything they were saying or doing; I started to wonder if I was allowed to be in here. People were looking at me strangely—or maybe I was looking at them strangely? I didn't know.

It felt, all of a sudden, like air was thick in my throat, and I just couldn't seem to get enough of it, no matter how hard I tried, so I just stood there in the foyer, crying and gulping for air, and telling myself loudly in my head to *stop being such a fucking idiot! PULL IT TOGETHER!* A moment later, when a lady approached me, asking me if she could get me anything, I tried to speak, to tell her I was fine, but the only words I could choke out were 'Thank you'. And then I was so embarrassed, I just . . . fled, back down the steps, out onto the street, leaning over in the sunlight, crying and trying to catch my breath.

This was not like me. I never cried in public. Not like this. I mean, I cried when I was a kid but it was always for a particular reason, like I grazed my knee, or someone called me a mean name. This crying felt like it was for a million reasons and, at the same time, I couldn't pinpoint even one. This crying felt like there was no use talking about it because it wouldn't make any sense, ever. Maybe I was missing Joffa? Or maybe I was just disappointed to discover that it was true what everyone said: it doesn't matter how far you run, you really do take your feelings with you.

All I knew was I needed to work this out. I had not come to London to cry. I was here to start my amazing life, for fuck's sake!

Further down the street I found a seat, pulled out my diary and a pen and did what I always liked to do when I needed to get my life under control: I made a bloody good plan.

How many months until February? Six months. Okay. If I worked from now until December and saved some money, I could then spend two months travelling through Ireland, France, Italy, the Czech Republic and Spain, then maybe stop in India on the way home, where I would enrol in the course that Libby had done: the Bachelor of Creative Arts at Melbourne Uni. This sounded really, really good, I thought. Good. Good. I wrote list within list within list and, soon, this was looking like a plan. I was beginning to feel better.

But what about my diet? I needed a new plan for that, too, because whatever I'd been trying up until now just wasn't working. I had to get serious about this. I needed something bold. A goal.

In my diary I wrote:

Q. What is my goal?
A. To become the healthiest person I know.

Q. What are my vices?
A. 1. Shit food and too much of it.

   2. Animals—as in, eating them.

   3. Cigarettes.

    4. Coffee.

    5. Tea.

    6. Alcohol.

Q. What is my plan?

A. 1. Give up <u>shit food</u>. No more animals! (Only fish.)

    2. No more <u>coffee</u>.

    3. No more <u>tea</u>. (Go the herbal!)

    4   Give up smoking and drinking forever.

As I wrote, the bad feeling gradually began to subside, and in its place I felt a sense of calm, a sense of hope. I could do this. I could do this.

Q. When will I begin my plan?

A. MIDNIGHT TONIGHT.

I added more detail at the bottom of the page, instructions. With each new directive, I felt that little bit better:

Also:

    i. Drink large quantities of water.

   ii. A minimum of 30 minutes exercise per day.

  iii. 15 minutes of meditation per day.

  iv. Only three meals per day plus two snacks.

Underneath that I wrote:

Goodbye binge drinking!

Goodbye cigarettes!

There. Better. I had made for myself an anchor, and now I could rest easy.

I don't know quite what was different this time, perhaps the level of desperation, but I did stick to that plan. Through headaches, fluctuating emotions and dizziness, I gave up what some would call life's pleasures but my mind at the time was calling vices. I'd given up coffee and tea, and, after limiting myself to three meals a day with such success, I'd even decided to cut it down to two meals a day. I just wanted this over and done with and so, I figured, the less I ate, the quicker we'd be sorted. I must have had some sense that this was a dangerous approach to take to food, because I joked in my diary that it was lucky I was too fat to be anorexic, otherwise I'd be worried right now! I didn't know then that size isn't actually an indication of whether or not you have an eating disorder. I didn't know that an eating disorder is an illness of both the body, and the mind, and you can't look just look at someone, and spot whether or not they have one.

All I knew was that I looked forward to fitting into normal-sized clothes bought from normal-people shops.

I looked forward to being thin.

*

The day before my twenty-first birthday, the phone rang at Phil's place: a call for me.

It was Joffa, ringing to say happy birthday.

I couldn't believe it—how had he got my number?

That day, his voice was light and happy; he sounded better than I'd ever heard him sound. I told him so, and he said that he had changed. He was turning his life around. He'd virtually given up dope now, he said. And then he just talked about all the stuff that was on his mind, like gigs that he'd been to and how he was looking for a job. He said life was a bit boring without dope but, then again, sitting on the couch watching TV all day sucking back cones wasn't really that much fun either. I bit my tongue. It was so weird to hear him talk like this, as though . . . as though he really wanted to talk to me. It had been so long since I'd felt that from him. I got excited, I think. What if . . . ? What if we . . . ?

That night, I lay in bed reading *The Little Prince*, pondering the question of self-determination, and what kind of adult I wanted to be when I turned twenty-one (a truly grown-up age). In this famous book, the narrator (the Pilot) tells the story of his first drawing at age six, which he describes as a picture of a boa constrictor swallowing an elephant. When he shows his masterpiece to the adults around him, they think it is a hat, and he has to re-draw his picture, with less mystery, so they understand it more clearly. That night, I thought hard on this concept—on whether it was possible to be both a grown-up with your shit together and, at the same time, continue to see past boring concepts like 'a hat', and into the possibility of a boa constrictor swallowing an elephant. Was it conceivable to retain the imagination of our childhoods, and be a successful grown-up at the same time? I wasn't sure. All I knew was, I hadn't had the easiest day of it.

That morning I'd tried to cash a traveller's cheque, the last of my money, but I'd been denied for some reason—the wrong ID or something—and I'd spent the rest of the day feeling like a *pathetic LOSER with no money*, trying to work out what I could eat that cost less than two pounds. I knew I could have asked Libby for help, but I didn't want to.

I gave myself a big talking to. *What the hell was wrong with me? Why couldn't I ever seem to make anything work? Why had I even come to London in the first place? What did I think would change?*

That night, I decided, things *were* going to change.

I was going to take more risks.

I was going to put myself out there.

And if the chance came up, I was going to do some more singing. Not just on my own in my bedroom, but out there, in the world.

The very next night, at a bar with Libby celebrating my twenty-first, that chance did come up. The singer of the three-piece band playing in the corner asked if anyone knew the words to this old jazz song—'Summertime'—and, without thinking, I stood up and yelled, 'Me! Me!', ran to the stage, grabbed the mic and sang my little heart out. It felt so good. Libby took a photo of me afterwards, in the car park with the band, arms around each other's shoulders, and I am smiling ear to ear.

At home, however, after the buzz had worn off and everyone had gone to sleep, I started missing Joffa again. I hadn't been able to stop thinking about him since he'd called. I knew it was crazy, but imagine if he and I did end up together after all?

So, using my long-distance calling card, I rang him, just to say hi. He answered the phone, said, 'Hey, Clare! Sorry to be rude, but I'm just on my way out.' Nothing else. *Fuck, you're a loser,* said the old voice in my head.

I called Mum after that, and thanked her for giving birth to me. 'Good work, Maria.'

She laughed.

After that, I went to the kitchen and ate some cake, wondering what the fuck I was going to do with my life.

Not that I would ever have admitted it to Mum, or anyone, but I wrote a prayer in my diary that night.

Dear God,

I want to be a tool of peace: I really, really do.

I want to do something good with my life, make the most of my life, but I just don't feel like there is a place for me.

Please please please—uncover my eyes so that I can see where I belong. Let me see beauty in something again.

God—give me a sign, please. Tell me what I'm supposed to do with my life. I mean, I feel PATHETIC asking, but really—what the fuck am I supposed to do with my life? Why did you put me here? Give me a sign so clear that I cannot deny it. I am so thick, God: you need to make it very clear. Where do you want me?

With thanks,

Clare (of Melbourne)

✳

Phil had two new housemates: two noisy Spaniards with a penchant for red wine, who then stayed up all night doing acrobatics in the room next door. That is not a euphemism, by the way. Libby and I could never quite work it out, but from the sounds of the thumps and crashes and laughter we concluded they were, actually, practising acrobatics. We never got to the bottom of the story. They didn't speak English, we didn't speak Spanish. They seemed to think that everything we said was funny. No matter how many times we asked them to please keep it down, they did not.

In the morning, Libby had planned to take a train to Paris. Phil and I went with her on the Tube to see her off. Phil had been out drinking the night before and had arrived home only a few hours prior. He was carrying Libby's big backpack, and we were talking, and as we stepped into the carriage I glanced at Phil and saw something I've never forgotten—his eyes rolled to the back of his head, and then the rest of him fell backwards, like a big tall tree, and collapsed onto the floor of the train. I was closest so I got to him first. I leaned over his face, saw his eyes were open, that he was not moving, checked his breathing, but there was so much noise behind me I couldn't be sure. In my head the old voice was saying: *He is dead. Dead. Dead. Dead.* And with that thought the most enormous electric shock of horror flowed through my body, although my voice stayed calm enough. I said something like, 'AMBULANCE, NOW!' Some stranger held open the door, another helped me remove his backpack and drag him off the train. Once on the platform, as Libby ran for help, Phil surprised us all by quickly springing to his feet, like a jack-in-the-box, before falling down again.

I cradled Phil's head in my lap, could see he was breathing, drifting in and out of consciousness, and as I stroked his head and tried to reassure him that everything was okay, there was a stillness in me, a feeling similar to the one I had the day Rowena died. All around was panic but in me there was stillness. It was shock, I suppose.

Soon, a first-aid officer arrived. Libby fetched some water for Phil, he drank it, he got up, and the first-aid officer checked him over and said he would be okay. I can't explain why, but at that moment my calmness left me and instead I was overwhelmed by the feeling of something being very wrong, so wrong that we could never make it right again.

In the cab to Golders Green Phil blacked out again, then woke up, breathing erratically. I felt like an ill-equipped mother, trying to smile at him, hold him up, tell him everything would be all right. My mind kept flashing back to memories from my childhood, to the Royal Children's Hospital, to Rowie, and Mum, and Mum reading stories to Rowie, and the sound of the life-support machine beeping—all the things I had tried for so long not to think about.

At home, Phil drank some water then started to fall asleep. My anxiety grew; I didn't think he should be sleeping. What if he slipped into a coma? I gave him a stir, told him I thought it would probably be safer if we did just go to the hospital, and have him properly checked out. Back in the cab we went.

At the hospital, they confirmed that Phil was suffering from a serious case of—wait for it—suspected dehydration. Could it have been the booze? It was possible. More tests would be needed. And, yes, he needed more sleep. Nothing more serious than that, they said.

Phil was fine. Absolutely fine. But for reasons I did not understand, I was not fine.

I called Mum and Dad, trying to sound calm, but they heard it in my voice, heard my shock, and Mum said, 'You must have got a fright', and she was right. I had. I'd really thought he was dead, I said, and then—without wanting to—I just cried and cried, trying to find words to explain what was going on. Mum kept reassuring me and, eventually, I stopped crying and apologised for making a fuss. They were so far away. There was nothing they could do. I didn't want them to worry.

After that phone call, it still felt like half of me was stuck in a bad dream—like I couldn't quite seem to wake up.

And it bothered me, that day, how loud the passing trucks sounded, how strong the dinner smells from the kitchen were. I looked down at my hands, and they were shaking. I couldn't seem to make them stop. I told myself I'd feel better after I'd had some sleep.

In the morning when I woke, the bad feeling was still there, my mind was racing with dread already and, I thought to myself, I've got to get out of this city.

The noise, the expense, the smells, this feeling of dread; I wanted it all behind me. I needed to be around trees. I wanted to be somewhere quiet for a while. What about Oxford? I'd always loved the idea of one day visiting Oxford. Why not today? Excited, I pulled out my diary, and got to work planning exactly what I was going to do next.

After a shower, I put my things in my backpack, closed the lid on my guitar case, drank a quick coffee, left a note for Phil thanking him for his hospitality, and went off to the bus station to buy a ticket to Oxford.

On the way there, I saw a butterfly on a statue of an angel, and thought of my mother. I wondered if this might be a sign of good things ahead. I'd been looking for signs ever since I got to London; looking for some idea of what I was supposed to do next. The signs I found seemed as good a flag as any.

Oxford in autumn is breathtakingly beautiful, just like the movies. Blue skies, golden trees, gothic spires overlooking you from every corner. Walking from the bus station with my backpack and guitar, I felt hopeful. Maybe this was just what I needed: a few trees, a little peace and quiet, some old buildings to inspire the imagination. Who knows? I thought. Maybe I'll end up loving this place so much, I'll move here.

When I checked into the backpackers—the cheapest I could find mentioned in my Lonely Planet guidebook—the lady behind the counter saw my guitar and asked if I played. A little, I said. She told me that I was in luck; there was an open mic tonight at the local, the Catweazle Club. I felt my heart beat fast in my chest with excitement. This was one of the promises I'd made to myself: that when I was twenty-one, I would start playing my own songs in public. I couldn't play well—I only knew the names of a few chords—but that was no excuse. You didn't need to know the names of chords in order to play your own songs. Maybe I'd try the new song, I thought: the 'Amazing Life' one. It wasn't finished, but I guess I could just play the bit that I had? And if it was awful, who cares? No one knew me here anyway.

And so it was that I ended up that night at the Catweazle Club in Oxford, which was really just a cosy room in an old fire-lit Oxford pub, with tattered red velvet curtains covering the windows and a tiny stage in the corner. Inside this room, the world felt exciting and intimate and new. The event organiser, a friendly fellow called Matt, introduced himself and smiled warmly as I wrote my name on the list. He said when it was my turn I'd hear them call out my name. I leaned my guitar against the bar and, even though I had technically 'given up drinking', I bought myself a beer. Dutch courage, because . . . I felt like I'd need it. I could already feel the heat building in my body. My frosted pint of beer trembled in my hands. What even was this feeling? Was it excitement? Or fear? Both, I suppose.

Once I heard them call my name, heard 'Clare from Australia', the feeling inside me changed. Before I knew it, I was up there on the stool, shaking still, wanting very much to *run, run away!* but I stayed put, and once I was past those first few awkward chords, there it was, that feeling of rightness, as though I was telling the truth for the first time in my life. What a relief it was, to sing my truth, and no one else's. I could do it here in a way that just didn't feel possible at home, where people knew me, might worry about me. It felt . . . vulnerable, and brilliant, like I was doing the exact thing I was born to do. As I sang, it was as though—for the length of the song—all the wrong feelings in me, and in the world, were suddenly put right. The audience was so kind, whooping, clapping, encouraging me when I missed a chord. There were only about twenty of them out there, but that was all I needed: just a few kind people who seemed to get me and my song.

And, still, the applause afterwards came as a shock. It was loud and generous, and someone even whistled. Matt, I think.

How did it sound? No idea. *Probably terrible*, said the voice in my head, but I didn't care. I felt proud of myself just for getting up there. I'd never played my own song in public before; I had faced a fear. It felt . . . exhilarating.

I rushed off stage clumsily, and was almost finished packing up my guitar when Matt came over with a beer for me and said something that has stayed with me all of these years. 'You've got something special about you,' he said. Then he smiled and patted me on the shoulder, as though we were both . . . soldiers. He told me he hoped I'd be back, because they could do with my sort around here.

I was speechless, and embarrassed, and wanted to change the subject, so I asked him where he lived. It turned out he lived on a barge with his girlfriend; a long boat with a fireplace and a bedroom, narrow enough to fit through the canals in Oxford. I'd never even heard of a barge before.

It sounded a hell of a lot nicer than the backpackers, that was for sure. I wasn't looking forward to going back there. Even if they did have private rooms, I couldn't have afforded one. From now on, I'd be sharing my bedroom with ten other girls. Ten strangers—I was dreading it. So, I stayed at the club late that night, watching the other acts perform, feeling too shy to speak to anyone but sensing for the first time in a long time that here in this room, with these songs, I was in a place that felt like home.

*

I didn't sleep well that night, or for many nights to come.

My roommates—girls from all around the world, with no parents and no rules to stick to—came and went at all hours, turning on and off the lights, slamming the doors, tripping, giggling, snoring like drunken sailors.

I lay there in the dark with my Walkman, listening to the joyful music of Nusrat Fateh Ali Khan, just loud enough to block out the sounds in the room, drifting in and out of sleep.

In the morning, I hired a bicycle, and, without any map to speak of, just rode it around the streets, eventually finding myself at an entrance to the university. Wheeling my bicycle down its laneways, walking past places with history, colleges that were grand and old, I once again felt less like a stranger.

Ever since the incident with Phil, I had felt . . . different. For a start, my hands still trembled constantly. Even more curiously I had, for the first time in my life, lost my appetite. Sometimes at night I'd have something hot to eat, like a meal at the pub but, mostly, I just drank coffee.

I registered my name with a few employment agencies that day, and was immediately offered some work in aged care.

It paid five pounds an hour, which was better than nothing, and I could start the following week.

I don't know why I stopped at the chemist to weigh myself. I knew it wasn't a good idea. But for some reason, I did it anyway. To my disappointment, I'd put on a pound. A whole pound. I'd been feeling so happy before and now I just felt gutted. More than that, I felt like an idiot for even caring. I tried to talk myself around. *Stop making a big deal out of it!* But the feeling of failure came upon me strongly and, with it, my missing hunger. I binged that day, going from shop to shop buying food I couldn't afford and shoving it in my mouth with little regard for pleasure or manners or anything really. I ate so much food, I wanted to throw up.

On the ride home, the bad feeling got stuck in me. The old voice in my head. *You absolute fuck-up. Pathetic. No wonder he dumped you.* I let it roll for a bit, that voice. I think I believed it might do me some good, might help me pull myself together. But I noticed somewhere on the bike ride back to the hostel that the voice had gotten crueller than usual, harsh.

I felt the very strong urge to write a list. I wasn't far from the hostel, but I didn't care—I stopped the bike by the kerb, pulled out my diary and began writing anything I could think of that might make me feel better about myself.

THINGS THAT ARE GOOD ABOUT THIS SITUATION:
1. If this was a famine situation, I would be WINNING!
2. Despite the way I trash my body, I am SO healthy and SO strong.

3. I have fair and balanced judgement for almost everything (except myself).

4. Um . . . I possess moderate intelligence (?).

5. Apparently, I have a pretty face. (I'm not trying to be up myself, this is what people tell me. Whatevs!)

6. My family love me.

7. I am a privileged woman born in a lucky country.

8. My friends love me too.

9. I have a voice that sings.

10. I have enough money to live for at least another two weeks without needing to get a job.

11. I can write.

A list like this would normally make me feel better straight away, but that day it just didn't work. The bad feeling, the old story, came back again and again, as dictated by the voice in my head, which was making a full-time job of reminding me: *You are a loser. You are pathetic. You can't even stick to a fucking diet. What the fuck is wrong with you? Fat fuck. You're a big fat fuck. You're an embarrassment. What are you even doing?*

Three nights later, still desperately tired, I was sitting in the common room on my own listening to my Walkman and writing in my diary when a tall skinny greasy-blond-haired stranger walked over and waved something in front of my face. I thought he was asking for a light, so I offered him one. He shook his head and motioned for me to take off my headphones. 'Hey!

How can I help?' I said, just as I would have at Martin Dawes Telecommunications, which now felt many worlds away.

With a thick accent that might have been Polish he said, 'Hey, would you like to come back to my room?'

I was genuinely confused. 'Why?'

'Oh, you don't know?' he said, and smiled, raised his eyebrows, as if I did know. But I didn't, and I felt scared then, and his face changed too—a combination of anger and embarrassment—and he said, 'Ah . . . sorry, I thought you knew.'

Knew what? Something was clearly getting lost in translation here. 'Sorry,' I said. 'What is it you're asking?'

'For you to come back to my room to make love.'

'WHAT?'

The old electric shock of fear ran then from my chest to every other surface of my skin, signalling that I was in danger.

'What the hell are you talking about?' I said loudly. It was just him and me in here. I wanted him to go away, now. He got the picture, loud and clear.

'Sorry,' he said. 'I misunderstood.'

Then he just walked away.

I didn't know what to do, but I knew I didn't feel safe there anymore. My mind was racing a hundred miles an hour. Maybe it was just me? But there was something very creepy and not right about that guy. I wondered if I should say something at the front desk, but it was all so odd—would they think I was making it up?

For a few moments I remained on the couch, alternating between fear and anger. Who the fuck was that guy? Why didn't we have locks on our room? What if he tried to rape me in the middle of the night? (*He's not going to rape you. Why would he rape you? If he was going to rape you, he'd have raped you already. Besides, you're a fat fuck. As if anyone would rape you.*) But I just couldn't make sense of it. I had never seen that guy before. What had I done that had made him think I wanted to have sex with him? Did I look at him funny? Was it my fault?

My body told me to get up and leave, so I did—I walked out onto the street, casting nervous glances over my shoulder, a key in my hand ready to stab anyone who came near me. My mind continued to race. Was I being paranoid? I *was* being paranoid, of course I was. But he was so creepy. What the fuck had he meant when he said, 'Oh, you don't know?' as though . . . what? Was this hostel actually just some big fuck-party? Had I missed the memo? Was that why it was so loud at night with so many people coming and going? What the fuck was I doing there?

That night, as I walked, and raged, a feeling of unreality walked with me. At one point I pinched myself, not quite sure if I was awake or asleep. I wish my father was here. I wish I could hold his hand, just for a second. But he wasn't here. No one was here. No one was looking out for me. What if something happened to me? No one would know.

The voice in my head kept telling me to *get a grip. No one is going to hurt you. It was just a misunderstanding. You're being a fuckwit. Get a grip.*

What I wanted in that moment, more than anything, was Joffa. I wanted him next to me. I had travelled all this way to get as far from him as I could, and all I wanted was to hear his voice again. Just the thought of hearing his voice made me breathe a little easier.

I stepped into a phone booth and called his number. My hands were shaking so much that it took a few attempts. When he answered the phone, my heart dropped. He did not sound happy to hear from me. He sounded stoned. I didn't tell him what had happened at the backpackers; I told myself it would probably sound so stupid, and besides, he'd probably think I was trying to make him jealous and he'd get pissed off at me. He barely said a word, and I didn't have enough credit on my calling card to wait for him to care. As I replaced the receiver on its hook, my hands still shaking, I started to feel faint, dizzy. The voice said, *Maybe someone spiked your tea.*

That night, in my bed, I lay awake yet again, this time with my mother's rosary beads in my hand. I tried not to make noise as I cried. *Pathetic,* I said to myself. *You are fucking pathetic. You are a baby. Grow up.*

I must have dozed off at some point, but when I woke, it was with a startle. It was early still. Dawn was only just breaking. I got up and headed to the shower. I opened the door cautiously. *What if he is in the bathroom?* I looked under all the stalls. Nobody was there.

I hadn't really noticed it before, but the smell of mould in the bathroom was so strong it made me feel ill. My head hurt too. As I showered I recalled a story I'd read once in a magazine about a girl who died from inadvertently inhaling bathroom mould. Cold panic prickled my skin. Was I going to die here?

I then did a thing I'd seen other people do in movies: I slapped myself on the face, turned off the hot water, and stood under the cold water trying to shock myself awake. It worked. *Pull yourself together, Bowditch. Get out, go for a walk.*

So I did. It was quiet at that time of morning. I remember hearing a bird singing. I remember feeling happy then, for just a second, as though things might be okay. As though I might be okay. But a passing truck disturbed my peace, and once again the bad feeling shadowed me, told me I'd need to be careful to make sure I got through the day *without dying*. I had Mum's rosary beads in my pocket. I walked and prayed, said, 'Please, God, protect me.' But from what? This was the most confusing part—that there was no obvious threat to speak of. Just a feeling in me, a bad feeling, like something very wrong was either happening, or about to start.

But that night I could not sleep, not at all. I rang the employment agency after-hours number and told them I was sick, that I wouldn't be able to start the job. I knew I wouldn't be offered another one, but I was beyond caring by then.

I resolved to go to the chemist to get some sleeping pills, but once I'd bought them I became so scared that I might accidentally overdose I decided it wasn't safe to hang on to them, and put them in the bin.

That night, awake, quivering for *no good reason, you idiot,* it seemed I had only one thing on my mind: death. It was the last thing I wanted to think of, but there it was—the feeling of

131

death. So close. I kept thinking of Rowie, imagining how it must have felt for her to no longer be able to move—to know she was going to die. I cried then, as quietly as I could, and couldn't seem to stop crying, no matter how hard I tried. Clearly, there was something wrong with me.

The next morning, I walked into reception and told the young man behind the desk that I was not well and I needed a doctor. 'Can you please help me?' I begged. And then I started crying again. I had never felt this thin-skinned in my life—never felt this afraid. Every bit of me ached.

He moved quickly out from behind the desk and put his arm around me, told me not to worry. He called the doctor and then an out-of-hours number and gave me the phone. A receptionist answered and asked a series of questions. What seemed to be the problem? (I didn't know). Had I lost my appetite? (Yes.) Did I have a fever? (I didn't know.) Was I having headaches? (Yes.) I had stopped crying by this time. Her voice gave me something to focus on. She reassured me that it didn't sound like anything serious. There was a virus raging through Oxford, she told me, and no doubt that's what it was, but I should pop in to the surgery later today for an appointment. It felt so good to be told that everything would be all right. For a moment, I even believed her. But then I heard it again, that voice in my head, the one that said, *she's lying*.

The guy on reception's name was Ian, like my father. A sign, I thought. Being with Ian made me feel safer than I had in weeks. Very kindly, he moved me from the dorm into a private room, told me to get some rest, and for the first time in weeks I did manage to sleep for a few straight hours. In the shower afterwards, I smelled the mould again, but I was able to remind myself not to stress. *You have a virus. You're just feeling sensitive.* It was easier to tell myself a better story after sleep. Ian kept an eye on me. Told me to call my parents. 'I'm telling you, they would want to know. Go call home.'

My sister Anna answered the phone. She asked me if I was okay. I tried to talk calmly but within thirty seconds, I was howling. Mum got on the phone, asked me if I was drinking enough water, eating enough. I couldn't remember the last time I'd eaten. I felt too nauseous to eat. She said I needed to eat something, and also I needed to get myself to a church and light a candle and just sit there and let the grace of God settle on me for a little bit. It had always annoyed me, the way Mum talked about God so much, but this time I didn't mind at all. Any tiny little piece of comfort I could get, I was taking. She asked me if I wanted to come home; she could arrange it in a flash, she said, that's why credit cards were invented. When she said that, I felt bad. The voice in my head told me what a *bad daughter* I was, *worrying my Mum like that*, and I stopped crying, and said, 'Mum, I'm gonna be fine. I just miss you. I'll call you later.'

When the doctor agreed I probably did have a virus, and prescribed paracetamol for pain relief and pink chalk liquid to stop my nausea, I felt relieved. But then she said something else, something that terrified me. She said, 'Clare, I realise this may come as a surprise to you, but I think there may be more going on here. I think you might be depressed.'

I didn't want to believe her when she said that. I told her that, sorry, she'd got it wrong. Trying to hold back tears now, I told her that, in fact, I was a very happy person. Ask anyone. There was no way I could be depressed. It seems silly now how obvious it all was but, in 1996, I was as ignorant and fearful about mental illness as the next person. In my mind, the word 'depressed' had always been synonymous with 'crazy'. The only books I'd read on the subject were Sylvia Plath's *The Bell Jar* and J.D. Salinger's *Catcher in the Rye*. The only stories I'd heard were of Plath putting her head in the oven, Vincent Van Gogh cutting off his ear, Virginia Woolf walking into the river with stones in her pocket.

The doctor was patient and kind and said, 'Perhaps I am wrong, Clare, but either way I am going to prescribe you some Valium to help you sleep, and also to help you on the plane home. I really think you need to go home. I think you need to be around people who can help you to take care of yourself.'

I didn't take the Valium. Didn't trust myself to take the right amount. I was quite sure that if I took even one I would become an addict, or accidentally overdose. But I did get the prescription filled, just in case. In case . . . I really did go mad. I put the bottle in the very bottom of my bag, so I wouldn't have to see it or think about it.

I told myself I probably just needed to eat something, like Mum said. By now, just the thought of food was enough to make my stomach churn, make me run to the toilet and have to empty my bowels, but I decided enough was enough: it was time to eat. Something healthy, I said. Not fattening. Just a little bit.

I entered a cafe, found a seat in a quiet corner and looked at the menu. But when the waitress came to take my order, I couldn't decide what I wanted. Everything sounded too complicated, too expensive. But I spotted a jar of yoghurt-covered muesli biscuits on the counter—surely they were healthy? I would only eat half, I promised myself, and no more.

On my plate, I cut the biscuit in half with a knife and started to eat. Before I knew it my hand was reaching for the second half—the half that I had promised myself I would not eat. This is the moment that something inside me seemed to snap. Suddenly the voice, the bad feeling that had been with me for as long as I could remember, said something more vicious than it ever had before, and not just as a sticky thought, but an instruction, a threat, a demand. It said, *If you can't even stick to a diet, you might as well kill yourself.*

Any other day, a thought like that would have registered as a dark joke, a dumb thing to say. On that day, however, that awful day, it registered as an ultimatum. In my tired, fragile mind, the words 'Kill yourself' felt loud and real, and utterly terrifying. Oh my God. Is that where all this is leading. Am I about to kill myself?

From this moment onwards, my illness began to escalate. I had tipped now from anxiety into danger. I didn't want to hurt myself; I didn't want to do that to me or my family, and yet image after image flashed before my eyes: ropes and knives and cars and trucks and trains and guns. Blood and more blood. Horror and more horror. All I could do was sit there and weep, as quietly as I could, covering my face so no one could see me.

I had no name for what was wrong with me. I had no language. Just feeling. Instinct. Terror. Shaking.

I must have paid for my biscuit, but I don't remember it.

I remember being in a church next, on my knees, praying to an icon of the Madonna, asking that something please stop me from killing myself.

And then I remember being outside the church, starting to walk back to the hostel, feeling too tired to continue, sitting on a bench.

I saw Matt from the Catweazle Club walking towards me, or was I imagining it? No, it was Matt and, when he saw me, he stopped. He told me I looked terrible. He kept asking what was wrong.

I tried to talk, but I didn't know what to say. All I could do was cry, and mumble about being scared, about having a virus. I didn't say anything else. I didn't want anyone to know what else the doctor had said. I just wanted to be home, with my parents, and never leave the house again.

He took me to the tearooms for a cup of Earl Grey. I remember the red-and-white-check tablecloth, the smell of the tea, how his voice was so kind and steady, and slowly, slowly, I stopped crying. For a second, I pulled myself together to say, 'Thank you', and then had to look down because I'd started crying again.

He said that whatever was worrying me would pass. He said we all suffered sometimes, it was just the human condition, and besides, I was a songwriter: I'd probably use all of this and write an awesome song one day.

I thanked him again, told him he was making me feel more normal, that I felt so grateful—each sentence broken by sobs that I just could not, for the life of me, stop from coming. And he said, 'You are normal, you're just really far away from everything you know. What you need is a good home-cooked meal.' He invited me to dinner on his barge, drawing a map on a napkin, with directions on how to get there. Then he paid for our tea, walked me back in the direction of my hostel, and told me he'd see me at six. Said he'd have the pot-belly stove cranking, and I could borrow his guitar. I said, 'I can't really play.' 'Yes, you can,' he replied. 'I heard you. Remember?'

That evening as I walked along the canal I was scared I might lose control, and jump in and drown myself. But when I reached Matt's boat, it was like a scene from a movie: dusk, a long blue boat, smoke coming from its little chimney and, inside, a jam jar of red wine, and lovely music playing, and a warm dinner waiting, kilims and cushions, a guitar, and even though I could not eat, what I felt that night was enough to remind me that I was still here. I was not dead yet. And I dared to hope maybe that night I would sleep. Maybe I would go to sleep, and wake up in the morning, and feel like my old self again.

That night, lying in my bed in the dormitory once more (the private room Ian had allowed me to rest in was now back being used by paying guests), I tried to imagine my father's deep voice saying, 'All will be well, all will be fine,' and for a few hours I drifted off, only to be woken again and then again by the churning of my stomach, by the half-felt feelings of my childhood rattling around inside me.

It was about Rowena, mostly. I saw it clearly that night, the horror of how long I'd been trying to remember to find places to hide these feelings, to somehow float above the sadness, the injustice, of what happened to her. I'd used every tool I had—religion, logic, humour, fantasy—to try to make sense of it all somehow, but on that night all I had left in me was the cold horror of the truth—a truth I had, up until this point, been able to avoid.

The fantasy I'd been harbouring since the day she died—that everything was okay, because she hadn't really died—was not actually true.

And it struck me on this night, clear as a death knell, that it was never going to be true.

As far as this world was concerned, my sister really was dead. She really was gone. There was nothing, absolutely nothing, that I could do, now or ever, that would make that right.

In that moment, an abyss of despair opened up so wide inside my chest that I wasn't sure how I was supposed to go on breathing, and I wasn't even sure I wanted to.

I can't remember how many nights I lay awake in that back-packers in Oxford. I can't remember whether I ate, or drank. Whether I talked. What I do remember is that one night, after I had almost drifted off, I was woken so suddenly by one of the girls coming into our room that my heart started racing in my chest, and it scared me so much that I just gave up on sleep after that. I was too tired to keep trying. The old me would have grabbed her diary and written a list. Maybe had a cup of tea. Eaten something. But those comforts were beyond me now. They felt too hard, required too much effort. All I knew is that I could no longer stay there, I could no longer stand these feel-ings, so I got up, got dressed, and decided just to walk, and keeping walking, until something changed.

Every nerve in my body seemed to be on high alert that morning. I was aware of every moving thing—cars, ants, clouds. When the clouds went grey, I felt greyer. When the sun popped out, so did a fleeting burst of hope. A passing car sounded so loud I felt it in my chest like a train hurtling right through the middle of me. I leaped back in fright, and had another disturbing thought: what if I had jumped the wrong way? What if I was under that car now, my head all squashed on the road, and they had to call my parents and say, 'There's been an accident,' and they never recovered?

That morning, the unspecified, all-encompassing dread was no longer shadow, it was in me. I was in it. And as I paced I felt there was no separation, no skin at all, between myself and the people I saw. An old lady in a blue coat walked past me and I felt, bizarrely, as though I knew her, could feel what it felt like to be her. Of course, I didn't but, in that second, I felt that I was her: felt that I knew every pinprick of her hope and sadness, that there was no separation between what she felt and who I was.

Later, much later, I would find a name for this feeling and a way to live with it. I would write songs about it, songs about being 'born into this skin, that feels just a little too thin, skin I'm never sure if I belong in'. I would draw on this depth of feeling, this acute sensitivity, this ability to imagine, to write every song, to fuel every tiny act of outspokenness, of passion, of courage. But in that moment, in Oxford, I had no way to imagine anything so bold as a future. All I had really was one step, another step; that was as far forward as my mind would allow me to think.

None of my memories had walls that day. They bled into each other, made a mess inside me: pictures of my childhood homes, schoolyard, the hurts, slights, things I had done badly, the angry words. Most of all, the times I'd stood next to Rowena in her bed in the hospital, knowing something bad was happening, trying to ignore the barnacle of my guilt, the voice in my head saying *I could have done something, but I didn't*, and the impossible question of why I had lived, and she had died. That day, and for many to come, these memories flew around inside me like a colony of bats that I could not swipe away, could not see through.

Too many feelings. Too much.

My mind was getting stuck that day on words, on one word in particular—'dead'. I didn't want to die. I didn't. But I couldn't seem to stop thinking the word. I kept repeating it, in cycles of three: a song, *dead, dead, dead.* So I walked close to the houses, as far away from the road as I could. I stepped over cracks, counted house numbers in my head, matched fence colours, rearranging them in colour order in my imagination, looked at angles and shapes, sorted them into stacks, anything to crowd out the bad words, the bad feeling. These sorting games had always worked, until today. That's when I got really scared, actually; when I thought, *There is nothing left to help me now.*

I walked over a bridge and, although I willed myself not to look down, I couldn't resist and imagined my body flying over the edge, breaking the surface of the shallow water below. *Dead dead dead.* Terrified, I ducked my head, put my hands on the sides of my face like blinkers, and bolted as fast as I could to the end of the bridge.

My last memory from Oxford is of standing at the bus stop, the one I'd arrived at only a few weeks before. I was shaking so much by then that I felt I would surely fall over. I knew I needed to be around people—to be reminded of life, not death—so I had come to the bus station for the company of mothers, fathers, children, old people. I was sure they could see that I was crazy. I was crying again, and praying too, perhaps even aloud. *God, I believe, help my unbelief.* It was a prayer from the gospel of Mark, one of dozens that my mother had taught me when I was a small child, in case I ever needed them.

It was then that I accepted that maybe the doctor was right, and it was time to go home. I did not want to die here in Oxford, alone, fighting a voice in my head that felt as real as a floral wreath atop a coffin.

It no longer mattered that I was not yet ready, that I didn't have money left, and that I would have to ask my parents to help, and asking them for help would worry them.

I know now that Ian was right—it is worth worrying your parents over certain things, and this was one of them.

*

My friend Libby got me home; Libby and her mother Madeleine, who was visiting, and their friend, allowed me to stay with her until the flight left.

At first, after I asked for help, I was so ashamed that I begged Libby not to tell anyone. And then, as I deteriorated further, I wasn't even ashamed anymore. All I knew was that I needed to get home.

Madeleine drove me to the airport.

The last thing she said to me echoed what Matt had also said: 'Clare, you will write songs about this one day. That is what you need to do.'

I couldn't imagine it then—couldn't imagine I would ever write another song, or another word, ever again.

My life, said my head, *was over.*

*

I don't remember much from the flight home. I certainly didn't pack my own lunch. I doubt I ate at all, in fact. I remember that just the thought of eating—the thought of the battle of it—was too much.

I know that I sat by a window, that my hands shook as we took off, that I put them over my eyes, that the bad voice in my head told me *You are going to die*, and that I believed it.

I wanted to sleep, but I couldn't, my head told me, in case something went wrong. *It might, you know.*

I wore earplugs to block out the noise.

There were televisions in the plane, up high, attached to the roof. When the news came on, I slipped low in my seat. I didn't think I could handle any more sadness.

In my head, I had my own horror movie running, 24/7, the one about how we never made it to Melbourne, because we all died in a plane crash. I'd see it in my mind, imagine the feeling of the plane falling, freefalling, nose down into the ocean below, my skin so thin I imagined I could feel it already, feel the cold as we plunged into the water. I imagined I heard a mother screaming, a child crying, felt the cold horror again as the water came in, the lights went out. I would see our bloated bodies, our bones underneath, a time lapse, now the breaking of the fibre of our clothes, the fish eating our bodies, and there we were, just skeletons in seatbelts, never found.

I had other stories too, worse than that—dozens of them. The worst of all was the one where I didn't just get hurt, I also hurt everyone else around me. *If I was not very careful*, said the voice in my head, *I might lose control of my mind, my body, might, in my madness, run to the plane doors and release them, mid-air, and all the lovely people sitting around the doors would get sucked out after me, and I would be so so sorry, and yet absolutely unable to take back the thing I had done.* That was the most insidious story of all: that if I allowed myself to relax, to drop my guard for even a second, I would put innocent people in danger.

All I really remember from the flight are that those stories came to mind again and again, and, along with them, wave after violent wave of horror ripping through my body, a cold whoosh in my knees, shoulders, head and toes. I tried to sing the songs of my childhood, just quietly to myself, but was too tired to remember the words. The hum died in my throat. I needed very badly to go to the toilet, but refused to leave my seat. *In case.* I did not want to walk past any of the plane's doors. *Can't trust yourself.* There was nothing for me to do but hold on, and pray to the hope of the existence of God: a God I both needed and resented.

How pathetic, said the voice in my head. *All these years you've been quietly mocking your mother and father for the strength of their faith, and now that you're all in a tizz, what's the first thing you do? Pray.*

When I finally saw the early-morning lights of Melbourne, felt the tilt of the plane, the racing of my heart (*We are going to die, we are all going to die*), the bounce of the rubber on the runway, and heard the stewardess tell us we were in Melbourne, I could hardly believe this was real. I was alive! The thought of my parents waiting to see me acted like an invisible string that drew me up and out of my seat, hopeful for the first time in what felt like forever. This would all be behind me soon.

I must have collected my backpack, my guitar, must have put them on a trolley and pushed it right through Customs, but the only bit I really remember, and still sometimes weep as I do, is the moment I exited those gates—went from before to after, inside to outside—and saw my mother's face waiting for me. She was as pale as a sheet. Crumpled, somehow, with worry. She carried yellow roses, and when she saw me, she started smiling and crying and running. Dad was there too, but Mum got to me first, held me tight—oh, the relief, I was home, I was alive, I had made it—and I heard her whispering, 'Thank God you're home, thank God you're home—sweet Jesus, thank you for getting my baby home.' Too weak to care anymore about the promise I had made to never worry my parents, I heaved with sobs and the gratitude of having made it home alive. I had no energy to pretend. I was done with pretending.

After Mum hugged me and we had both calmed down a little, she pulled back to look at me, said, 'Darling, where have you gone? You are so thin. Ian, she is so thin.'

And I'm not sure I had noticed until then. I had been avoiding mirrors. I could see I was changing, and it scared me. It didn't feel like my face, my body, belonged to me anymore.

But, as Mum said it, I knew she was right: I was now thin. Very thin. Thin as a rake, thin as a pancake, thin as a willow and so far away from the girl I had once been. Here it was— my dream come true. I'd expected to feel happy. Instead, I felt insane. After all those years of longing to be thin, of planning, dieting, restricting, failing, starting again, of imagining how it would feel to finally 'win', how happy it would make me, here I was, thin, and . . . now what?

Now it was just me and the bad feeling with nothing in between to protect me.

This was not what the box had promised.

6

Storms and other weather patterns

Black dog

Thick the fog

Yellow fog that rubs its back against your window.

'YOUR OTHER HAND'
(*The Moon Looked On*, 2007)

Perhaps this will come as no surprise now that you know me a little, but in the lead up to my return home to Melbourne, there was a part of me that had hoped that as soon as that plane landed, as soon I saw my parents' faces, I would somehow magically become well again. Everything would make sense, and I could just pick up where I left off.

Apparently, it doesn't quite work that way.

The morning my plane landed, when we headed out into the crisp Melbourne air, walking to my father's Nissan Bluebird, everything still felt too bright, and not quite real, and I kept blinking and wondering what was going on. I knew I was alive, but it was as though every other shred of my identity was now gone. My ideas of myself as resilient, bubbly, unbreakable and strong were all gone. My lists—gone. The fantasy of how, when I got thin, I would feel better—gone. Finished. *Dead.*

In the back seat of Dad's car, him smoking a cigarette out the window, me resting my head on my mother's lap, still crying, I did feel an enormous sense of comfort and relief. But when Dad turned on the radio and I heard the opening theme song of the ABC news, the bad feelings began to stir once more. I could feel it coming, feel it building in me, and in my fear of what might happen next I began to shake, and could not seem to stop.

Mum said, 'Ian, turn on the heater, please,' and he did.

She was talking fast. I could hear how worried she was, and how she was trying to hide it. The voice in my head told me I was a *terrible daughter* for doing this to my family. It told me *how weak I was to have needed to come home and worry everyone with all this fuss.*

The noise was all too much for me. I needed silence. I was too tired to speak loudly, so I asked Mum to tell Dad to please turn off the radio.

Even though I spoke quietly, Dad must have been on full alert, he heard me, clicked off the news, and started talking. I noticed he wasn't using his normal speaking voice, he was using his special voice, his barrister's voice, the one he normally reserved for the art of convincing a jury.

'Your mum is so happy to have you home,' he said. 'Look at her. Scared as a pussycat she was. But you're a tough girl. I knew you'd be fine.'

Mum said, 'Ian, shh. Not too much talking.' Mum said she wanted me to settle, to rest.

Dad knew what to do, though. He just carried on talking, confident in what he had to say. I suspect Dad would have been every bit as scared as Mum, but I also suspect he would have worked out in advance that some part of me would be relying on some part of him to hold the fort, to mirror back to me an image of life that was still robust and not just a husk. So he just kept talking about this and about that, moved on to minor matters, the garden and so on, and with his deep reassuring voice murmuring in the background, I think I might even have dozed off for a minute.

Yet, once home again in Sandringham, once the reality of my situation hit me—that I still felt weird, that I was a stranger to myself—it was as though my despair tripled.

That first night home, and for dozens afterwards, I lay awake in my childhood bed, shaking and terrified by the thought that, any minute now, I was going to start hallucinating, start seeing things or, worse still, I was going to lose control of my mind all together, and do *something terrible*. I felt like I was walking through a nightmare, or trapped in a computer game, and all the while my mind kept telling me I needed to stay vigilant and keep watch of my thoughts, that that was the only way to stay alive. So that was what I did, all day, all night: I watched my thoughts. For some twisted reason, I believed the most danger-ous thing I could do was fall asleep, and lose control.

I remember feeling so tired that even talking seemed to take too much energy, so I barely spoke at all. Eating felt equally difficult, but my mother insisted, told me I really needed to eat, darling. She started me on Dad's broth and, later, on his vegetable soup.

I remember time itself was a torture to me. Every moment felt like a year.

I still could not make sense of why I was shaking so much, or why any passing thought or noise seemed to set it off: the phone ringing, a bird chirping loudly at my window, even the sound of my own voice in my ears was enough to shoot bolts of fear down my spine.

The worst part of all of this was that I had no real idea what was actually wrong with me. I didn't even know where to start. The doctor in Oxford had used the word 'depression', but I didn't like it. Doctors scared me; everything did. There was no relief. Things that had once brought a feeling of fun, or distraction, now held no interest. I no longer sang, or played my guitar, or listened to music, or wrote in my diary, or watched television. Just thinking about doing them seemed to take more energy than I believed I had. Trying even to read—to make sense of words on a page, lines in a sentence—left me feeling nauseous with exertion.

There is no easy way to say this, but I will say it anyway: in those first few weeks at home, my only hope, my *single* hope, was that I would get to the end of the day without somehow killing myself or—as the voice in my head kept warning me was possible—*hurting someone I loved.*

The last thing a girl like me would ever, ever want to do is hurt anyone, let alone someone I loved. As I said, this was the most insidious part of the illness. This, I am heartbroken to say, is what I suspect to be one of the fears that lies behind so many of the unexplained suicides that our community has to grieve: the thought that just by being alive we are running the risk of somehow causing harm to the ones we love most.

Inside me, even in this darkest of times, there was still a quiet voice that floated up sometimes, telling me I would recover. It would only bleat in for a few seconds, but it was there.

Mostly, however, what I heard was: *I am broken for good. Whatever this is, I will never recover. My mind is gone. There is a devil in me, and if I am not very careful, I will end up dead. They would be better off without me.*

In the dead of night, I felt the pull of these stories, I felt the temptation of them, but the one grace of this situation is that I really did know better. I knew these ideas were lies—tempting lies dressed up in dark sparkles. I knew that my own death was a line of thinking that, although I could not seem to stop it, I must never, ever indulge. I knew—had always known—the truth of what grief really does to a family. Despite my obsessive thoughts, despite the story in my head that my own death was unavoidably close, I was not, under any circumstances, allowed to die.

And so, at first, to make sure I stayed safe, I refused to leave the house at all.

After a few weeks, however, I did finally agree to attend a charismatic healing mass with my mother. It was in the middle of the day, in a church hall half an hour away. At least here, I reasoned, the devil could not get me. In the car, I told Mum to slow down—she was driving too fast. She said, 'I'm driving thirty kilometres an hour.' Still, the motion, taking in all that information from the outside world—sounds, smells, colours, billboards—felt like too much. I closed my eyes, put in my earplugs, and hummed to myself until we were there. I don't remember much about the prayer meeting except that it was very, very loud, and I was very, very scared, and there were lots of older people who raised their hands in the air and said, 'Thank you, Jesus,' and it was, frankly, far beyond anything I was capable of processing. In the end, the only thing I could think of to do was stand up when everyone else was sitting down, and cry. Mum quickly got the cue; 'I'm sorry,' she said. 'Let's go home.' So we did.

More nights passed and, still, I could not stay asleep. Sometimes I dozed off, but I never seemed able to pass over into the next level of sleep. Again and again I woke with a start, my heart thumping. This feeling of panic in my chest stayed with me from the moment I got up in the morning to the moment I lay my head on the pillow at night. I felt like I was walking on a knife-edge between life and death. My sensitivity was so heightened that, even at home, smells overwhelmed me: the spice in an Indian dish or a strongly perfumed shampoo— both pleasures I'd previously enjoyed—now made me nauseous. Bright colours made me furious, like a personal assault. And a glimpse at Dad's morning newspaper could send me into a spiral of panic for hours. The missing persons headlines haunted me; when I pictured the missing people and their families, all I could think of was Rowena. I've only ever had one recurring night-mare; one in which the child I was supposed to be caring for is kidnapped and I cannot, despite every effort, get the police to take me seriously. I am yelling, 'Where is she? Where is she?' and no one will take me seriously. In the weeks after I got home, this dream visited me often.

I was eating more now: still Dad's soup, mostly. 'Good for you,' he said. Still, progress was slow. Even just getting dressed and leaving the house felt impossible. Mum encouraged me to try anyway. The local weekday morning mass was a gentler place to begin, she said. 'Why don't you join me?'

'All right,' I said. 'But don't drive so fast.'

When we arrived, there were only three or four people in the pews, mostly elderly parishioners from the nearby nursing home. That suited me just fine—I wasn't there for the entertainment. The less I had to talk to people, the better. Going to mass gave me something to do, something to think about besides the sleep I wasn't getting. I went for the peace of mind, and for the routine, and because the blessings made me feel safe.

There is no doubt that one of the very first things I should have done when I got home from Oxford was to visit a doctor but, for reasons I find difficult to put into words now, I refused. I did not want to think of what I was experiencing as a 'medical issue', as a mental illness. I preferred, instead, to think about my experience as a problem with my very soul itself. The thought of taking any medication terrified me. What if they gave me the wrong medicine? What if I took it and never woke up? Or, worse, what if I took it and then took too much of it and lost all control of my mind, and accidentally hurt some innocent person on the street?

I told no one about these worries; I just refused to go to the doctor. I was not willing to take what I thought of as 'the risk'. People weren't as open about mental health in the 1990s. We really didn't talk that much about it, and I just couldn't seem to get over the feeling of shame. I wish I had known that the only way to get well is to speak the truth, and that a good place to start would be with professional help. But I didn't even know help was available. In my mind, all a doctor was going to do was force me to take meds, or have me committed—knowledge I had gleaned purely from watching daytime television in my youth.

Also, do you remember that story about Rowena and the psychiatrist? That story stuck with me, and I guess—fair or unfair—some childhood part of me was not yet ready to trust a psychiatrist.

And perhaps psychiatry as it was practised in those days wouldn't have offered me what I needed; back then it was extremely rare to find a psychiatrist who practised an integrated approach to self-care, one that incorporated lifestyle recommend- ations, such as diet and exercise, or was open to the idea that spirituality (or even this crazy thing called yoga) would play a role in people's healing. It was almost unheard of.

Other than going to church, I did try once or twice to leave the house on my own, but barely got further than the corner without finding myself shaking. The world just felt too big and dangerous. In my mind, something terrible could happen at any moment, and the effort of being on guard was just too exhausting. Once, in the car with Mum, passing a suburban pool, I saw children laughing, laughing, then, in my mind, drowning, dying, crying for help. A simple, sweet sight—like a mother in the park pushing her baby high on the swing—suddenly became, in my mind, a potential decapitation, just waiting to happen. I reeled in horror with the images my own mind created. I didn't know then that this is exactly what a tired brain does: it tries to keep us safe by warning us of all the things that might go wrong.

Mum tried her best to encourage me to look on the bright side. She kept saying, 'There must be something for you to learn here. This can't be for nothing. This must mean something.'

But despite hours ruminating on what was happening and why, I didn't have any answers, only questions and more questions. What could this all mean? What is wrong with me? What am I supposed to be learning here? Why is this happening? What is the meaning of life? Why was I born? The biggest questions, of course, were about Rowena. Why did she have to die, God? What the *fuck* was with that? Why did she die and I live?

Sometimes, in the middle of the night, when I couldn't sleep, I got mad at God. Told him off, good and proper. What kind of joke are you playing? I'd say. What, we're born and then we die? What's with that? I noticed that when I expressed my anger like that, I felt . . . better. Felt, at the very least, like I was saying something true. But as soon as it was out, the guilt would creep upon me, and I would begin to worry that perhaps, if I was rude to God, I might go to hell so, to be safe, I tried instead to keep my prayers polite and indirect. I was not yet ready for a full confrontation of any kind.

Mostly, I felt like no one in the world had ever been this scared before, this crazy.

It was a relief to discover I was wrong.

One day, Mum and Dad gave me a set of cassette tapes of the ABC radio program *The Search for Meaning*, presented by Caroline Jones. The program was interview-based, and all the conversations centred on (you guessed it) the search for meaning, spiritual purpose, and stories centred on the concept of hope. It was one of the few places in the world at the time where you could hear true stories from people of every faith—or no faith—who had made something of their suffering. I cannot tell you how important it was for me to hear that I was not the only one. One story in particular—of a woman who had gone 'technically mad' and come back better for the experience—brought me more solace than I knew how to express (mainly because I still wasn't able to talk much. I was still too tired). What I did notice was that when I listened to stories like these, the bad voice in my head fell quiet, and a new thought took over: was it possible that I too might one day recover from whatever this thing was?

Although Mum has never admitted it, I'm pretty sure that even before I came home, half of Sandy was on prayer duty for me. I was so embarrassed about what had happened that I couldn't even bear the thought of seeing friends who had known me before I left. But, for whatever reason, I felt okay around Mum's friends, who were especially kind to me during this time.

Her dear friend Fay, a songwriter, left a message for me on the phone, told me I could call her back anytime and, when I did, she shared stories from her own life, from a time when she was young, and had gone through her own suffering, and also shared with me the things that had helped her. She told me that sometimes, when we're feeling fragile, what we need more than anything is a good hero's journey for our mind to latch onto. We need wisdom and gentle reminders that this is all part of being human. I told her I couldn't read, that it felt beyond me. She said, 'Why don't you start with children's literature? Something old and beautiful?' She dropped over a book called *The Little White Horse* by Elizabeth Goudge. Many years later, I would learn that this was a favourite childhood book of J.K. Rowling, author of the Harry Potter series. At the time, all I knew was that I liked it. It was gentle and sweet and it made sense to me. I didn't want anything complicated or overwhelming: what I needed, what I craved, was a less direct approach. Metaphor, and symbol, and story, and hope. This book provided all these things.

Mum had another friend, Cath, who—it turns out—had once been through a very similar experience to mine. I still wasn't being honest with Mum about exactly what was going on in my head, mainly because I didn't want to scare her, but when Mum repeated back some of the thoughts Cath had mentioned as being quite common in this kind of illness—crazy thoughts of driving off bridges and into trains and so on—I felt a little moment of relief. At the very least, I was not the only crazy one! Best of all, Mum's mate had recommended a book that really helped her and, she said, she was going to send it to me.

For the next three days, the only time I left the house was to check the letter box. I was desperate, absolutely desperate, to find some way of getting better. But, then, when the book did finally arrive, I wasn't sure what to make of it. For a start, its title was *Self Help for Your Nerves*—a title that would have made the old me giggle. So quaint! And in the photo on the front of the book, the author, Dr Claire Weekes, looked a lot like my grandmother. To be honest, if I hadn't been so incredibly unwell, I think I would've dismissed it as 'not for me'.

Fortunately, I was desperate enough to try anything. And, as it turns out, this was the book that would save my life.

While Dr Claire Weekes might have struck me as old-fashioned, it was quite clear from the outset that she was in fact rather a progressive sort. The introduction explained that she had cut her teeth helping war veterans recover from what at the time, and in the book, they called 'bad nerves' but is now known as post-traumatic stress disorder, or PTSD. She was a pioneer in her field, and not at all prone to beating around the bush. I liked how direct she was.

Until opening the cover of this book, I had assumed that my bad feelings would be with me for life. I wasn't sure I would ever truly recover. Or, if I did, I assumed it would involve thousands of unpleasant hours of psychological muck-raking on the therapist's couch, not to mention lifelong medication and occasional visits to the psych ward. I had been thinking of late that the most I could ever hope for was that I didn't kill myself.

From the very first page, Dr Weekes *utterly, utterly* disagreed, and what a relief that was.

She was not here to tell me to do anything complicated, she said, and it felt like she already understood that, right now, what a girl like me needed was something clear, and simple, and practical. She said that if I was reading this book because my nerves were 'in a bad way', I'd come to the right place. She was going to talk to me directly, as though she were sitting right beside me. She promised me that even if I had suffered from a complete 'breakdown' (and it was quite clear now—I had), I would not only recover, I would thrive. All it would take was a little time, some courage and perseverance, and the application of her simple, self-administered technique. With a little bit of practice, I would once again be able to enjoy life to the full. I would find happiness again. 'You can do it,' she said. And for just a second, I believed her. And one second was all I needed to begin.

She gained my trust early on by explaining that the terrifying symptoms I was experiencing—the acute sensitivity to sound and smell and colours, the feeling of shakiness in my heart, my obsessive ruminations (mainly about Joffa and Rowena), my overwhelming feelings of guilt, the insomnia, my inability to read adult books, my sudden weight loss, shaking hands, constant feelings of unreality and entrapment, my obsession with death, my compulsive tapping, uninvited violent thoughts, inability to engage in normal social activity or even to muster the courage to leave the house—were all very common and highly treatable symptoms of a condition she called 'nervous suffering'.

Using simple language, she went on to explain how the parasympathetic nervous system works and how, under extreme stress and fatigue—states of mind that she said could be triggered by emotions, travel, traumatic events and even extreme dieting—we tricked our bodies into displaying symptoms that were really just stock-standard survival responses: just surges of adrenaline running through the body with nowhere to go, because most of the danger was just in our imagination. And no one ever died from a silly little thing like a panic attack, she said. Although I might think that I was suffering from 'an illness of how you feel', I was in fact just being duped by my own thoughts, and that 'thoughts that are keeping you ill can be changed'.

Dr Weekes said this was perfectly normal—when triggered, when nerves were raw, our survival brain mistakenly thought that the best way of helping us to survive was to ruminate again and again on the saddest times of our lives. For whatever reason, this seemed to trigger the hormones that kept us alive and alert. But it was just a little trick of the brain, she said, and we weren't going to fall for it anymore, were we?

You're kidding? I thought. I was hooked. I couldn't read the words fast enough.

She wrote that although such suffering could make us feel frightened, there was really nothing terribly wrong with us—it was only the fear of fear itself which perpetuated the cycle of fear, and therefore the symptoms. Fear of fear itself! Of course! That made sense!

Since this dreadful business first set in after Phil collapsed on the Tube, I felt as though I hadn't been able to remember a single happy thing. It was as though every joyful, relaxing memory from my childhood had been completely erased and all that was left were the saddest bits, the scariest bits, and all the memories around Rowena, and her illness, and her death. I was at an absolute loss to explain why my brain kept going back there, and I had no idea—night after night, day after day— how to stop it. Here, in Dr Weekes's words, the explanation became clear. The only reason my mind was thinking this way was because in its exhausted state it had somehow mixed up the hormones of sadness and anxiety with the hormones of survival. This anxiety—and its subsequent cascade of fight-or-flight hormones—was just my brain's misguided attempt to keep me alert and, therefore, safe.

Even just that—this reminder that it was perfectly natural to be thinking so much about the sadness of Rowena's illness and death at a time like this—felt like a hopeful place to start.

Dr Weekes's writing on the page, her clarity, her confidence, made me feel safer than I had felt in months. All of a sudden, there was an expert in the room. An adult. A coach. Someone who knew exactly what I was going through and exactly how to come out the other side. She was not at all patronising; just very clear and confident that she could tell me everything I needed to know in order to recover. She said it would be up to me to do the work but, if I decided to do it, I could, and would, recover.

When I read this I wept with relief.

Yes, of course! I wasn't nuts, not really, I was just being duped by the symptoms of panic, by adrenaline, by the constant shocks and starts. My reaction to what happened with Phil, and then later at the backpackers, was exaggerated, but also normal. I was not sleeping, I was not eating—my body was doing everything it could to shock me into taking care of myself. It's not that

I was a bad person, or that I actually wanted to kill myself; I was mainly just a tired person who needed some sleep. She said again and again that, given time and rest, I could and would recover, and the moment I believed her was the very moment my true recovery began.

For the first time since I'd come home, I felt not only happy, I felt excited—so excited that I yelled out, 'Mum! This book is amazing!' She ran up the stairs and said, 'Yeah?' and I said, 'I think it's gonna help me!' and she made a face like she was trying not to cry and said, in a high voice, that she was going to go and get me some soup now.

That night, instead of staying up worrying about why I couldn't sleep, I just read and read and read, my heart full of hope for the first time in such a long while. It wasn't that my panic wasn't there, it's just that I wasn't *quite* as afraid of it as I had been.

By the morning, I was clear: It was me and my thoughts and my stories that had triggered my breakdown. And it was me and my thoughts and my stories that were going to get me well again.

The solution Dr Weekes offered was simple and achievable.

She wrote that recovery did not come from sitting at home, hoping to get better. She said that it came from getting up and out into the world again, and allowing yourself to practise facing and floating through those feelings of panic and unreality. Not flinching. Not backing down. Not clenching up in dread. Just accepting. Panic may come, but panic would not hurt me, and feeling it did not make me a bad person.

In short, what she instructed me to do the next time fearful thoughts and feelings came up, was simply to:

162

1. Face (don't run away)
2. Accept (don't fight against)
3. Float (don't freeze)
4. Let time pass (let go of your impatience).

As tends to happen when my brain is in learning mode, I read that sentence and then went straight for the acronym F.A.F.L. I was going to FAFL my way through this!

But, where to start? Perhaps, anticipated Dr Weekes, I could try something simple, like going for a walk. It would give me a chance to practise my FAFL, a chance to remind myself to just breathe. As I read this, a new determination rose in me. Damned if I was going to stay inside all day, slowly going mad. I had a recovery to make! And with that, I went looking for my walking shoes.

It wasn't a cold day, but I was still shivering, so I put on two layers, told Mum I was going for a walk—no idea where—and I'd be back soon. Just around the block, I supposed. I headed out the front door, and hit my limit at the end of the street. Exhausting. But at least I'd made a start. I spent the rest of the day lying on the couch, eating soup, and rereading the words of the woman I had started to call The Weekes.

The next morning, I did the same thing, this time venturing a little further. I just walked and walked and walked, up and down streets close to home, picking sweet-smelling flowers and crushing them in my hands. Lavender and rose geranium were my favourites. They lifted my spirits. I walked from bush to bush. Many young flowers were sacrificed in the pursuit of my recovery, and I did feel a little guilty about that, but what I also felt was deep relief. Finally, I was making some progress.

✳

Only a week before, I had still thought my life was over. Now, I had hope. In taking The Weekes's advice to stay occupied, I had returned to an old hobby of mine: crafting, making beaded necklaces, drawing, knitting, sewing, anything really just to stay occupied.

And this, friends, is the week I mark in my mind as the beginning of my recovery from what—thanks to Dr Claire Weekes—would turn out to be my one and only genuine authentic nervous breakdown.

My gratitude was beyond words.

I still had a long road ahead of me, but this was my turning point.

I started watching television again after that. Just a little. I was still too fragile for things like The News. All I was up for at that stage was gentle stuff, which is how—close to Christmas—I came to watch a little movie starring James Stewart called *It's a Wonderful Life*. I'm not the first person in the world to feel that, somehow, this story came to me at just the right time. If you haven't seen it, I won't spoil it for you except to say, if you're ever at a low point and wondering whether it's worth going on, you might find something hopeful in this movie, as I did.

One night that week after re-reading *Self Help for Your Nerves*, and again feeling grateful for the gift of it, I made myself a crazy promise—one that would inspire me for many years to come.

The promise I made was this: that one day, when I was well and I had something hopeful to offer, I would take the baton—the hopeful feeling that movies like *It's a Wonderful Life* and books like *Self Help for Your Nerves* had given to me—and I would pass it along to someone else who needed it. I had no idea who that person was, or how I'd find them—all I knew was that, if and when I came out of this, I was going to write a book. I was going to share this whole story—the bad bits, and the good bits—so that whoever was reading it would know that they were not alone, and that recovery was possible.

I felt so inspired, making that promise. It felt huge, and for a moment, that was exciting. But before the hour was over, my fear had returned, as had my habit of self-doubt, and with it stories like: *Don't get ahead of yourself. As if you'll ever be well enough to write a book? Anyway, who the fuck would want to read your book? Who do you think you are, the Queen of Sheba? You really want people to know this about you—that you're nuts? Have you really thought that through?*

Maybe it was a stupid idea? It really did scare me, I'll give you that much. And, yet, it also made me feel hopeful. A tiny bit excited, even. For whatever reason, this promise felt important, more important than the stigma I risked attracting if I ever did fulfil it, and more important than listening to the voice of all that fear. This promise felt like a link to a future where maybe my life would, after all, mean something. It felt like a bridge, actually: one that I could step onto and walk along every time I wanted to remember the way I felt as I first read The Weekes's books—that I must never ever give up, because recovery is possible, even for someone like me.

So, in an attempt to shut down the cycle of rumination and self-doubt, I added a concession. I said that, yes, I would one day write this book, but I wouldn't make myself do it until all this was behind me, way behind me. I wouldn't do it until I was really old. Say, *forty*.

And it helped me, that night, to just leapfrog ahead like that, to imagine myself at that age, at forty. To imagine, just for a second, that things had worked out. That I had lived. That maybe I even had a family, and a house, and a dog.

✳

Two decades later, the year I did turn forty, now a grown woman with a family, and a house, and a dog, I was reminded of that promise.

I was in my car listening to the ABC, and was surprised and delighted to hear them roll out a radio documentary about a radical Australian doctor called, you guessed it, Claire Weekes. I was amazed!

In all my years of recommending her books to friends and their kids and strangers on the internet, I had never ever met anyone who had heard of her, or of her theories around 'nervous suffering'. Her name, it seemed to me, had been forgotten by history. But this doco proved otherwise. I learned that, in certain circles, Dr Claire Weekes is still regarded as one of our most influential pioneers in the discussion and treatment of mental ill-health. Long before words like mindfulness or cognitive behavioural therapy were popular, there she was, walking the talk. My sense of her as progressive had been correct. I learned while listening that not only was she the first woman ever to receive a doctorate from the University of Sydney, she was also a singer, a soprano, who had once been awarded a Rockefeller Foundation fellowship and travelled alone by boat to London to study zoology. And I learned something else new: something I don't think I'd ever heard her disclose despite now having read every single word of hers that I could get my hands on. I learned that the reason she was able to empathise so brilliantly with her patients was because once—after a long convalescence—she too had suffered from a severe case of 'bad nerves', and this was the very technique she used to cure herself.

That is why she could speak so confidently about recovery.

Dr Claire Weekes really was the OG—original gangster— of mindfulness.

I used to wonder if there was a name for whatever it was that was wrong with me. I suspect there are quite a few names a psychiatrist could have given to the set of quirks I lived through when I was twenty-one, and still sometimes have flares of to this day.

But the truth is, I didn't want to hear it. I was too scared. I thought that when a doctor gave you a diagnosis, that was it, you were stuck with it for life. I thought that if I gave it a name, it would change the way I thought about myself. I thought names were cages.

I think about these things rather differently now.

Today, I think of the names we give mental illness more as a shorthand to describe the weather pattern our mind is stuck in at any one time. These names are not used to describe a sunny day; they are used to describe the storm. These days, when I think of 'diagnosis', I just think of it as a word or set of words explaining what's happening for us right here, right now. They say nothing of the strengths, or sunshine, the gold in them hills. They're just here to help us predict the kind of weather pattern that might be ahead; which route we should take, and what we should pack if we want to stay dry.

I have a prediction of my own; one that will either sound really obvious, or a little bit rude. But the truth is, on paper, as lists of symptoms, it's sometimes hard to tell one mental illness from the next. There's a whole lot of Venn diagram going on. The medications that help for one, often help just as much for the other, and the truth is, we don't even know why they help, just that they can. Even when two people with the same illness are given the same medication, their reactions to it can be vastly different. It's all a bit crude, really. The stigma remains.

My prediction is that within the next few decades, we will have found a much better way of talking about, thinking about, and treating what we currently call 'mental ill-health'. As our understanding of brain science, genetics, epigenetics, well-being, empathy, creativity, and the thing we call 'brilliance' continues to develop, we will begin including in our conversations not just the storms, but also the sunshine that always follows rain. I am in no way attempting to glamourise mental ill-health— not for a single second. What I, and perhaps also you, have observed many times is that the traits we think of as indicative of mental ill-health often just happen to exist in concurrence with the very same traits our world thinks of as genius. Name for me a genius who has never known suffering? Name for me a human you admire who has never known suffering. You can't. They don't exist.

What seems obvious to me is that so-called illness and so-called strength are somehow related, are woven fine, in the same way love and grief are woven fine, in the same way sunshine and storms are woven fine. We need to keep striving to invent better, clearer language through which to have this conversation, and I believe we will, and I want people like you, and me, to be part of that development.

So, yes, the story I used to tell myself about mental health and the one I tell myself now are very different.

Looking back, do you know what I wish I'd done then?

For a start, I wish I hadn't wasted so much time and energy feeling ashamed. There really was no need.

I wish I'd tried harder to find a therapist who 'got me'—someone who (to steal a quote from my friend Ilka and her father Terry) could act like my ticking clock in a thunderstorm.

At the very least, I wish I'd taken just one of those bloody sleeping tablets and gotten myself a good night's sleep much sooner than I did. (Paranoid thinking can be *such a drag*!)

7

The thing about grief

The thing about grief is,
Few people know if the I goes before the E
And it's hard to give away because it's
The last thing you gave to me.

'THE THING ABOUT GRIEF'
(*What Was Left*, 2005)

Discovering and adopting The Weekes's simple, uncompli-cated approach to curing 'nervous illness' marked a dramatic turning point in my recovery. You will notice my use of the word 'curing'—that's the word The Weekes used. I liked that bit. At the same time, she was clear that there would be setbacks; that they were, in fact, an important part of learning from my recovery. I didn't like that bit at all.

I practised FAFL every day, dozens and perhaps even hundreds of times a day. My progress from this point felt excruciatingly slow but . . . noticeable. Mine was most certainly not an overnight recovery. My nerves were a little too frazzled to magically un-frazzle just like that. My habits, my ways of thinking, were old. Their grooves were deep.

But I was on my way.

✳

I still struggled to sleep. If I did manage to nod off, I'd wake almost every morning with a feeling of the dreads, with a cloudy mind (The Weekes called this Brain Fog) but now, instead of lying in bed wallowing, letting my feelings build into storms, I got up immediately (whether I felt like it or not), put on the kettle, made a cup of tea, cooked some porridge, had a shower, got dressed, put my walking shoes on, and every day I'd walk a little further than I had walked the day before. I would follow this routine—wake up, shower, eat something, go out for a walk, crush some flowers, come home—for the next few months. Although it wouldn't have looked like much from the outside, I counted every walk as a chance to practise my FAFL. And as the days went on, I began to get glimpses of my old self. It was slow work, but I was no longer in any rush.

Sometimes, if I was feeling particularly brave, I would go on a second walk in the afternoon, and one such afternoon, instead of heading in the direction of the beach, I went the other way, in the direction of the cemetery—the one where Rowie was buried. By the time I arrived there it was getting a little late, but I was so close now I felt it would be wrong not to pay her a visit. I picked some yellow daisies that were hanging over a neighbouring fence, and entered the cemetery, careful to avoid cracks (bad luck thinking), then walked over what felt like kilometres of green grass until finally I found her.

Rowena Jane Bowditch
1973–1980
Beloved daughter of Ian and Maria
Loving sister of Anna, Lisa, James and Clare. Always close to us.
Thank you, Father, for this beautiful child who showed us how to live.

By the time I reached Rowie, I was so tired that, though it sounds odd now, I figured it would be a good idea to just lie down flat on her grassy grave for a while and have a little rest. A little chat, really. I wasn't sure what to say, but once I started talking, I just kept going. I talked and talked and talked. Then I cried and cried and cried. I told her everything in my heart—all the guilt, and all the horrible intractable feelings I still lived with, every day, in her absence. I had no idea where she'd gone, I said, but I hoped Mum was right: I hope I got to see her again. I told her I didn't get any of this. Why were we even here? Why were we even born? What were we supposed to do here? Any clues appreciated.

And after that, I rolled off Rowie's grave, looked up at the passing clouds, and had a little chat with God directly, telling Him or Her or It that even though I was not going to mass with Mum anymore (because—sorry to be rude—I found it a bit boring) and, even though I still really had no idea if He or She or It existed, right now, in this vulnerable state, it was probably best if I just acted as if He or She or It *did* exist, and stop with all the rumination.

As always, I noticed that once I'd spoken these doubts and fears aloud, a peaceful feeling came over me. Relief. The relief of speaking the truth. It made me feel more like myself.

By now some time had passed—a fair bit, actually, because all of a sudden it occurred to me that it was dusk now and well past time for me to head home. I felt the panic rising in me then. I hadn't taken a mobile phone with me. Mum would be worried.

I walked quickly back the way I came, only to discover with a flash of horror that the gates to the cemetery were locked. The panic started fizzing in me then. I walked faster, and then started running, all the way to the other side of the cemetery, where I discovered—Jesus help me—those gates were locked too.

Are you freaking kidding me? I'm locked in a cemetery? Are you serious? Am I going to have to sleep here? I looked around but there was no one else about. Oh my God! What the hell was I going to do?

I had still been a little on the fence about whether I wanted to live or die, but this was the moment I realised that I wanted to live. I really did. I would really, really like to live, and I would really, really like to get out of there.

These were very good things to know.

But the problem remained: how the hell *was* I going to get out of there?

There was only one way. Yes, the wall surrounding the cemetery was tall. Yes, if I fucked this up I was probably going to break some bones. But damn it, I was going to try!

So I did—I tried. I ran straight at the fence, jumped up and, with a strength that surprised me, somehow clambered to the top. With my legs straddled either side of the fence, I looked over the edge. I really didn't want to do this, but what choice did I have? I got myself into position, counted backwards from three, and let myself drop. A second after my feet hit the ground, without thinking, I jumped into a little Superwoman pose. 'Well done, Bowditch!' I mumbled, proudly. It wasn't graceful, but I was out! I dusted myself off, and ran as fast as I could all the way home.

A new courage was born in me that day, a reminder of the old me, the one who knew I was powerful.

When I got home, it was dark. Mum was waiting out the front, worried.

'Where have you been?' she asked.

Still huffing and puffing from my run, I said, 'You're not going to believe this: I just got locked in the cemetery!'

The look on her face was so confused, I could not help but laugh. And then she laughed. She laughed so much she had to run inside to use the toilet, and that made me laugh some more. Laughter! I'd forgotten how this felt! I like it, I said to myself. I should try and do this more often.

Although I now had a practical way of dealing with the symptoms of panic and anxiety, I hadn't worked out how to stop crying. My mind still felt full of the sadness of Rowena, and Joffa, and the world at large. All the feelings I used to be able to keep at bay simply by keeping busy, and overeating, and dieting, were now present, demanding to be felt. My parents and I agreed that, as I was making progress, it was probably a good time to go and see a therapist. A family friend recommended Ron. Apparently, he had once studied at a seminary in preparation to become a priest.

'Perfect!' said Mum.

At our first appointment, it occurred to me that Ron looked familiar. He was an older gentleman. He had a mostly bald head, a white beard, and he wore a grey skivvy, grey slacks and glasses that made him look very much like my dad in his 1978 driver's licence photo. But it wasn't Dad I was thinking of. It was someone else. Then it came to me—of course! He looked like Graeme from *The Goodies*!

At first, every appointment I had with Ron felt like Groundhog Day. He'd open his door, invite me to lie on the couch and ask me how I was; I'd try to tell him, and then I'd just weep and spend most of the session trying to stop crying so I could speak.

Rowena, Joffa, Rowena, Joffa—my grief felt like a racetrack that I was cursed to loop again and again, with no exit in sight.

It was more than that, though. Up until this point, the only people I'd really spoken to about the thoughts in my head were, well, God. I had tried to talk to Mum and Dad but because I didn't want to worry them, I wasn't able to tell them the whole truth. I wasn't writing things down either. That still felt beyond me.

Saying the words aloud—talking about the things I felt, how bad things had got—still brought with it a very strong sense of shame. How dare I feel, or have felt, these things? And one day, through tears, I managed to get this out: that I was ashamed, so ashamed, of how weak I was. I still could not quite believe that I—Clare bloody Bowditch, of the Sandy Bowditches—had had a bloody *nervous breakdown*.

Ron thought about this for a moment and then said, 'What if there was a different way of thinking about what you went through? What if, instead of calling it a *breakdown*, you started calling it a *breakthrough*?' A breakdown becoming . . . a breakthrough? I'd never heard of such a thing (although it must have been common language in therapist circles because, years later, watching Brené Brown's famous second TED talk, I was surprised to hear her tell the world that her therapist had said exactly the same thing to her!).

A *breakthrough*? When he said that, I wanted to laugh, and I would have, were I not still weeping (with some force) all over his couch. How could this—the disintegration of personality, my inability to eat, sleep, think, read newspapers or even just stop shaking—possibly be thought of as a breakthrough? It certainly didn't feel like one. Didn't look like one either. Unlike in the movies, the start of my breakdown just looked like a young woman in the corner of a cafe in Oxford quietly weeping over a slightly dry but otherwise perfectly edible yoghurt-covered muesli biscuit. Nothing to kill yourself over, surely?

Ron explained that from what he understood, I had spent most of my life to date trying to live up to other people's expectations of who I was, trying to please people, to fit in, to change myself in order to make sure I belonged, and to keep everything I really thought and felt, all my fears, to myself.

What if, he said, this is a chance for you to just be who you are? What if this is a chance for you to listen to yourself? And what if this is a chance for you to tell the truth, for the first time, about what you really want to do with your life? What *do* you want to do with your life?

Singing, of course. I wanted to write songs and sing. But . . . as if!

Like every kid everywhere, I had spent most of my life trying very hard to make my parents proud of me. And I don't really know why, but I had always thought that if I pursued my dream of being a singer, I would somehow be disappointing them. They didn't like pop music. They didn't approve of the music industry. They didn't value fame, or money, or prestige. I didn't either. But I did want to sing. I did want to perform. I did want to make my own kind of music.

And at this stage in my recovery, it was still hard for me to imagine I would ever regain the confidence to be able to do that. My sense of self was still very small.

That is okay, said Ron. Slowly, slowly.

Then he said something very, very interesting. He said, 'Have you ever considered that these fears you have, these stories you are telling yourself, are actually just that—just stories? Have you ever considered that this experience—the breakdown—could actually be a new starting place?'

Week after week, on his couch, crying—I can't tell you how pointless I thought it all was. I tried to cancel almost every appointment.

But every time I walked out of Ron's office, I felt a little stronger, a little closer to who I was, and who I wanted to be. A little more confident about telling the stories I longed to tell, even if just to myself. And the truth is, if I was being really honest, what I still wanted more than anything was to one day do all those things I'd sung about in that half-finished song of mine called 'Amazing Life'.

Even though sleep was still proving elusive, now, at the very least, I had a routine in place; one that I followed to the dot, every single night.

After dinner, I'd take a shower, put on my pyjamas, put on a relaxing CD (of Canadian loons singing. *Ka KAAAH*). Then I'd do some stretching, something approximating yoga, make two hot drinks (valerian tea, then a Horlicks malted drink). Just before hopping into bed, I'd dab marjoram oil on my pillow, add a splash of lavender oil, do a little light reading, and then turn off the light and tell myself, 'Goodnight now. Sweet dreams.'

Did I sleep?

No, I did not.

But I was now at a point where I had realised, thanks to The Weekes and Ron, that sleeping itself wasn't really the point. The point was learning not to give so much of a fig about whether I slept or not. I mean, this had been going on for months now, this non-sleeping business, and I hadn't dropped dead yet, had I?

Night after night, I used my awake time to experiment with the possibility that maybe Ron was right—maybe there was great power in deciding what story I was going to tell myself.

Was my lack of sleep going to be a big deal, or not a big deal?

When Ron had first proposed this theory to me—that we have a choice in what we feel, because what we feel is based on how we think about things—it had felt radical, and wrong. Absolutely wrong. What choice did I have in feeling sad about Rowena, for example? Anything else would make me a monster. He gently urged me to pull out my little shovel, and dig a little deeper. In detail, he explained that there are some things we get to choose, and some we don't. Those we can't choose are circumstances. I could not choose whether or not Rowena lived or died, for example. But I did have some choice in what meaning I made, based on those circumstances.

When he said that, I cried and cried. 'Why are you crying?' he asked. I choked it out: 'Because I feel like I should have been able to help her, and I didn't.' Slowly, over time, I came to understand that there is something comforting about guilt. It sounded bizarre to me when he first suggested that by choosing to feel guilty about Rowena's death, to think guilty thoughts, I was in fact trying to exert some modicum of control over my situation. I was trying to contain, somehow, the horror of her illness and death. I was also using my guilt to keep her close.

I hated hearing that. But I came to realise, over time, he was right. For years I had been carrying a big sack of bad feelings, one that acted in a way as a proxy for my missing sister.

Although this is a deeply common grief response, in my case it also proved deeply destructive. My sack of rocks was just too heavy. Now, because of my collapse, I had been given a chance to look at what I was carrying and work out which parts were mine, and which parts I could leave behind. As I allowed myself to feel the grief of my childhood, my resentment, my fear, my horror, I began to see that underneath it all was one simple truth: I loved my sister. I didn't want her to die. And if I was going to get well, I was going to need to find healthier places to put all this love I was still dragging around for my big sister, Rowena.

I make it sound simple when I say it like that. In truth, it would take years. And it is still hard to this day. I can't tell you how easily I default to this habit of grief, of powerlessness, of refusing to accept what was left.

But this lesson with Ron would have far-reaching implications—this lesson that although we cannot change circumstances, or the weather, the thoughts we have about them creates our feelings. If I wanted to fight that, I could. But there was another way.

Now, as I lay awake at night, my mind running its fake-news-banner of all the things that scared me the most, I would remember what The Weekes said: that every supposed failure was an opportunity to practise. As my mind presented my greatest fears, I started to use them as an opportunity to practise not fighting, just accepting. At night, my fears didn't travel in any order I could make sense of, they just rolled out randomly, jumping from one to the other, like this:

You will never get well.

I accept the possibility that maybe I will never get well.

You will never be well enough to be a mother.

I accept the possibility that maybe I will never be well enough to be a mother.

You should have done something to save Rowena.

I accept that Rowena died, and there's nothing I could have done about it.

You are too fragile to be a singer. It would kill you. You would be terrible at it.

I accept that I may never be well enough to be a singer/songwriter, that the demands of performing, touring, self-promotion may be too much for me.

You are living at home with your parents, you loser.

I accept that I am living with my parents, and that's fine for now, actually.

I accept that I don't know how to prevent another holocaust happening.

I accept that I feel guilty for having lived at all, but that I can let that go.

I accept that I have no money, and no idea how to make money.

I accept that my stomach is churning and my heart is pounding.

I accept that I may not get to sleep tonight.

I accept that I will no doubt un-accept all these things a million more times in the years to come.

And so on.

This was well beyond my comfort zone. In learning to live with the voice in my head, I had to practise accepting lots of things that I wish had never happened, and lots of things that I didn't want to happen. I had to stop fighting with the past, and the future. I had to come back again and again to the story that felt true, and hopeful: I was in recovery from a nervous breakdown. This would take some time. But I would get there. I was no longer going to live in the shadow of the bad feeling that had haunted me since childhood.

And then the sun would come up.

More often than not, I was now getting at least three or four hours of sleep a night, even if it was interrupted.

For a long time to come, my first feeling as I woke up, my go-to feeling, was still a shudder of dread and shame. I was getting better, however, and just carrying on with my day anyway. And slowly, slowly, week after week, my body remembered to sometimes forget itself. Bliss. Some days, I felt okay for only three minutes out of every three hours, but I practised accepting that too.

I still had a long way to go. It would be months, for example, before I felt able to catch an underground train, or be part of a crowd, or play my guitar and enjoy it. It would be months until I could watch television without feeling nauseous. I still, to this day, jump at the sound of a passing truck.

And it would be a year or more until I could sleep the way I used to. But, thanks to The Weekes, I just chalked all those sleepless nights down to training. I didn't know it then, but I know it now: there is always something good waiting on the other side of fear.

✳

Thanks to my local bookshop, I had now ordered and bought every book and audio cassette that The Weekes had ever made. I was, let's say, a superfan. Turns out, The Weekes had one of the sweetest old-fashioned cultivated Australian accents you've ever heard in your life. Her tape began with: 'This is Dr Weekes speaking. I am very happy to have this opportunity to talk to you personally.' What a character! In every one of her works, she spoke of the need to nurture internal courage. She told me I'd need to do this regularly, and purposefully, until it was an established part of my schtick. (She would never use the word 'schtick', but I'd read her book so many times now, I was starting to take liberties.) She made it clear that if, at first, I needed to trick myself into little acts of courage, that was fine. My yearning would kick in at some point. That was the key, in fact. She said that in order to cultivate courage, we must *want* it.

And I was actually beginning to want it.

I had noticed that after I made the promise to one day write a book, and then jumped the fence at the cemetery—both things that terrified me—I felt happy, and alive.

So what else was I afraid of?

With pen and paper, I made a small list, discovering that, in fact, it was not so small after all. It was long. Very, very long. Looking at it made me feel sick.

And so, I decided to tackle it slowly. I decided I needed to just do one thing at a time, deal with one fear at a time. Okay, maybe two. Two fears at a time.

The two fears I decided to confront first were:

1. Swimming at the beach.
2. Applying to uni.

That creative arts course Libby was doing really did sound perfect for me, but there was no way I was going to get in; I hadn't done the right subjects at school and, besides, I was a mature-aged student now. However, as Ron would remind me, there was no harm in trying, was there? I said to myself, if I *didn't* try, there was every chance I'd still be living with my parents at fifty-seven. Is that what I wanted? (Although Ron said to watch my habit of 'catastrophising', I must say, I did sometimes find it rather motivating.)

I decided to start with the easier, more practically faceable fear: the one about swimming.

What exactly am I afraid of? I asked myself.

I am afraid of the cold water, because it hurts, and I am afraid of being in my bathers, because I will feel embarrassed.

I am also afraid of being eaten by a shark. (That was unlikely, of course but, nonetheless, I said it because it was there.)

So I decided that the next morning I would march down to the beach and, despite not owning any bathers that fit me, despite the cold weather, despite the stranger who would no doubt be jogging, or the possibility I might get attacked by Jaws, that I would go for a swim anyway.

On the shore, wind whipping, me shivering, stripped down nearly bare in my too-big bra and my mum's small undies, I tried again and again to walk into the water, without moving much at all.

Did my mind keep telling me there was definitely a shark in there, about to eat me whole?

Yes, it did.

Was there a shark in there, waiting to eat me whole?

No, there was not.

There was an upturned boat that looked like a shark, that my mind told me could well be a shark, but it was not a shark. Through my work with Ron, it was becoming clearer and clearer to me now that there wasn't just one voice in my brain, there were . . . at least two. There was that fearful voice, but there was also a calmer, more rational voice. The question I kept needing to ask myself was, which voice was I going to choose to believe?

After a number of false starts (running an inch into the water and then running out again when my heart felt too loud), it occurred to me that I was . . . swimming.

I was swimming, in the water. And I was alive! This was great!

I spotted a group of half a dozen older women and men swimming nearby. They must have been the famous Icebergers—a group of over-sixties who swam here every morning, no matter the season. Without thinking, standing up tall in the water in my bra and undies, I waved. A few of them waved back. They looked happy. I felt happy. This, I thought, is what happens when you spend every day facing your fears: you end up happy.

And exhilarated.

And then just cold.

At home, I had a shower, and felt warm again, and more myself than ever before.

✳

I don't know how many times I told Ron that with a brain like mine perhaps I would never get to live out my Jeff Buckley dream. Even the thought of standing on stage made my cheeks go pink and my hands start shaking.

What if I just started smaller? suggested Ron.

What if I just started with something other than music?

Over the course of the last few months, at the suggestion of The Weekes, I'd begun working on small art projects, the kinds of things I used to do as a kid, just as a way of filling in time. I'd been picking flowers and arranging them in vases, pressing them in books, drawing, painting, knitting, playing with clay, planting seeds and writing down my favourite quotes, especially anything that might also double as a metaphor for hope. These were all things I could do without using too much energy, that I could get carried away in, which made time pass. The voice in my head often still told me that the only way I would ever feel better was to hang on to my fears, ruminate over them, stay alert. But as I became better and better at observing the relationship between the stories I was telling myself and the feelings I was experiencing, I began to realise that the opposite was true.

The less I thought about my own existential worries and the larger worries of the world, the more peaceful I felt. Of course, the voice in my head told me that I was being soft, that I wasn't facing up to reality, that I was selfish and self-centred.

I practised accepting. That might well be true, I conceded, but for now, for today, the best way forward was to keep dismissing those rumblings with statements like: 'You know what? There might be a day in the future when I get to tackle those things. Right now, I'm recovering from a nervous breakdown, so I'm just going to craft for a bit.' At first, I needed to spell things out clearly like that, as though I was talking to a child—that was how Ron explained it. Okay, I said. In a way, I was learning a language—the language of self-kindness, self-support, naming emotions, finding ways to alchemise them. It might take a while.

And finally I felt able to face the second fear on my list. I was not qualified to get in to the Bachelor of Creative Arts. I had no folio, had done no arty subjects in Year Twelve, but with Ron's encouragement, I decided to apply anyway. I wrote a letter— in fact, a rather long letter, a story, explaining why I thought the course would suit me. I took it as a sign of recovery that— in writing my application—I let my sense of humour through. I titled the essay:

THE SIMPLE AND TRUE STORY OF
CLARE BOWDITCH
WHICH AIMS TO EXPLAIN WHY SHE IS AN
EXCELLENT CANDIDATE FOR ACCEPTANCE INTO
THE BACHELOR OF CREATIVE ARTS.
(Otherwise entitled, 'Please accept me or I'll cry'.)

I had no real idea where this new confidence came from, all I knew was that facing my fears felt good. While the prospect of rejection was nearly paralysing, Ron said we could deal with that later. For now, my only job was to apply. And so I did.

Sometimes at night, I'd find myself thinking about my future. Not too far ahead, just a few months or maybe a year or so. The voice in my head kept telling me that it was silly to have applied to the Bachelor of Creative Arts. As if I was someone who could survive that kind of chaos. The sensible thing to do would be to just live a small life from now on—get a job, stay at home with my parents, do things that were safe, enjoy my little crafts. I didn't want to have another breakdown, did I?

And for a small while, I did just that. I stuck to my routine. I kept things simple. I let my nervous system settle. I took my time. I practised FAFLing every day with small challenges, like walking around the block. I walked, I ate well, I took deep deep breaths, I entered and exited bed at the same time every day whether I could sleep or not, I swam in the ocean, I went to therapy. As the months rolled on, I developed a new identity as a quiet person, a person who didn't say that much, who didn't do small talk. A mostly serious person. I listened more, and observed more, and I quite liked these qualities. It took so much less energy to be the quieter one in the room. I felt quite different to the person I had been. In fact, I began to judge that person rather harshly. Old Icarus—that's how I now referred to the 'pre-breakdown me'. Too much ego. Flew too close to the sun. I still thought that I'd failed—at travelling, at university, at relationships, and with my mind—and this breakdown was the playing-out of my failure. Aiming high still terrified me. The thought of ever travelling again was off the cards. I just wanted to keep things low-key from here on in.

My sister Lisa did not quite buy it. She knew me very well. She must have observed that if things kept going this way that I was probably going end up a rather bitter old lady. She didn't believe me when I told her that I was too fragile to go out anymore, that I didn't like being around people. She said that I just needed to start getting out again. I told her that I'd have another panic attack; that I couldn't follow conversations properly anymore.

You know what Lisa said?

'Tough titties! You're coming out!'

She was not impressed by my little story. She said I was coming out with her and her friends that night. Nothing challenging, just Christmas carols in the park. Be ready by 6 pm.

That night she arrived at Mum and Dad's with a fully packed picnic basket and told me to shush and just get in the car. We drove to a park in the middle of Malvern, which was hosting their annual Christmas carols concert.

In my pre-London life, I would rather have died than attend a Christmas carols concert—death by boredom. Now, curiously, the thought of attending said event filled me with terror! The voice in my head kept scouting all the potential disasters that could happen at any moment. My mind could not seem to help telling me wild stories that I, and all the people there, were not safe. But, as instructed, I practised my FAFL, applied a little rationale, a dash of humour even ('Clare, it is highly unlikely a gunman is waiting in the bushes in the leafy suburbs of Malvern, just saying!'), and I was able to enter the park.

Lisa's friends were waiting for us on a blanket, and when I sat down with them, they were all so kind to me that I started crying. Lisa didn't skip a beat; she kept the mood up and even though I was too depressed to be able to make much conversation, it was good for me to challenge myself. They must have known what had been happening because none of Lisa's friends asked me about Europe, or told me how well I was looking, or asked me how I'd lost the weight. Someone handed me a candle and a booklet and I heard my voice singing for the first time in months, which (surprise) also made me cry. I'd missed that feeling of singing with other people so much. It just calmed me in a way that nothing else seemed to.

It was a simple night out, but my spirits were lifted. My hermitage was broken. I went out, and I didn't have a panic attack. This was good, I said to myself.

One day, a big white letter arrived in my letter box addressed to me. In it, I was remarkably surprised to find a letter confirming my, wait for it, acceptance into the Bachelor of Creative Arts at Melbourne University and the Victorian College of the Arts! I was so surprised, I screamed!

I was going to art school!

And . . . I was excited!

Or was that terror?

Either way, all good!

＊

When I first came back from London, I thought my life was over. I thought I would never be well again. But in my recovery, in my work with The Weekes and Ron, I was learning to tell myself a different story: that every time I spoke the truth about what I knew, or thought I knew, I felt stronger. So, as long as I was willing to keep doing that, and keep fronting up to the things that scared me, there was nothing so wrong with me that couldn't, in time, be set right.

And what I also learned was this: it might sound daggy, and you might have heard it a million times before, but Ron was correct when he told me that, sometimes, what starts at a breakdown really can become the moment you look back on as a breakthrough, as the moment in which you started to live your own kind of life.

8

God and Frank

I thought you were God
And I believed in you.

'I THOUGHT YOU WERE GOD'
(*What Was Left*, 2005)

I'd always known my family were Catholic, but I don't think
I realised quite *how* Catholic we were until the first time my new
best friend Defah came over after school for band practice. We
were fifteen then, nearly sixteen. We met at Preshil, the school
I went to after I left Star of the Sea. There were many interesting families at Preshil, and Defah's was one of them. If I had
to describe her family in a sentence, I'd say she was from good,
solid, rational, liberal, entreprenurial, bohemian, artistic, Jewish
stock. In short, Defah was pretty fricking cool. I suspect now
that I may well have been the very first Catholic she'd ever really
crossed paths with, which I suppose explains the animated smile

on Defah's face the first time she walked through the entrance of my family home.

'Fuck!' she said. 'You never told me your family were so religious!'

'What do you mean?' I asked. I was genuinely confused. What had given it away?

'What do you mean "What do I mean"? Look around!'

I guess I'd never really noticed it before, the water I was swimming in, but as I looked around that day, and in the days following, it became clear to me that, yes, Defah might have a point.

Inside the front window, looking out on the street for all to see, were two child-size statues—one of the Madonna, and one of Joseph holding a toddler Jesus. In the hallway, there was a small holy water font, and a poster of a biblical quote of an old tree, and at the bottom of it were written the words: *Lives rooted in God are never uprooted.*

In the living room, I looked with new eyes at what had always been there—Bible quotes on the wall, crucifixes, smaller statues of Mary, the postcard of the *Pietà* by Michelangelo, and the large framed picture of a young bearded Jesus in contemplation, looking down at his palms.

Turning my gaze to the bookshelves and the windowsills, there were clogs and little statues of Dutch windmills, and blue-and-white original Delft pottery, and lots of art books and cookbooks and a dash of philosophy, but most of the decorations and most of the books were about Jesus, God, saints and faith.

It had never really occurred to me before now that Defah and I were different in this way—me Catholic, her atheist. How embarrassment! 'Not at all,' she said. As always, her openness and curiosity led the way. She wandered around our house like an anthropologist, and asked my mother just the kind of intense questions I tried, very hard, to avoid. Defah participated in all of our rituals—prayers before dinner, mass on Sunday, weddings, confirmations, baptisms. She did so eagerly and without judgement, and she and my mother grew very fond of each other, and they remain so to this very day.

I asked Defah recently, 'Was that weird for you?'

'Not at all,' she said. 'It was fascinating.' She told me that what she felt in our house, more than anything, was that we were people who knew how to laugh, and how to love—and what else really matters in the end but that?

Joseph Campbell once said that most religions begin with the word 'help', and that makes sense to me. It was when Rowie was ill and dying that Mum—in a cry for help—felt her true faith was born. Dad went with Mum, although his own faith always remained much simpler. As an old man he still said the same prayers he'd said as a child, on his knees, morning and night, thanking God for the day and asking for the strength to face another one. It truly was thanks to the strength of their faith, and the support of our parish and school community, that our family was able to hold together as it did after Rowena died.

But despite my inheritance, I am, myself, a bit of a shit Catholic. I always liked praying, and lighting candles, and sitting quietly in churches, and singing, and feeling good hopeful feelings in my chest, and being loved and approved of, and doing the right thing, and being with my family, but with very few exceptions I have never been able to make much sense of the mass, itself.

Ironically, these days, every mass I attend leaves me feeling as though, by being there, by taking part, I am betraying the very same values I was always taught to uphold.

When I came back from London, thin-skinned, I did lean rather heavily on the framework of my childhood faith. I took comfort, I suppose, from the ritual of attending mass with Mum, and of praying morning and night. I was very grateful to have somewhere to go with my terror and my fear. Faith proved to be a great consolation. I was too tired to question anything. I was happy to follow the rules.

Alas, it was not to last.

One day, not long after I'd discovered The Weekes, the phone rang. It was Jenny Brookes, a childhood friend from Girl Guides who I hadn't been in contact with since, well, the last I'd seen her was about five years ago when she was sneaking into the toilets at church during mass to smoke out the window. I remember admiring her guts. She had a very friendly voice, and spoke very quickly, saying she wouldn't keep me for too long, but she'd bumped into our old Girl Guides leader at the shops and heard I'd been having a bit of a tough time (gosh, news travels fast!), and she was just calling to invite me to this thing that she and her friends went to—kind of like a youth gathering for young Catholics, but cool?

Catholic and cool: not words I'd ever really heard spoken in the same sentence before, although I'd always secretly hoped that somewhere, in some corner of the world, there existed a crew of Young Catholic Rebels—people who were artistic, curious, philosophical, intellectual, open and, preferably, really really good-looking. In my dreams, it would be kind of like Defah's house on a Saturday night—coffee, wine, music, dancing, people snogging in corners, and so on. The only difference was there would be just a touch more God talk, if you know what I mean. I wasn't quite sure if this was the kind of meeting Jenny had in mind but, hey, I was willing to give it a crack.

Three minutes into my car drive with Jenny and her fiancé, Tom, I realised that maybe I should have asked a few more questions before I agreed to this. The meeting was about an hour away—a long time to make small talk, which was a skill I had lost in Oxford, along with my mind. Fortunately, Jenny could talk, and she did, first about her engagement, then about her wedding plans. She told me that from the moment she and Tom met they knew they were meant to be together, that their families shared the same Catholic values, but then—and I don't know quite how this happened exactly—she jumped into a rather detailed monologue about her and Tom's sex life. Or, to be clear, lack of. Without any prompting, she proceeded to tell me how they had been saving their virginity for marriage, how much they were looking forward to it, but how sometimes when they were kissing, things got out of hand (she added much detail of the stuff they did to each other that wasn't technically sex—*Sweet Jesus and Mary, help me now, make her stop*) so much so that it could probably still see them both in hell unless it were properly confessed, which wasn't easy these days, because half the priests didn't even know how to take a proper confession, not like in her parents' generation, yadda, yadda, yadda. I was sweating by now—s w e a t i n g. As hard as I was trying to do my FAFL, my breathing was getting shallower and shallower, and eventually I squeaked, 'Could someone please roll down a window?'

This was not the conversation I'd imagined. At most, I'd anticipated perhaps a light brainstorm about whether there was any evidence of early Catholic feminism in the writings of, well, I didn't know—I thought maybe they could tell me. I was hoping the experience would leave me feeling better about the church, feeling there was more openness, not less. I wished, for a moment, I had not come.

But as we arrived at the gathering, which was at a church, I decided to keep an open mind. It wasn't a pretty church. There was none of that old-school Oxford charm. It was one of those 1970s-designed brown-brick affairs with an oddly angled roof and a carved wooden cross hanging on the wall behind the altar. All I needed was one little sign of kinship—perhaps someone with a facial piercing, or sporting a beret. But, alas, the only remarkable thing about this Catholic gathering was that everyone was young and, also, there appeared to be a rock band setting up next to the altar.

Turns out, this was not so much of gathering—it was in fact just a mass. Friendly people filed into the pews, I along with them. The service began with a bang—loud Christian rock music, blaring out across the crackling speakers. I quickly realised I was trapped. I felt the old panic start to gurgle inside me. Then the priest began to welcome the congregation. The last thing I needed was more fire and brimstone, there was enough in my head already, but too late—here it came. I tried my best to maintain normal facial expressions, to sit and stand at the right times, but when the charismatic healing portion of the service had arrived, and Jenny asked me if I'd like to take part, I knew I had to get out of there. The crescendo of the Christian rock grew so loud that all I could think to do was stand up and run. I said, 'Excuse me, excuse me,' as I fled the pew, going straight to the toilet cubicle, where I locked myself in. To myself, or perhaps aloud, I said, 'Face Accept Float, Let time pass. Clare, you are not in any danger. You are just over-whelmed. Face Accept Float, Let time pass.'

I heard the door creak open, heard Jenny's voice say, 'Clare, honey, are you okay?'

I lied, told her I was just fine, just feeling a little sick, a little dizzy—I was just going to sit there for a while, on the toilet seat. All good.

She stayed quiet for a while, and then apologised. She said she'd thought it was going to be really low key, but it was sur-prisingly intense, even she felt it. She kept talking then, saying she also needed to apologise for what she had said in the car about her and Tom, about sex. (*Not again!* I thought. *Please God, spare me!*) But this time, she did not go on. She waited for a while, then just asked if I wanted her to take me home, and I squeaked, 'Yes, please, that would be very nice.'

The drive home was dark and long, and my panic was loud, and I couldn't seem to think of anything to say but I didn't need to, Jenny was talking, talking, talking, careful this time to keep the topics chilled.

I was pleased to arrive home. I thanked them as I closed the car door. As kind as it was for Jenny and Tom to invite me, my fervent hope as I walked into my house that night was that we would never have to speak of this night again.

Upstairs in my bedroom, my relief felt soft and sweet. I did something then that I hadn't done since I'd got home from Oxford—I took out my writing book and jotted down everything that had happened. Every detail. It felt so good to write, and to remind myself that it was okay not to have enjoyed myself, it was okay that I didn't want to force myself to sit and listen to things I disagreed with anymore, nor should I feel compelled to argue against them. It was none of my business, really, what other people believed. None of their business what I believed, either. Was I going to hell for thinking the way I thought? I couldn't say for sure but I doubted it.

What else did I believe, or not believe? That night, I wrote it all out. I believed in love. I believed that two people who loved each other, and enjoyed that love, had not done anything wrong. I didn't believe there was only 'one true faith'—words they uttered at mass. I didn't believe that at all! If there was a God in whose image we were made, and that God was clever, I didn't believe He or She or It would be so arrogant as to insist that every human should think of Him or Her or It in the same way in order to feel connected to goodness. That would be no fun at all.

I wrote down my fears that night, and my beliefs, and it felt good, as always, to tell the truth. And the truth is, I wasn't going to do things like that anymore—go to places like that mass, places that made no sense to me, that made me feel weird and sick and as though I was doing something wrong.

I was no longer going to fight to define what God was, and what God wasn't. Instead, I was going to start small. All I had to do was continue moving forwards in the direction of my heart's deepest longing to stay connected to the grace and the truth that I knew did actually exist, because I could feel it.

And I wasn't going to pretend anymore that, just because the Catholic Church was full of good people, it had the right to tell me what was good and bad. I already knew what was good and bad. I was going to live according to *my* values.

For now, I was not going to wrestle with the religion of my birth, not going to try to be a good Catholic, not going to suppress, or even speak, my opinions, to make other people feel comfortable. I would no longer keep pretending that this religion, and the way it was practised in the modern age, made sense to me, just because it made sense to my parents.

I would let them be them and me be me.

This would disappoint them, and I hated disappointing them. But I was not, and never would be, a good Catholic.

There—I'd said it. What a relief!

And so, from that day forwards, I committed to keeping my faith rather simple, and rather practical. Where I could do good, I would. If something made sense, I would adopt it. If something made no sense, I would waste no time trying to work it out, or excuse it. Where I could find thoughtful answers, I would take them.

As my recovery progressed, and my moods stabilised, I became braver in my determination to live true to what I knew to be right and wrong. I gave myself full permission to untangle from what I felt as the heavy expectations of my childhood faith, and to explore spirituality and meaning and philosophy and wisdom in whatever form took my interest. Thanks to Caroline Jones, and her ABC program *The Search for Meaning*, I had become interested in interfaith dialogue and had started to look for the common good in all paths, to listen out for perennial philosophies, the places we agreed—and that was how I first fell in love with the stories of author Jack Kornfield.

Jack had once been a Buddhist monk living in a cave. Now he was a Buddhist monk living in New York. His writing had such humour and wisdom and life on the page, I was hooked. Like so many other writers I've never met, Jack Kornfield would become my teacher, and his lessons would light the path of my recovery.

My favourite chapter in his book *A Path with Heart* was the one called 'Naming the emotions', which contained an exercise called 'Naming the demons'. Jack explained that peace could never be found by running away from difficult emotions; it could only be found by sitting with them, and letting them pass through us. He said that when we meditated, the trick was to observe our emotions and then name them in threes (for example, 'anger, anger, anger' or 'lust, lust, lust'). It was a bit like training puppies, he said. We needed to train our mind, to tame our thoughts.

This theory made sense to me, although I was no good at the practice. Everything I felt was still so entangled. Most of the time, I was very much working on instinct. Whenever I went beyond that in my search for The Correct Name For This Feeling I would find myself trapped back in the ping-pong of anxiety, and my fear of *getting it wrong.*

At a certain point, it occurred to me that, yet again, I would need a workaround.

Ron had once said to me that perhaps this whole breakdown had been about giving my head and heart a chance to catch up and create language around what really were incredibly complex early childhood feelings and experiences, and their long tail. This was, in a way, like a very poorly orchestrated yet highly essential system update. Because so many of these feelings occurred around the time I was just learning language, they clustered together, and I really didn't know how to untangle them, which is why I called them the Bad Feeling. But through my work with the FAFL exercise, I was beginning to understand the benefits of being able to simplify and name my experiences. Maybe I needed to apply that same attitude to the Bad Feeling?

And so it was that one fateful day, after failing yet again at this exercise of naming, naming, naming, I decided to do something weird: I decided to put a little distance between me (Clare), and that voice of worry in my head, that inner critic that had been at me since I was a child. I decided to give that voice a name all of its own. I named him . . . Frank. Not sure why—perhaps because it was the first name that came to mind. Could have been any name. But Frank it was.

When I heard the bad voice, felt the bad feeling, I began calling it out, challenging his authority. At first, I would say, 'Hello, Frank. I see you.' I tried to be reasonable, collegial, but Frank always seemed to need the last word.

And so, one day, instead of engaging in battle, I decided that I was, in fact, the boss. The next time Frank arced up, here's what I said: 'Fuck off, Frank. Go sit in the corner.'

And lo and behold, for a second, my busy mind fell quiet.

That's the day I got it (although I often forget, and still need to practise): I am the boss of my brain. Inner critics can be tamed. Although occasionally Frank said something useful, mostly, he was just being naughty. The words 'Fuck off, Frank'— or FOF, as my friends and I call it—is, quite literally, the secret of my success.

I didn't realise this at the time, but it's clear to me now—Frank was never really my enemy. Frank was just my survival brain, gone rogue. Somewhere in that heady mix of genetics, circumstance, imagination and expectation, listening to Frank had become a familiar habit, and that was pretty much the sum of it. All I had to do to start my recovery was to disrupt my old habit of listening to my fear.

Now, when Frank popped up, I just named him, then dismissed him. As I practised, as I grew more skilled in my ability to deflect his arguments and drama, I started to feel lighter inside. I wanted more of that in my life—less worry, more play. I saw my habit of worry was like an addiction—reminding myself of what was wrong with me, instead of what was right with me. Jack, and Buddhism, spoke to that in a way that I could understand. His writing reminded me that, as a human being, I was not just an original sinner, I also had access to original goodness, to dignity, to nobility of spirit and to humour. He reminded me that despite the rigidity that our inner critic tries to impose, we can be reborn every single morning at breakfast. In this new day, he would ask, who is it we want to be?

The Dalai Lama was once quoted as saying that, where possible, don't change religions. All religions have within them a path to wisdom. He said to stick with the religion of your childhood, which is easy for him to say, because he wasn't brought up a Catholic.

I used to tell myself I wasn't allowed to have my own relationship with God—that if I thought differently to my parents, I was doing it wrong. I don't feel that way anymore.

When it comes to spirituality, I changed my story.

I am not at peace with the religion of my childhood. I'm not sure I will ever be, not unless something drastic changes. I am tempted, quite often, to completely overlook its good deeds—the way it remembers people that the rest of society, and governments, would rather forget. The way it cares for them. That is still going on, even today, and I'm glad it is.

But I want the Catholic Church to be different, and it seems to want the very same thing from me. Neither of us seem to be budging. We are like members of family who don't really see each other, except at Christmas, where we try our best to get along. And I feel sad about that sometimes. I really do.

Probably worth noting, my feeling about the church is quite different from my feeling about Jesus. I will always have a crush on Jesus. Just the idea of the man, of his pace. He was loving, and brilliant, and radical, and he wasn't scared of dresses—just my kind of guy. But I no longer worry myself about whether or not he was The One, The Only, because that's just not an argument which makes any sense to me. As with music, I think it's actually okay to appreciate both classical and jazz. I don't see the point of arguing over which is better. Shit hot music is shit hot music. And I have the same attitude to my faith.

I suppose this makes me one of those much derided cherry pickers. I light candles in churches all over the world, of all denominations, and I attend philosophy classes and, when invited, I join my friends to eat dates at Iftar, to eat challah on Shabbat. And most days of the week, you'll find me sharing my meal with a bunch of heathens, atheist, free-thinkers. I'm good with all of that.

Is it possible that, with my open attitude, I am missing some additional layer of religious richness, and joy?

I may well be, and if I am, well, who knows what might be ahead for me and the Big G. I've already warned my husband: enjoy me now, my love, I could turn pure at any moment! I could wake up one morning, sit up in bed, with the spirit of the One

True Catholic God so big inside me, I would never question it again. And then you could come to mass with me! Would that be fun?

My husband doesn't say much, just clears his throat. Changes the subject. God bless the man, and what he puts up with.

For now, however, when it comes to questions of faith, I guess I just think of myself as a bit of a bower-bird: I hunt, fossick, find the blue things, the bits that make sense to me, the bits I love; I test them, keep what I like, and I waste no time arguing with anyone about what's blue, or what's not, because isn't that kind of obvious?

And I'm not asking anyone to agree with me. I'm just asking that you respect my nest, the same way you want me to respect yours.

9

Empty pockets

I think I found a path
Won't you walk with me
Said the fox to the prince
You tamed me, now I'm lonely.

'EMPTY POCKETS'
(Red Raku, *Sweetly Sedated*, 1999)

You know how much I adore my parents, and they me, but it will come as no surprise that six months after I moved back home from London we were just about ready to, shall we say, 'let go'.

I was so sick of them worrying about me, and they were no doubt so sick of needing to worry. It was probably time I got a place of my own.

Ron—my ticking clock in a thunderstorm—said this was a sign of good health, and progress.

*

Financially speaking, the timing could not have been better. My old call centre rang—they'd moved to South Melbourne, just around the corner from my uni—and they needed new staff.

Say what you like about people who work in call centres, that job was good to me. They gave me as much work as I wanted, the pay was three times what I would get as a waitress, and it was a job I could do with my eyes closed. Win, win, win!

I would need to buy a new suit, of course. Like those people in the weight-loss commercials, you could now have fit two of me inside my old one. But that was easy enough, because buying a new suit when you are thin is as simple as walking into Target and choosing from the available items. Life is just easier when you fit the clothes on the rack.

I worked up to twenty hours a week, fitting my shifts in between my uni classes. Some of my old mates still worked there, but many had moved on. The company was now about ten times its original size. It wasn't like the old days. These days, before they let you on the phones, they made you sit through a week of corporate training. We did trust exercises, role-play, and spent an entire afternoon reflecting on a corporate meta-phor about a man who threw washed up starfishes back into the ocean, one by one. The week was both rather boring, and rather fun. I suppose I've always had a bit of a soft spot for 'teamwork'.

Things had certainly changed since those early days at the start-up call centre in Footscray. As the company expanded, it also 'professionalised'. We were now subject to far more rig-orous KPIs. We were asked to swap leisurely chats with our customers for very short ones. Efficiency was king. That didn't make sense to me. Wasn't it more valuable to make sure your customers felt cared for?

The company had changed, and so had I. Now, at my cubicle, wearing my headset, I didn't need to make up voices anymore. I was no longer spilling over the side, no longer tripping over all my unlived dreams. It didn't look like much back then, but my amazing life had already begun.

My first share house after my 'breakthrough' was on a busy Fitzroy street, just on the lip of where the freeway began. Cheap rent, good location, bloody noisy. My housemates— dear friends, a couple called Jill and Dave—knew I was having trouble sleeping, and they set me up in the back bedroom: dank and dark with purple walls but far away from the traffic. Still, I stuck to my routine: early to bed wearing earplugs and an eye mask. Jill and Dave would laugh at me as I walked out from my bedroom in the morning, eye mask still in place. Their lightness and laughter were a balm. They were my age, but so grown up, so together. They slow-cooked legumes, baked polenta, fried haloumi and gardened. They had wonderful taste in world music, and didn't ask questions when they knew I was tired. I was almost always tired. They let me be who I was, in that moment, and the routine of their lives, their stability, their generosity, gave me the freedom and space to start feeling my way into my new life as a uni student.

Over the next few years, I would move in and out of half a dozen share houses, all in or around the suburb I still call home, Fitzroy. Later, I would have the good fortune to settle with my teenage friend Ilka, who by now was a weaver, and invited me to live with her in a long-standing, urban permaculture-focused community in Thornbury which the founders—a bunch of free-thinking Methodists—called Compost (a joke that stuck). There were nine houses with no back fences and a shared garden. Our housemates were two of the original founders, Gil and Mem, who were educationalists, and then sustainable bush-food farmers, and, when I met them, nearly three times my age. For whatever reason it worked beautifully. I would live there for nine years, and raise my family there too. Of course, I could never have predicted that then. I was still busy trying to work out day-to-day things, like how to drive a car without having a panic attack.

I took my time at uni, finding my feet, practising telling Frank to fuck off. I was not in a rush, I told myself. I began, slowly, to rebuild my confidence. Every day, I recited the same things—there was no race to win, there was no way to do this wrong, there was no one else I needed to be, just me.

In the first six months at uni, all I really did was make sculptures of objects that symbolised hope. As the year went on, I also studied creative writing, theatre production, Butoh dance theatre, painting, film studies. Later I would study ethnomusicology and radio production. By audition, I was also allowed to take some additional classes in singing (improvisation) down at the Victorian College of the Arts, which was affiliated with my course. I took the tram there twice a week. It was next to the National Gallery of Victoria, where my mother used to take me sometimes after we visited Rowena.

My heart was raw with Rowena that year; raw with all the uncried tears of childhood, and all the guilt that—through my crying sessions with Ron—I was only just beginning to name and understand. I can't tell you how much time I spent frightened, or how much I prayed to The Universe to please give me the strength to follow my calling, to do something useful with my life, to take this pain and transform it somehow—to help me learn to hope again.

Although I was making progress, I was still very thin-skinned. All it took was the sight of a newspaper headline, or the flare of fire and heat in a metalwork class, and my mind moved quickly to images of destruction, violence and emergency. Death, potential death, was still everywhere I looked. Sometimes it was too much, and I had to just hide in a toilet cubicle with earplugs in my ears and practise my breathing, coming back to the present moment, centring myself, asking for help, for the feelings to move. I may have been fragile but, fuck me, I was determined.

In class, I was quiet. Shy. I kept to myself that first year. Although I was practising challenging my fears, I still couldn't think too far ahead. I wanted to keep my life as simple as I could. And, still, I was often overwhelmed, mainly by my own feelings. The students around me appeared confident and gung-ho. They wrote books, put on plays, made films. One made a plaster cast of her whole body, nude. I admired them all terribly. But I was not there yet—I was still too timid and prone to panic to claim my place in this coterie of creative people. I thought they were fearless. I thought they had something I didn't.

Even though I was still scared, still jumping at shadows, still doubting myself, here is the point: I showed up anyway. My FAFL and my FOF (Fuck off, Frank) were enough to get me through those first days, then weeks, then months, and soon, I had started making things. I modelled tiny angels out of wax, melted silver with a blowtorch and cast the angels in metal using a centrifuge. I sewed tiny little pods of seaweed to sequins, to costumes, to stories. When my fellow students in film studies talked over intense storylines—youth suicide, murder, rape, terminal illness, even some Greek myths—and I felt too many feelings (these days you might call this triggered), I excused myself, found that toilet cubicle, and sat there until the feelings passed. I worried that my fellow students would think I had a bladder problem, but no one ever seemed to notice. Truth be told, we were all a bit odd.

Some days were more difficult than others. Some days, when I felt scared for no reason, I would just leave, go to Dad's chambers, and sit in his office with him quietly as he prepared his cases. I still needed my parents, very much. Dad was such a comfort to me, always. He never asked me anything. Nothing. He just let me sit, and be; if he wasn't busy be would buy me lunch, I'd feel better, and then back out into the world I'd go.

Around this time, in addition to my studies and my jobs, and therapy with Ron, I also started going to weekly group therapy at the Cairnmillar Institute in Melbourne. Dear God, it was awkward, sitting in that room in a circle with strangers who

were much older than me, with much more complicated lives—
kids, divorces, addictions, and so on—and I don't remember
much about what I added to the group. My main memories are
of watching the facilitators, their skill, the way they used open
questions and active listening to try to include all of our voices,
all of our feelings. I had almost nothing in common with any of
those people and, yet, we were all there for the same reason—
we were looking for wisdom and purpose and peace. These
groups were real and raw, and gave me an insight into adulthood
that was truly formative. We didn't have to be best friends. We
didn't even have to like each other. We just had to learn how to
get along and, in general, that is exactly what we did.

Slowly, slowly, the thin membrane between myself and
the outside world grew thicker. Slowly, slowly, my confidence
returned.

As the months rolled on, I grew braver, more experimental
with my clay work; they were still only small-scale pieces like
boats and bowls and goblets and masks, but I started playing
now with different materials and glazes and styles of firing. Raku
firing was my favourite. It's a Japanese style of low-heat firing
where you add combustible items to the piece; you can't predict
how it will look when it comes out. I appreciated the symbolism
of this. The way it allowed for artist and magic/fate/randomness
to create something together, which allowed for the possibility
of a happy (or, at the very least, rather interesting) ending. I also
fired my pieces in wooden boxes stuffed with seaweed (saggar
firing), just to see what would happen, and was so delighted
with the result I did it again and again. I called these kinds of

harmless experiments my Random Creative Adventures. I found the less attached I was to outcomes, to the future, the better I felt.

I was still very much inspired by the hope of a future further off—the one when I was forty, and a writer, and a musician, maybe a mum, with a lovely man—but any other timeframe (such as imagining what I would do next year or the year after) made me feel like I was choking.

So I kept things open. I explored. I allowed myself to do just one thing at a time. My only real hope for my time at uni was that I would survive (Fuck off, Frank) and that somewhere along the line, I could make something beautiful, hopeful, true—that I could take the straw of my life and somehow make gold of it, and that maybe, just maybe, I would one day remember what it really felt like to forget myself. I did not yet allow myself to think bigger than this, and sometimes I felt ashamed of how small my ambitions were. I thought it made me less of an artist, less talented than my fellow students, less bold, less brave. This was Frank's argument, anyway, but time and again I FOFed and gave myself new stories to believe, said it didn't matter whether my art was worthy or not, I was going to make it anyway. The new voice of strength in my head, the graceful voice, reminded me: *You are doing the best you can. Just keep going.*

At home each night, what I did more than anything else was read and read and read—books by Anaïs Nin, and Carl Jung, Julia Cameron and Andy Goldsworthy. All of my spare money was spent on either therapy, or books. I think I read every single word ever written by Australian author Stephanie Dowrick (most especially her classic, *Intimacy and Solitude*, which I read again and again). I cut out Leunig cartoons and pinned them to my diary. I did whatever I could to remind myself that I was not broken. It was okay to feel things. It was okay.

I took a while to adjust to my new small body size, to my new way of being treated in the world, to my thin skin. I did not tell anyone from my new life about my old life. I never talked about my weight, or my breakdown. For that first year, I mostly just listened. And slowly, over time, I worked out who my friends were, and I started taking tiny little chances, like saying 'Hello', and 'Yes' when they invited me for coffee, and a few of these people are still dear friends to this day. Even now, I'm not sure they know how unwell I'd been as I just didn't talk about it, because every time I did, I felt like I was going backwards. I wanted the freedom of a new start, and I claimed it.

Even though I now fitted into clothes from regular shops, I discovered quite quickly that I didn't really like modern clothes very much. Turns out, I liked old op-shop clothes. They suited both me *and* my budget. For the first time in my life, I was able to play around with my body, and what I wanted it to say. I wore tight cords and scarves wrapped around my head. I wore short dresses with stockings and boots. I dyed my hair red, dyed it blonde, then red again, and eventually at midnight with friends at a party where there may or may not have been alcohol involved I shaved it all off. My long blondish reddish hair, all gone. I felt as free as a bird. Just as it had when I was a small child, my body once again felt like a fun place to be.

That year, on campus, I decided to do extra classes in whatever I pleased. When interest sparked, I followed it. That's how I ended up learning skills like basket-weaving, African dancing, jew-ellery design, puppeteering, felt making, herb propagation, body percussion, and slow cooking for beginners. And as time went on, I took more chances—chances with things that don't seem so frightening now, but were then. Things like elevators, and planes, and escalators and mountains. I remember camping, walking with friends through dense bushland, heart beating jungle drums in my chest, Frank screaming at me that I would be bitten by a snake, by an ant, by a spider. And afterwards—look at that—I was still alive! With FAFL and FOF, prayer and hope, good fortune, good family, good friends and good food, I made my way through that most tender of years. The voice of grace reminded me that I didn't need to have it all worked out. I didn't have to be living some amazing life just yet. All I needed to do for now was start, and I had done that, by following my instincts and doing the things I love.

And can you guess the thing I still loved more than anything else? Singing, and writing songs, and recording them on tapes, and putting them under my bed for 'later'.

It may surprise you, even concern you (as it did my parents), to know that during that first year at university I did get back together with Joffa.

I know, I know, I know. You don't have to tell me. I know now, and I knew then.

But listen, his brother was sick.

Really sick. In hospital. Intensive care.

I could not *not* be there for him.

He needed me, and his need took me away from my own. And, to be honest, that was quite a relief.

I needed him too, I thought.

I was lonely. I missed him.

As always, it wasn't like he was hiding who he was.

Yes, he had given up the drugs. That was no easy feat.

But he still did not have a job.

He still did not have a licence.

We were both still just twenty-one years old, nearly five years on from our first kiss.

When he said he wanted me back, I said yes.

I was not ready yet to live with the guilt of no, which I felt would be a betrayal at the very moment he needed me the most.

To not be with him in this moment would be, I thought, an act of cowardice, disloyalty.

Maybe this was what God had in mind the whole time, I told myself.

When it came to family, and to the people I loved, I was still very unclear of where I ended and where they began.

I put him above my own recovery.

I told myself that he was a part of my recovery.

And maybe that was true.

I did sleep better when he was next to me.

But it was a dangerous move.

I am amazed, sometimes, that it happened, and at other times I'm not surprised at all.

My way of loving Joffa had nearly ruined me. I had acted like a wave crashing against a rock again and again and again, trying to prove again and again and again that I would not fail, that I was here, that I wouldn't leave him. That I would save his life, without realising that it was his life to save, not mine. It was not my job; it is never our job to ruin ourselves to try to save the men we think we love. Never. But there were older forces at play: the guilt I felt about Rowena's death, the desire to make it right. I wanted so much to save someone. I didn't know it then, but now, as an adult, I can look back and see it. There it was—clear as day.

Although Joffa had given up the drugs, he had not given up the drink.

Two weeks after we got back together, he cheated on me at a nightclub with a friend of ours from school. When he told me the next afternoon, I cried and I raged, but in the end, after he begged for forgiveness, for one more chance, I stayed.

Maybe some couples come back from brinks like ours. But I see now why my parents were so upset. We were absolutely not right for each other. I would not want this for my own daughter.

It was a much better relationship than it had been—I will give it that. But it was still horrifically sticky. Just like my relationship with the church of my childhood, I felt like he wanted me to be someone I wasn't, and I wanted the same for him. He was a quiet man, and getting him to open up to me felt like pulling teeth. I always wanted more, more, more. More connection. More truth. More love. More attention. All the things I felt I had missed out on last time, I looked to him now to repay.

Again and again, I ended my day feeling disappointed, and wondering what I was doing here. I retreated to a quiet room, turned to my diary, wrote out my feelings, then picked up my guitar to see if I could put them into some kind of order. Something that would help me make sense of them. Something that would reveal the secret language of my heart to the one person who needed to hear it: me.

I wanted a baby, you know. I played with that idea. What would it be like if Joffa and I got pregnant?

One day, after we'd been camping, I re-read my dog-eared copy of *The Little Prince* by Antoine de Saint-Exupéry. And I wrote these words:

I wanted to have his baby, but not too soon.
Through the roof of our tent I sent a wish to the moon
'Please let me really know you.'
The clash of yin against the yang
My big fat love for a quiet man
I know you, I don't know you.
Empty pocket filled. Empty hearts trying still to forgive.
I ask you to ask an angel for me, but you don't believe.
Think I found a path—won't you walk with me?
Said the fox to the prince: you tamed me, now I'm lonely.

These words marked the start of a new style of songwriting; one where I just spoke the truth, even when it was awful. I called the song 'Empty Pockets'.

I didn't play it for him, or anyone, except myself and, when I did, I felt as though I was getting stronger. I did, I got stronger.

Six months passed. Joffa was making an effort. He was doing his best. I could see that. He got his licence, got off the dole, got a trade apprenticeship, and then a car. When he invited me to come for a drive in the country with him, to go apple picking, I felt like my heart would burst open with happiness. This was exactly the kind of date I had hoped he might one day suggest, and now he had.

But when I showed up at his house on the morning of our would-be date and knocked on the door, no one answered.

I felt something shift in my heart.

I knew, in that moment, I was done waiting. Done trying to change. Done trying to make him change. I was done.

I wanted more. So much more.

And by now, it was clear: he would be more than okay without me.

He did eventually answer the door. He was not, as Frank had suggested, in the bed of some other woman. He had just slept in, he said. Sorry. He was in his boxer shorts, and while he had a shower I made myself a cup of tea and sat on his couch for what I already knew would be the last time. Although my panic was high, and Frank was loud with a particularly cruel story—that if I left him, he might kill himself, and it would be all my fault—there was something strong in me helping me float just a little above: helping me find the strength to say the thing I knew needed saying.

Joffa got dressed, held me in his arms, smiled at me, and I looked at him, smiled back at him, tears streaming down my face, and he must have known then because he paused, and he hooked his arm through mine and said, 'Let's go for a walk around the block,' and we did. I rested my head on his shoulder, said the words; he told me he loved me but he understood, he didn't blame me, I had stayed longer than he thought I would. And when we returned to his house, I kissed his soft pillowy lips, nuzzled my face into his neck and breathed him in one last time, and said, 'Goodbye. Thank you.'

It was time.

*

You already know this, I'm sure, but heartbreak—the grief of a true goodbye—is not really something you ever truly forget. Even today, as I pause to reflect on that time in my life, I can still feel it—the ache of missing him, of wanting to see him, of wanting to hear his voice tell me that he's okay now. It's okay.

The pain was not like before: not like the shame and revenge that had fuelled my adventure to London, and not like the pain of being cheated on or lied to.

This was just the ache of pure grief, and what I discovered by not running from that ache was that grief can change us for the better, can bring out an honesty in us that will connect us to the whole of the human race, but only if we allow it to.

It's been almost twenty years since I last saw him.

It's incredible we've never bumped into each other, but we haven't.

As far as I know, he's not on Facebook. And he changed all his numbers, his address, all that.

I tried calling his mum once to say hi, to check if he was okay—she didn't call back.

I guess that was the only way it was ever going to end for good: to treat it as a death and mourn it, which was what I did.

I mapped my way through my heartbreak as simply as I could: by sticking to the basics, just making sure the dog and cat were fed, I was fed, slept, watered, and that my journal and my guitar were close at hand.

This was also when I finally accepted that, although I was terrible at meditating, I was going to do it anyway. I suppose this marks the moment I first began my highly imperfect meditation practice.

That summer, I wrote my heart out; just me and my guitar, night after night, sitting on a leather couch by a bookcase, writing songs about all the things I didn't want to be feeling, but was.

Through tears and more tears I recorded and recorded and re-recorded those songs onto cassette tapes, listened back, changed lyrics, went in again.

What was different this time was that I was telling my story, from my perspective, my lens, to myself, for myself, without hiding or apology.

If you have ever wanted to write a song and been paralysed by your own self-doubt, begin here: your story, to yourself, for yourself. No one ever has to hear them. That is what I told myself anyway, and it sure did help.

My dream, my songwriter dream, began to trickle back in. As I wrote I noticed something interesting. Although Frank would often show up before and after I'd written a song, he would rarely appear while I was writing a song, nor when I was singing it, or playing my guitar or piano. For some reason, when doing the work, my anxiety seemed to dry up.

Perhaps that's why I played so much that summer; because when I was playing, I felt at my best. I sometimes just played the same three notes for an hour at a time, because, when I did, it made me happy, or gave me a place to be sad. Music did for me what it does for all of us: it took a pain so great I did not think I would survive and made it into something else. I must have written thirty songs that summer, starting with songs about the pain of goodbye ('Sweet Pain'), and, later, the guilt of moving on ('Another Love'), but this time, I kept going—I did not allow myself to get stuck in the drama—and I wrote songs about other things, like Defah's dog Mozzie ('Doggie Song'), and the ocean ('Tide'), and sailing boats ('Sailor's Song').

But the one I liked the most was the one about empty pockets. That's the one that gave me the best feeling—truth and beauty, sadness and resolution.

And I suppose that this was the summer I finally worked it out . . . Well, look at that, I'm a songwriter. It didn't matter to me that maybe no one else would ever hear my songs; what mattered was that I'd done my part. I'd written them. They existed. I had done my part.

This was also the summer I finally remembered what it felt like to get a good night's sleep.

10

The story of music

Let it all out.
Go on say too much
Let someone know you.
Go go go.

'ONE LITTLE RIVER'
(*The Winter I Chose Happiness*, 2012)

I can't remember exactly when it was that I first began to sing; all I know is I have been singing for as long as I remember. It was just a thing I always did, and always loved and, for some reason, I just kept doing it, and kept loving it, and I still do to this very day.

That I got to grow up, and make my living doing this thing I love? Still, to this day, that fact absolutely blows my mind. And the way that all rolled out? That is a story so fortuitous that I'm not even sure you'll believe me when I tell it.

But I swear—every word is *true*.

Without music, I'm not sure I'd be here. No really—my very origin story, the story of how my mum met my dad, is entirely thanks to music. Legend has it that one day my father was walking through the suburban streets of Melbourne when he heard rather exciting Hawaiian music coming from within one of the houses on the street. Curious as ever, he walked over to where the music was coming from, peered inside the window, and found himself face to face with a small band of young Dutch beatniks playing ukuleles. Naturally, as happens in all stories of this nature, my rather handsome young father was invited inside. This is how he made friends with my mother's sister, Clascina, who later became his secretary, and it was because of this connection that, when my mother came to visit Australia for the first time, my dad met my mum.

I hope this comes out the right way, but there is nothing unique about the fact that I sang, and wrote songs, from an early age. So do all kids. That's how we teach ourselves to talk, and make sense of the world, and language—through making sounds and shapes with our mouth, our tongue, our throat, through mimicking, through hearing or seeing sounds repeated back. This is how we lay for ourselves part of the foundation of language, and meaning, and belonging: through call and response, through watching and copying. This is why I have always insisted, and continue to insist, that if you can speak you can sing. At the very least, you can make sounds with your mouth in time with music. That's as good a place to start as any.

So, yes, as a little girl I did love singing.

I didn't think of my singing or my made-up songs as something separate to me—they were just part of me; invisible, like a bone under the skin, but just as real and easy to feel.

I knew a song was mine to write not because I heard it fully formed or anything of that nature, but more because of the way it *felt* in me, the way it settled into me, and then rattled in me, the way it told me, *it's go time.*

To this day, writing a song feels a little like scratching an itch, I suppose. First comes the feeling—a need of some sort, a request, a restlessness, an awareness of something new in the room, or something unspoken and important that wants to be spoken— and then, once I begin writing it, I can breathe a little deeper, because I know that whatever was wrong or unhoused is now in the process of being set right. That's the way it always was for me and songs. Songs were homes for things that needed containing.

My own songs have always appeared this way: not so much as fully formed sounds at first, but as feelings attached to colour and image and story and personality and temperature that need a little room to find their place with each other. A little like animals, in a way. They feel familial, familiar. Some are tame, some are difficult. None bite. All are welcome.

I feel like my songs and I are the same in this way—we want places to belong, to feel contained, but we do not like to be trapped.

I have learned, over time, to wait, to be patient. It is the song that needs to make the first move, not me. I learned through error never to rush them, or I will scare them off. I need to give them time to trust me. To spend enough time with them—around them—to earn that trust. I circle back in again and again, my attention being the thing that feeds them. I would never want to betray a song, never want to squash it into something it is not. In my mind, I am often checking in on them—is this okay? Are you okay? Is this right? Is this true?

As a child, memories sat in the same place. I felt I had a duty of care, somehow, to both the songs and the memories.

Sometimes, while singing in church on Sundays, I used to get so bored I thought I might die.

Perhaps that's why, as a child, I took it upon myself to liven things up a little, to—I mean, I don't want to be presumptuous— improve upon things a little. Without asking for permission, I started adding harmonies where there were none, and drum-beats too (played on my thighs). When I couldn't think of the right words, I just made them up. And I made sure that, at the end of every song, I was the one who held my note for the longest, so as to win (win what, I did not know; just . . . win). I can still feel the elbow nudge of my older sisters as they told me to stop it, stop embarrassing us, but, no, I would not be stopped! (Not unless Dad told me to stop—then, I stopped. Fear is good like that.)

One of my greatest pleasures as a kid was when the older ladies in the pews behind or in front would comment afterwards on my lovely singing. I would shine with pride, ignoring my sib-lings muttering under their breath, 'Don't encourage her!' I *was* encouraged. Clearly, I was talented (so I told myself). Why else would the older ladies tell me so? I suppose I was quite confident, at the start.

In the past, when I have listened back to those tapes of me as a child singing my little songs—songs about vacuum cleaners and Sam the dog and various fantasies, such as *'Livin' in the jungle because it's free, and all the animals talk to me. I like the jungle, it's very nice. The air is fresh, and it smells like spice!'*—it is quite obvious that my clear sense of being a talented singer right from the start was . . . a little misguided. Like all children, I did have a sweet voice, but the truth is I really had no special vocal talent to speak of. What I did have was a heart that wanted to sing, a body that felt good when a song was in it, and a brain that saw sounds as pictures, saw harmonies as streamers flying together, and I knew just how to arrange them, and just how to make them right—and when they were wrong, I knew how to turn that around as well. My relationship with my songs has almost always been excellent.

As much as my siblings found my voice rather loud, and told me to keep it down when their friends were over, I also suspected (perhaps incorrectly) that they rather liked it when I sang, and my parents were kind about my voice, and nobody ever really told me I *couldn't* sing, just that I shouldn't sing quite so much. All up, songs and singing felt good inside me and once I had started, I never stopped.

When I was nine, my first piano teacher, Mrs Anderson, gave our family her old piano. It had a big crack down the middle and could never quite be tuned, but it was good enough to start lessons on, and so I did. Mrs Anderson taught me the names of the keys and how to read music. We played small songs about Every Good Boy Deserves Fruit and Walking Up The Scale. She was patient and encouraging, and I was always sorry, every week, when I had to tell her that I had not really practised. I didn't mean to be bad, I just really didn't like practising. What I liked doing was pretending to be Liberace. I had seen him on TV once in a white sequinned suit, sitting on his stool, taking a deep breath, and then just running his hands up and down the keys in a fury. And, so, I did exactly the same. Oh, the noise of it! As a general rule, my family were able to tolerate my racket. But, over time, I like to think their tolerance paid off. I went from making terrible, loud, up-and-down-the-keyboard sounds to quieter, sweeter, more pleasant sounds. At a certain point I realised that if I closed my eyes when I played, I saw pictures, and colours. Certain sounds would seem to sit in certain colour groups, and I suppose this was the beginning of my habit of sorting sounds into families in my head—making happy sounds, sad sounds, crazy sounds and then chunking them together, laying them out again and again into themes and then, later, songs. The thing I loved most about playing this way was that I didn't have to think; all I had to do was follow the picture stream of the sound. Now the truth is, when I was a child, it was my sister Lisa who was the clearer talent. She was a bloody whiz on the guitar, and the piano, and the noises she made sounded like actual . . . songs. My noises didn't sound like much, not from the outside—a mess, really—but I was teaching myself something; I was making a little world for myself, one where I had a place, right there at the centre.

Back in reality, I was a terrible music student. I was told again and again, by several teachers over the years, that although I had a 'talented ear', I would need to work much harder on my theory, and my practice. Unfortunately, my brain just could not see the point of it. All that pausing and reading, learning rules and following them, reading and pausing, felt so awkward, so clunky, so annoying. I could not sit still for the life of me. Why couldn't I just play what I had heard the teacher play—listen and copy? I was good at that. Or why couldn't I just play the new things in my head, the things my hands wanted to say? Why did I need rules when I could just hear a song, remember it with pictures, and then play it back? And why did I need to learn those boring songs? Why couldn't I learn *good* songs? Of course, I said none of this aloud; I wouldn't have known where to start, really. Teachers tried to teach me the names of chords, where notes should sit on the stave, the upper and lower clef, and I did try to do what they said but, for whatever reason, I always seemed to default back to what worked for me—approximation, mimicking, filling gaps by following the feeling of which notes sat well together, felt good together. I was obsessed with trying to make everything feel good, like it belonged. I played with sounds and songs the way other children played with dolls and dollhouses.

I moved very slowly through the Australian Music Examinations Board stages, all the way up to Grade Four. I'm not sure how, really. But I *did* win one award once, for a recital, when I was about eleven, the summer after I lost all that weight.

Ironically, the prize was a slim book on music theory called *Rudiments of Music.*

I still have it, and do plan to study it—one day.

✳

One winter's afternoon when I was fourteen or fifteen, I came home from school to discover my mother swanning around the kitchen wearing a smart beret.

'What are you doing, Mum?' I asked.

'Setting the table,' she said.

'Mum, you're wearing a beret. What's going on?'

'Oh, nothing—just having a few friends over after dinner, that's all.'

At the age of forty-three, Mum went back to university to study psychology, sociology and, later, pastoral care. Even though she left school early, at age sixteen, to work in a bank in Amsterdam, she continued her education right throughout her life: first at night-school three times a week, studying business, business law and bookkeeping, and then, once she'd moved to Australia, she studied to became a nurse. Later in life, already a wife and mother, she went back and completed her high-school diploma and, now, here she was—a uni student.

Mum quickly made friends, younger friends, whom she would sometimes invite over for cheese and cask-wine and candlelight.

One of her friends was a songwriter called John Beavis. When I first met him, I remember thinking that I'd never met anyone like him in my life. He too wore a beret. He also brought his guitar. And after dinner, and red wine, after I heard him playing songs from the folk songbook, something familiar that I can't explain clicked into place for me. You would never have known it by looking at me (blonde, puffy fringe, going through a 'slightly sarcastic' patch) but, that night, when I heard John play, a new space opened up in me. And when I heard him sing the songs of The Beatles, and Simon and Garfunkel, and then, after that, even some folk songs he'd written himself, I found that I was singing along. And it felt so good.

It twinkled that night, the thought that songs do mean something, the possibility that perhaps there was a different kind of power to the one I had aligned myself with at high school, the power of being popular. I sensed that this was deeper, more nurturing, more giving, more honest.

I went to bed that night humming, just like I used to when I was a little girl.

*

It so happened that John Beavis had this friend, a fellow folk singer called Fay White who lived just around the corner from us. You've already heard me mention Fay—she's the family friend who got me reading again after my breakdown. You've also heard me talk about Fay's daughter Ilka—my dear friend who invited me into the Compost community in my twenties. One of the coolest things about Ilka and Fay was that, along with father Terry, and brother Tali, these guys had a family band: the White Family Band! I had never heard of such a thing! (At fifteen, the thought of singing in public with my parents was, well, not a prospect I'd ever considered.) When Terry's job as an environmental scientist permitted, the family would tour up and down the Victorian coast, playing gigs at festivals and church halls. I found the whole scenario absolutely fascinating! I hung around their house like a bad smell. They ate carob cake, lentil soup and, occasionally, roast lamb. It was almost as though . . . I wanted to join their band?

Around this time, I got into a little trouble with The Authorities.

For whatever reason, by the time I was fifteen, I'd decided that school sucked and I was going to stop going. No, this wasn't something I mentioned to my parents. So now, at least a few days a week, instead of getting off at Gardenvale Station to attend Star of the Sea, I'd stay on the train and travel to the city. There, after a quick cappuccino, I'd set up shop inside what was then auspiciously titled the Dome Reading Room at the State Library of Victoria. While there, I read, and some-times, when the mood overtook me, I even turned my hand to a dash of teenage poetry. It was terrible, but it was a start at least. Then I'd read some more. Any book, really. Didn't matter. I liked the old ones the most. Also, I just loved wagging. Most of all, I loved this room. The size of the dome, the way it let in the light, the feeling of being around smart people, acting smart—I just loved it all. There was also, of course, the story Mum once told me, about how when she first moved to Melbourne and took a job in the basement at Myers, this is where she would come at lunchtime. This is the room in which she taught herself to speak English. She did this by reading—mainly, she says, *The Diary of Virginia Woolf*—and then copying it. I can imagine her now, our little Dutch treat, back from her lunch break, in the Myers basement, making tea, talking in 'streams of consciousness'. It was Australia, 1962. I'm just glad she got out of there alive.

Once I was sick of reading, and poetry, I'd often go and buy myself a treat, something fancy like a pack of smokes. That's the thing—I always had money. Yes, I stole two-dollar coins from behind the couch (I admit that now, sorry, Mum and Dad) but I also always had jobs. I got my first school-holiday job when I was thirteen, down the road at the local hairdressers. There, I swept, answered phones and occasionally assisted with perms (I was responsible for handing the hairdresser the perm rods). For this honour, I was paid a grand total of ten dollars a day, which seemed like a princely sum at the time. After that, I worked at the local bakery, then the local pizza place and, later, at a cafe, a surf shop, an Indian import shop, a museum, a jazz club and at an organic fruit and vegetable market. I always hated asking my parents for money. I have always loved working. And that, I suppose, is how I could afford to buy my own smokes.

But when I got sprung wagging and smoking by the station-master at Sandy train station and he called my parents, it seemed like the jig was up. Small mercy: neither of my parents were home. My sister Anna answered the phone. She had recently returned from Japan, where she had been working as a model. She is, in fact, a photographer (who do you think took the photos on the front and inside cover of this book? Anna). Modelling was just an easy way to make good money on the side and, as fate would have it, she kept getting booked. Five years later, tired of being bloody fabulous, she'd moved back for a while to catch her breath.

I loved having her home, loved sitting with her in the backyard in the morning sun as she drank her coffee, painted with watercolours, practised her calligraphy. I was in awe of her.

But when I got home, and her first words to me were 'What the fuck are you doing?' I very nearly shat myself with fright. Uh oh, my hero Anna was not very happy. 'What are you doing ruining your beautiful lungs like that?'

'What do you mean?'

'The stationmaster called. Said you'd been smoking again.'

'But you smoke!' I said.

'Yes, and I told you not to! You are too smart for that shit, Clare!' She ripped into me then, called me on my lies, and my games, and on the way I was acting just to impress a bunch of 'bloody bitches' who, let's face it, didn't really know me, because nobody knew me, because I was lying so much that no one could work out who the fuck I was.

Then she pulled out a striped paper bag and put it on the table. 'Also, what the hell is this?'

The bag looked slightly familiar, but no bells were ringing. I peeked inside. Oh, yeah! Little black balls—dozens of them.

'Lollies,' I said.

She didn't believe me at first, but it was true. I ate one to prove it. She looked relieved.

'What did you think they were?' I asked.

'We thought they were drugs. Mum found them in your schoolbag, along with these.' She pulled out two squashed Indonesian-leaf cigarettes.

I turned pink. Looked closer. 'Why are they half smoked?' I asked.

'Because me and Mum wanted to find out if they were dope, so we lit one each and had a puff.'

I cracked up. That was the most hilarious thing I'd ever heard. My mum, smoking?

It turned out there was a lot I didn't know about my mum—like the fact that she was more open-minded than I thought. When Anna told Mum she had to let me leave Star of the Sea, because it just wasn't going to work for a Year Nine like me, Mum surprised me by letting me swap to a school over the other side of town called Preshil—an alternative school, one where the classrooms were among the trees and you could call the teachers by their first name and wear what you wanted, and it was full of creative types. Fay had recommended it once. I'd wanted to go there from the moment I first heard about it, and after a tour with the handsome headmaster, who charmed my mother with stories about what children can become once they've been empowered to make their own choices, direct their own learning, my parents agreed. It would take me three hours a day on public transport to get there and back, but I didn't care. I knew from the second I started that tour and saw kids playing guitar in a large sun-dappled music room that this was where I belonged.

※

Nevertheless, I got off to a little bit of bumpy start. I now had more freedom than I could ever have imagined possible, and it took me a while to work out what to do with it. It wasn't that there weren't rules, it's just that, as far as I could see, you were under no real obligation to follow them. I was intimidated by the other kids, who seemed so confident, so aware of who they were, so different to my old friends. And then I met Defah.

Boyfriends are all good and well, but it was Defah who was the true love of my teenage years. When we first met, I thought she was tough and scary, and more. What I realise now is that she wasn't scary, she was just opinionated, and she had no fear of sharing that opinion, and I suppose . . . I hadn't really met many girls like her before. As the year rolled on, I began to see that she was also honest and clever and lots and lots of fun, and when we first started to sing together as part of a school project, my world grew brighter. I was ushered into the warm heart of her bohemian family—and the fun of long dinners and late-night soirees in their warehouse off Brunswick Street, and boards of cheese and wine and large blue Le Creuset pots of slow-cooked beef bourguignon at Defah's big family homestead in Eltham. With Defah's encouragement I grew little wings of courage, and started confessing more and more of my big fat dreams. I allowed myself to imagine that, as Tracy Chapman sang in 'Fast Car', maybe I, too, could one day 'be someone'. In the bosom of the Dattner family, no dream felt too crazy.

In our houses in these years, there was always music playing—Joni Mitchell and Rickie Lee Jones, Miles Davis, Nina Simone,

Donny Hathaway, Debussy, Phoebe Snow. Our friends Aurora and Felicity shared our musical tastes and we started an a cappella band, spending Saturday nights busking on Brunswick Street, Fitzroy. We played our first gig at a garden festival in the leafy suburbs of Kew. It was an inauspicious start: it was raining, we were in a rotunda, and our only audience consisted of the two elderly festival organisers standing under umbrellas. But they were terribly encouraging, and it was a start, and . . . an end, too: we broke up not long after that, citing . . . well, none of us can really remember. Professional differences, one supposed. But it was fun. And we continued singing together, because it was the thing that brought us close.

I got a part in the school musical that year—I played Maisie in *The Boy Friend*. I loved being on stage. But as happened with my songs, Frank got loud every time I was anywhere near victory, with story after story about how I needed to be better than this, smaller than this and then, only then, would I really show the world who I was. In the musical, there was a beach scene where we were all told to wear bathers, but I refused, too ashamed. I thought I would lose the part, but I did not. The embarrassment of being 'too big', however, was right there in my head before and sometimes after every show—but *not*, I noticed, while I was on the stage, playing my part. How curious, I thought.

On the night of the final performance, in the middle of a Charleston, I accidentally kicked off my red high heel, sending it flying into the audience. Mortified, but in character, I put my hand on my mouth like Betty Boop, ran into the crowd, pointed to my shoe under a chair, and then flirted with the man who bent down and handed it to me. The crowd thought it was all part of the act and roared with laughter. This, I realised, might just be the best feeling in the whole world: making something good from our mistakes.

After the show that night, Defah's Aunty Fabian sought me out and told me something my sixteen-year-old self really needed to hear: 'You were wonderful! You sparkled up there! I don't know if anyone has ever told you this before, but there is something very special about you. I see something in you. I think you should consider taking this up professionally, don't you?'

I had no words then to tell Fabian how much this meant to me—this moment of her naming my dream, of talking to me as though a dream like that was actually possible. I was just a kid in a costume, and here was this grown woman looking me in the eye, telling me my dreams weren't too big at all. I have never ever forgotten that—of how much it meant, of how it made Frank go quiet, of how exciting it was to imagine that maybe, just maybe . . . I blushed and tried my best to fob off the compliment but, inside, I was shining. Maybe this *was* what I was born to do.

I joined a band not long after that, a real one. My brother-in-law Tim—a bass player—asked me to sing backup in his friend Matt O'Donnell's band. We were called Quarter Acre Dream, QAD. My bandmates were all men in their mid-twenties; I was sixteen when we started, then seventeen. Most of my weekends in my final two years of high school were spent playing gigs, under-age, in pubs and clubs around Fitzroy and Collingwood. We played at the Rochester Castle Hotel on Johnston Street, the Prince Patrick on Victoria Parade, The Club on Smith Street and the Evelyn Hotel on Brunswick Street. I didn't drink or smoke by then—this was, mercifully, a very clean-living time in my life—and, although the nights were long, I loved singing, loved being on stage, and secretly wished, rather often, that I was singing the main vocals, not the backups. That was probably another clue, right there.

Tim kept a close eye on me, picking me up from rehearsals and making sure I got home safe. Mum and Dad would sometimes come to gigs and stand at the back, Mum trying to charm the mixer into making sure the vocals were high enough so she could hear the lyrics and not just the instruments. Here's the thing: Mum and Dad didn't exactly *love* the fact that their under-age daughter was playing in dodgy pubs and clubs around Melbourne, but I suspected they were proud of my chutzpah.

For twelve months, we saved all our gig money for recording— we were going to make an EP—but when the day came I was so nervous, so overwhelmed by all the strangers in the room, and Frank was so loud in my head, that I could hardly get any notes out. The producer was a man in his thirties and, like every cliché I had ever read in *Rolling Stone* magazine, he was sitting behind the glass at a control desk with a big fat spliff, trying to get me to 'Open up, open up'. (*Open up what, exactly? I had no idea what the fuck he is asking, actually. Can someone just speak English, please?*) I was trying not to let it show on my face, but every word of his (possibly quite useful) 'feedback' hit me as criticism and I just could not for the life of me get it right. 'Do it again,' said the producer.

You deserve to die in shame, said Frank. This was the first time I'd ever sung into a microphone in a studio in front of the whole band, all on the other side of the glass. I felt incredibly exposed, and Frank got so loud that I had to excuse myself to cry in the toilet (*As per fucking usual, you fucking loser*, said Frank). Louder and louder he grew and I wish I had known then about FAFL, about how to manage such a moment, how to lead myself through, but I did not, and I guess this was the moment my childhood dream of one day being a famous musician died in me.

I couldn't do it. I'd never be able to do it. Who was I kidding?

I left the band after that. Apologised, told them it was interfering with my schoolwork. They were pissed off, disappointed, and fair enough, too—we'd spent a whole year leading up to this moment, and now I wanted out? The guilt was awful, but I didn't know what else to tell them. All I knew was that all my life I had imagined how good it would feel to stand in front of a microphone in a studio and sing my little heart out, and now that I'd tried, I felt like I'd failed. *You are a failure*, said the voice of Frank.

I dropped music after that. Drama, too. In Year Twelve I wanted to study slightly more sensible things: humanities. Renaissance history, English, literature, international relations and environmental studies. And I worked hard, too—wanted to make my parents proud, to make sure they knew their faith in me was not misplaced.

It wasn't like the dream of music didn't still call to me after that, it's just that I stopped listening. In the quiet of my room, when no one was home, I still wrote my songs. I didn't know the names of the strings on the guitar but I still played them, plucked them, recorded ideas on my tape recorder, hid the tapes under my bed, never daring to say it aloud but secretly hoping that one day, by some miracle, I would meet someone who could help me work out what to do with them.

*

When I was twenty and working at the call centre, I heard this guy singing on the radio and, although he sounded a little morose, I quite liked his voice. His name was Jeff Buckley. I've told you about this, haven't I? How I bought his album *Grace* and then went to see him play an instore?

There were only about fifty of us at Gaslight Music that night, including me, and Jill and our Preshil mate, Anna. The fluorescent lights were switched off, and in their place was a candelabra. When Jeff arrived—lean and small, a guitar strapped to his chest—he struck me as fragile, and sweet. What surprised me were the jokes he told us before the show, to warm us up, about the Melbourne weather, about the way we spoke—just shooting the breeze, all casual like, but *so* fun, and *so* cool. When he did finally sing, when that sound coming out of his mouth hit my chest, dear God, I thought I would explode with the beauty of it. Eyes as big as saucers, I could not *believe* what I was hearing, the power of it, the way it sucked all the loneliness up and out of my chest and put there instead the most remarkable feeling of connection and warmth and hope. It was this night, this feeling, that really changed things for me again—that reminded me, once more, of the brilliant power of song, of the way it can change a heart, change a feeling, change a life. I was reminded, yet again, that music matters.

Later that night, me and Jill and Anna made friends with Jeff's sound guy. We went out for a drink with him. At the end of the night, he asked for my number. The next time Jeff came to town to play, the sound guy got us seats right up the front, once even sitting on stage. We saw him in Melbourne, and we also drove up to Sydney to see him perform at the Enmore Theatre. But at this show everything felt different. At that first small instore, we felt like we were part of only a handful of people in the world who knew of Jeff. We'd seen him play twice more since then, and still felt part of a secret club. Now, at the Enmore, with every cool kid in town in attendance, it felt like the whole world wanted a piece of him—and it also seemed obvious to us that he was not enjoying the pressure. The thing I'd noticed first with my sister Anna, the model, and could see here too was that fame was not all it was cracked up to be.

Later that night, Anna and Jill and I were invited upstairs, backstage, for the after-party. It was a small room, there were only about a dozen people in there to begin with, and the feeling was quite calm, until Jeff walked into the room. As we watched strangers swarm around Jeff with their words and their wants and their need to be near him, a feeling of sadness came over me. Me and the girls hardly spoke, just watched. At one point our mate the sound guy called me over, and then introduced me to Jeff himself. He told Jeff that I was a singer, and he should hear me sing. I didn't know what to say. We exchanged just a few words, a joke. I think I may have even attempted to speak Spanish. (There is no logical explanation for this. It's possible I was trying to be funny. More likely, I think I was just freaking out!)

Another time, our mate tried to get Jeff and I together for a jam up in Jeff's hotel room. We went late in the afternoon before the Melbourne gig, and a bunch of us sat on Jeff's bed, me playing Jeff's guitar, waiting for him to appear; he was in the next room apparently, occupied with his lady. I remember feeling so scared I actually dropped his guitar, something my girlfriends still rib me about to this day—the way my hands go clumsy and weak when I'm overexcited.

Jeff Buckley and I never did get to play together. And what I saw behind the scenes of his fame, how people wanted a piece of him, wanted him to smile and dance and listen to their problems, scared me.

Just like in the movies, once Jeff's sound guy realised we were not going to fuck him, not going back to his hotel room, he dumped us. Stopped calling. Stopped inviting us to shows. What a sleaze. The whole thing—everything about being a young woman backstage at those shows—made me even more fearful of the music industry, of what lay ahead for those 'privileged enough' to sign record contracts.

But what did not leave me was that feeling of when Jeff stood up, heart on his sleeve, chest to the world, and let us have it—all of it. Let us have all the beauty and all the horror and all the brutality and all the joy in his soul, and it hit us in our faces and our hearts and this, I think, is when I returned in earnest to teaching myself the art of writing songs, and I longed then and forever more to keep looking for and trying to make moments through song that shimmered, and were true, and meant something.

When I returned from London, and for many months afterwards, I could not play music. It was too much for me—too much information, emotion, memory.

For even longer afterwards, I could not write songs, could not imagine I would ever write another song. Could not imagine I had it in me anymore to take a risk like that—of writing a song, of dreaming of a life in music again. I closed the door, I suppose.

But after Joffa and I finally broke up, towards the end of my first year of university, the songs came back, all grown up. More honest. Less angry. Dozens of them, one after the other, night after night. Music became my great love once again, and this time, I did not fall apart. This time, I was able to make something of my heartbreak, and this is when I got it—that songs are like containers. They are one of the only things in the world strong enough to hold emotions this raw, and this contradictory. A song is like a Tardis of meaning.

I still could not imagine what to do with these songs, once they were here. I had no idea where to play them, how to really finish them, make them complete, turn them into— God forbid—an album. All I knew was that this was my part: catching the songs when they showed up as feelings, writing them down, and hoping that one day I would look back and this would all make sense.

By the time my second year of uni rolled around, I was feeling braver, less scared, more myself—a 'myself' I had never felt before. I was getting better and better at telling hopeful stories, better and better at telling Frank to fuck off.

Also, I was making friends. New friends. Good friends. Friendships that started over cups of tea and coffee in between lectures, and went from there. We would do assignments together, have a drink after lectures, go to each other's art happenings. I was getting better at showing people who I was.

One fateful weekend, some uni girlfriends and I decided to go on a last-minute road trip to ConFest: a hippy festival on the banks of the mighty Murray River on the border of Victoria and New South Wales.

We were greeted at the gate by a leathery old chap who wasn't wearing any underpants. Later someone told me his nickname— Long Schlong Silver. By looking at him, that made sense. Long Shlong Silver was pretty much ConFest in a nutshell: just a bunch of friendly naked people, greeting each other in peace. I tried very hard to keep my gaze 'upwards' as I asked Long Schlong if he could kindly direct us to the quietest area of the campground. We pitched our tent near some majestic old gum trees, painted our faces with swirls and dots, stuck on some bindis, and I do believe this may have been the first time in my life where I shared the sight of my naked belly-button with strangers (that was about as far as I was willing to push myself, that night). As dusk fell, my friends and I walked over to the communal chai tent, and settled in for what we assumed would be a blissful night of drumming and drinking chai.

I brought my book to the chai tent, sat on a communal cushion, tried not to worry about things like scabies, or how many crusty pairs of toes had touched these cushions before me, and was just starting to relax into the cool evening when I heard someone in the corner of the tent yell, 'Amber? Amber?'

I looked up to see a young, handsome, dark-haired chap strutting around the tent like Elvis.

As it turns out, 'Elvis' and his mate were looking for an 'Amber', which was made clear by the fact that his friend would not stop yelling Amber's name. Elvis spotted a communal guitar—one of several instruments that belonged to the tent. Soon, he was leading a singalong. I was a little annoyed at first—I just wanted to read my book, thank you very much—but soon realised what I was feeling wasn't irritation so much as fear.

There was something in me that wanted to go sing with him.

There was another part of me that told me not to be an idiot—I didn't even know that guy. I heard it then, as clear as day: the voice of Frank, of fear, trying to keep me safe, yet again, but I was stronger now, and I wasn't having it anymore.

I watched the Elvis dude play the guitar and, it occurred to me, shit, he's really good. And he could sing, too. He was singing songs I knew, by The Beatles, and the Rolling Stones and Creedence Clearwater Revival, and before I knew it I was sitting a little outside the circle, but singing along with him. Strangers, singing together. This felt . . . awesome!

Turns out, Elvis's actual name was John. After the jam he came and introduced himself. Told me he liked my harmonies. Asked me where I'd learned to sing. I'm not sure: from my mum,

I think. He asked me if played guitar, and I said not much; he asked did I write songs, and I said not much. He sure did ask a lot of questions, I thought. I was twenty-two and a half by now; it was almost eighteen months since I'd returned from London as a thin woman, and I have to admit I still was not entirely comfortable with male attention. Sometimes, being thin is weird. If they didn't talk to me when I was fat, why were they talking to me now? But with John, things felt different— he was direct, but something about that set me at ease and, at the same time, terrified me. Or was it excitement? Hard to say. Lots of emotions. We talked and talked. To my surprise, not only did he know all of Jeff Buckley's songs, he also knew all of Donny Hathaway's songs and, most impressive, he knew the songs of my favourite local band, the Acapellicans. Who was this guy?

When he finally handed me the guitar, said, 'All right, play me something,' two-thirds of me wanted to run. But from somewhere within that third little corner of me came a voice that encouraged me to stay. To be brave. To try. What was the harm in that? I didn't even know this guy. Would probably never see him again. Something inside me said: *Go on. Try.*

So, in what felt like a little nod to the woman I one day hoped to be, I said, 'Okay.'

That was the first time I ever sang 'Empty Pockets'—the Joffa song—to anyone. I closed my eyes as I did it, just like I had when I was in Oxford playing the open mic night at the Catweazle Club. I couldn't stand the thought of seeing John's face, just in case it said something I didn't want to hear, such as 'You suck!'

But afterwards, when I opened my eyes, John looked at me funny, and smiled, and then he asked, 'What's your name again?'

I told him.

Actually, I told him my first name, but a fake surname (*Just in case*, said Frank). Like I said, I wasn't yet used to male attention. It tended to make me nervous.

'Got any more songs?' he asked.

'Yes,' I said. 'I suppose so.'

And then John said four little words that would truly change the course of my life, and his life, for the better. He smiled, and said, 'Let's start a band!'

And before Frank could butt in, I also smiled, and said, 'Okay.'

The following week, John phoned and left a message.

I was scared to call him back.

What if I'd imagined it? What if we didn't really sound as good as I thought we did?

Of course, Frank was adamant that I should ignore the call, but I thought about that for a bit and reminded myself yet again that fear and excitement feel almost the same and I was no longer going to let fear dictate my life—*remember?* So, as yet another 'override', I made myself a rule: when it came to creative risks, whenever I felt this feeling, I was going to try saying 'yes', and just see what happened.

I called John back and said, 'Hi John, it's Clare, from . . .'

And before I could finish my sentence, he said, 'Hey! Let's jam!'

I'll never forget it. No small talk, no pleasantries, just 'Hey! Let's jam!'

I found his enthusiasm very amusing. I couldn't help but giggle.

Turned out we lived around the corner from each other, me in Fitzroy, him in a share house in Carlton.

'What songs do you want to jam?' I asked.

He said, 'Can you bring your songs?'

That scared me a lot, so I said, 'Yes,' and swallowed.

The first time I ever showed up at John's door, I had a tape of my half-finished songs in my bag, and I was sweating. It was a cool enough day, but I was hot with fear, and before knocking on his door, I stood on his porch for some length of time, practising my FAFL and my FOF.

John invited me in and offered me tea. I was quiet. Mainly, I was just trying not to blow my own heart out with panic. Deep breath, deep breath, Face-Accept-Float-Let time pass.

John's bedroom smelled a lot like Nag Champa and beer. When he started playing his guitar I relaxed. He was an absolute master. He could play pretty much any song I suggested. I kept thinking, Is this really happening? Even from this first jam, it was clear that John was a rare young man. He asked questions, he listened hard for the answers, he named the gaps in between and, from the first moment I met him, he made me feel like I mattered.

I never mentioned to John the stuff I'd been through in Oxford, but I guess I didn't really need to. It was all there in the cassette I gave him—a recording of half-finished songs that I couldn't believe I had agreed to share. I can't tell you how sick I felt as I handed them over. I told him they were terrible, sorry.

He said, 'I bet they're not.'

The first time ever I saw Marty Brown's face was at our second rehearsal, he was walking into John's bedroom, ducking, because he was so tall and the doorframe was so low.

I had already heard of Marty; John had talked him up on the phone. They were housemates and bandmates. 'An animal on drums,' was how John described him. 'Marty Monster. You're gonna love him.' And he was right: I *would* love Marty very, very much.

When he walked into John's room that day, I had no idea of what role he would later play in my life. I was still singing. All I remember thinking when he entered was *Holy fuck, that guy is tall!* And John kept playing, said, 'Clare, meet Marty,' and the tall guy nodded shyly, said, 'Excuse me,' quietly as he swished past me, all limbs and grace, a centrifuge in motion, and before I knew it he was sitting on the drum kit, holding his brushes, playing along to my songs. No prep, no practice. Just instinct, and talent, and a touch of bravado. The three of us—John, Marty, me—this was the moment it all began. They were playing my songs back to me. All the bits that weren't yet working, John had somehow set right.

John also had songs that he said needing finishing, and there in the room—pen a paper, call and response—we made his half-songs whole.

The following week, we did it again, this time in Marty's bedroom, which was larger.

Marty was a self-taught sound engineer studying Arts and Commerce at Melbourne University, which was where he had met John. His bedroom was full to overflowing with . . . old stuff. Machines I didn't recognise. Second-hand recording equipment: reel to reel, sound desks, microphones. After we had finished jamming, he said, 'Okay, who wants to record a song?'

From a modern-day perspective, it is almost impossible to explain to you how rare it was to find someone who recorded songs in their bedroom the way Marty Brown did then. To put this into context, the internet barely worked, MacBooks had not yet been invented, and there were certainly no gangs of kids recording songs in their bedroom; the technology just didn't exist. There was barely email. The fact that I happened to luck onto possibly the only kid in a fifty-kilometre radius who owned a reel-to-reel tape machine, a mixing desk and microphones, and just happened to have the skills to use them was incredible. I had never heard of, or met, anyone like Marty Brown, and I had certainly never been asked, 'Who wants to record a song?'

✳

And that's how my recording career finally began—in Marty's bedroom. I don't even think we had a name yet, but eventually we did—we called ourselves Red Raku, after one of my favourite firing and glazing techniques. When firing raku, you never knew what you were going to get at the end, and that was us too. When I listen back to those recordings today, it's all still there—that sparky feeling we made in the room together. There was no Auto-Tune then. We had very little tape, and very little money to buy more tape. But you have to start with something, and that was where we started.

That first day, we recorded five songs, and went on to record five more another day. Some were John's songs, some we wrote together, and some were mine. Mine were the ones written in the wake of my painful break-up with Joffa: 'Empty Pockets', 'Another Love', 'Letting Go of Charlie', 'The Master'. These are the songs that would make up our first album, *Sweetly Sedated*. I was raw. So raw. In hindsight, how incredible—that it was young Marty Brown who would witness all of that. He was so quiet, you know—he hardly spoke. But he listened like no one I had ever met. He was so steady. Nothing fazed him.

Thanks to John's enthusiasm, his ability to 'just do it', our band grew very quickly, and without much consultation, which was fine with me. Marty ribbed me that it was my fault because I was always too busy basket-weaving or African dancing to actually come to band meetings. He had a point. I still hated practice. And also I was really shy. Every week there was a new player: Andy Crean on viola, Rachel Henderson on cello, Matty Vehl on keys and Warren Bloomer on bass. All incredible musicians. Each added a new strain of goodness, magic, to our Red Raku sound. One day, John announced that he thought the only thing we were missing was a flute, which was why he'd invited my best friend Defah to join the band. Cool! Before long, surprise surprise, the two of them were in love, living together, and making sweet sweet music of their own.

John told me that Marty had also invited someone new into the band: a harp player, a very beautiful harp player. But it didn't work out. After seeing us play, she said she was flattered, but where, exactly, would she fit?

Quietly, I was relieved.

What a lovely guy Marty was, I thought. So talented. And look at that face. Like a little cherub. A bit too good to be true really. Obviously, he had a dark side. *Only a matter of time before it comes out*, said Frank.

In those early gigs, in front of our friends and family, first at cafes and then pubs, I was still too shy, too frightened, to actually look up at the audience very much. Mostly, I just closed my eyes, looked down, and swayed. My family were there. So were John's. In a curious twist of fate, John's parents were also massive bloody Catholics. Turned out that the obscure Catholic Scripture Diary Mum had been ordering and putting under the Christmas tree every single year for me and all my siblings for as long as we could remember was invented by . . . John's mum. I know!

The White family also came to our gigs, and Fay and Terry told me I was doing great, to keep going. That meant the world to me. Sometimes, my 'Jewish godfather', our dear family friends Lionel Lubitz and his son Jessie played before us, as our support band. We played small shows but, soon, they started selling out. I told my friends at uni about our gigs. But by far the bulk of our audience were John and Marty's crew. They were just so organised with that stuff. They'd make flyers, and send them to people in the mail, and put them up on poles around Fitzroy. And week after week, our audience grew. As the gigs clocked up, I sensed a confidence building in me. I started taking more risks. Shaved my head. Wore shinier bindis and tighter clothes. Tried different notes. Found my feet as a singer, I guess.

This was such an exciting time in my life, but there was a part of me that was still terrified of trying too hard. Things felt like they were moving very fast, and I kept needing to put on the brakes. Within a year, Red Raku were already recording and releasing our second album. Marty had a friend at a record company who had seen us play, and said they would love to have a chat with us. It must have been a mystery to him why I never took them up on it. I still didn't know if someone like me was going to be able to handle what I knew would be the enormous effort, and potential rejection, of 'Going For It' with music. Even though I was now average sized, inside me, the kid who got teased, and who teased herself, was still in there. Frank was still loud, telling me not to get ahead of myself. Telling me I didn't have the talent.

But together we muddled along. I took over the designing of the flyers, and the album covers, and John and Marty booked the gigs, our photo shoots, our community radio interviews and, two years later, in front of a sold-out crowd at our second CD launch, I think I finally let myself say the words: Maybe there's something in this whole singing/songwriting thing. Maybe I'm an actual . . . musician.

And that thought twinkled inside me like a happy little star, and it still does, to this day.

11

On this side

I thought that nobody could love me
The way that I loved them.
That was before him.

'ON THIS SIDE'
(*What Was Left*, 2005)

When I was younger, I would never have admitted I had a type. My boyfriends were all so different, I would have said.

Looking back now, however, it is fairly clear to me that even if I did not have a 'type', as such, I most certainly did have a dynamic.

In short: I fell in love with boys, and men, who, I thought, needed saving—and I was just the woman for the job.

✳

The first time I fell in love, it was dark, and I was on a couch. I was sixteen years old, and felt close to ancient. I had been impatient with love, thinking it would never find me, and then, one night, it did. My beautiful mate Nicko, a red-headed surfer, would be my first true love. I think I knew it from our first awkward kiss, on the couch at Defah's dad's house. Electric. He felt it too. On the night he asked me out, he told me he loved me so much he would even give up dope for me. Was I even aware, at the time, just how much dope he smoked? I didn't think I was. But since he was offering, great!

It was a sweet gesture, the sweetest he could make, because he knew from our chats that I could not smoke dope without having what I now know to be a massive bloody panic attack. It just wasn't for me, and he said that he wanted to do things I wanted to do. How bloody sweet! And, still, our love was doomed to fail. In the end, it wasn't the dope that ruined things so much as the lying when he started up again. The drama of the whole thing became too much. When we broke up, it was a mutual decision, but I still took it all rather personally. It hurt. But when he asked me to please return his mother's album of Joni Mitchell's *Court and Spark* I was devastated. Frank, of course, had a field day. Even though Nick had never once mentioned or seemed aware of my little weight problem, it was, said Frank, the main reason we broke up. The habit of breaking up with a boyfriend and then going on a diet started here. I thought that if I were thin, I would be loved.

By the time the diet worked, there was Joffa, whom I decided I was put on Earth to save.

Did he ever ask me to save him? Not at all.

I think we're all pretty clear now on how that ended (not well).

Then there was the young businessman from the call centre. At first, he seemed very kind, a safe shoulder to cry on as I recovered from the heartbreak of Joffa. But time would reveal he was both kind and . . . a bit of a 'bull-dust artist'. Sadly, we were just not meant to be.

After that, I fell in love with a series of beautiful, brilliant lost boys: the talented musician who always called his over-bearing mother to say goodnight; the tattooed motorcycling poet who—by candlelight, on the floor of his warehouse—introduced me to Bruce Springsteen's *Nebraska* album; the beer-sculling mushroom-munching holy-fuck-he-was-so-good-looking cowboy singer–songwriter who taught me how to sing a heartbreak song like I meant it, because I really did. My love for him was so fierce, and so wrong, I thought it would break me, but it did not. I lived to tell another tale. In the words of Joni, at least I got a song out of it.

How ironic, in hindsight, that the man charged with recording and producing these songs about all these doomed love affairs was my friend, drummer and all-round good guy, Marty Brown.

What a great guy that Marty is, I'd say to myself. Supportive, kind, never judgemental. He let me be exactly who I was, no questions asked. When I cried over Tom and Dick and Harry, he was right there beside me, asking exactly *zero* questions, just pouring me a coffee, or a beer, and waiting for me to be ready. I guess he could see a good song coming before I did. He'd just wait it out, and then ask if I was ready for a take, and then he'd press record and catch it all. These were the stories, and later, recordings that would make up our second and final album, *Roda Leisis May*.

Before John and Defah fell in love, John and Marty lived in a massive share house on Rae Street, North Fitzroy, which served the dual purpose of also being Red Raku club headquarters (the poor neighbours). We rehearsed upstairs in the living room, and recorded downstairs in Marty's bedroom. It was not, let's say, a very large space. Often it was just the two of us in there, layering vocals tracks. Those photos on the wall of him holding his nieces were adorable! His huge mixing desk and huge bed were about a foot apart from each other and the only standing room was a corner in front of the microphone. In between takes, I'd lie on his bed and look at the back of his head, bobbing in time to one thing or another, and I can't tell you how many times I said to myself, Ah gee, what a great guy is Marty Brown. So steady! So talented! So kind! I bet we're gonna be friends for the rest of our lives.

The fact that I wanted to jump his bones was, I kept telling myself, but a minor concern. Irrelevant. Hormones. Silly. All that respect and camaraderie: who would give that away, just for a quick shag?

Not me, I told myself. Not I.

And yet, curiously, at the end of every recording session, when we said goodnight and hugged, there was always a part of me that just wanted to stay and, I wondered, was it just me or did he feel the same way too? We didn't name it, I didn't want to name it, but annoyingly, yes, we did have *something*. But by then I already knew through experience: you don't fool with your friends, not if you want to stay friends. Are we clear?

Not long after meeting Marty, I had a vivid dream that stayed with me when I woke up. It was about a visit from a beautiful little angelic creature, a baby, who told me her name was Asha—a name I'd never heard before—and it was so real, and I was so happy, being with her, that the feeling of happiness stayed with me for the whole next day.

'Asha' must mean something, but what? I tried looking it up on this new thing on the computer called Google, except it didn't work so well, so I went to the library at uni instead, and there, in a name book, I found out that Asha was indeed a real name, a Swahili name, one that meant hope and life. This name belonged to something. But what? On the front cover of *Sweetly Sedated* I drew a picture of a boat, and named it *Asha*. I suspected there was more to this story, but I could never work out what.

One night after band rehearsal, I was meeting a mate around the corner for a drink so I asked Marty if I could leave my bike at his place and pick it up on the way home. Marty said sure, but he was gonna have an early night. He took his key off his keyring and handed it to me. 'Just let yourself in,' he said. 'If you wanna crash, all good. Whatever works.'

I'd just broken up with a boyfriend I once referred to as a safe bet. In the end? Not so much. I'd heard he was shagging his swing-dancing partner behind my back (*eye roll*), a claim he vehemently denied, but by this stage things had deteriorated so badly it really didn't matter either way. We were done and, as far as I was concerned, all men *sucked*. That's what I told my girlfriend that night over wine, and she could not have agreed more, and on it went, wine after wine, whinge after whinge, and by the time we were through our second bottle, I was a whisper past tipsy, and more than ready for bed. It was raining that night. I fumbled my way into Marty and John's house, soaking wet, and did a little 'Marcel Marceau' down the hallway to the bathroom, where I hoped I could find a clean towel. Of course, there were none. Back I went, down the hall, and as I passed Marty's bedroom door and saw him in there snoozing, well, it's hard to explain it now, it was awfully out of character, but I just kinda thought: Yay! Marty! Yay! I need a Marty hug! He gives the best hugs! Before my rational mind could stop me, there I was, curled up under the doona in the arms of a pleasantly surprised Marty Brown, feeling such a deep sense of pleasure in my heart that, for reasons that made no sense afterwards— *because we were just friends*—I had to kiss him.

And when I did, dear God, it was perfect.

Absolutely perfect. And then we fell asleep.

Naturally, in the morning, when I woke up, sober, in the arms of my friend Marty Brown, my first thought was, *This is terrible!*

'Oh, Marty, I am *so sorry*!' I said.

No, really, I was. I had just had my heart broken by a swing dancer. I wasn't ready for this. I was putting on my jumper as I was talking. This could not possibly end well.

He said, 'No need to apologise. Are you sure you don't want to stay for breakfast?'

'No, no, no, no, thank you very much, off I go,' I said, and off I went, crashing my bike down the hallway, Frank loud in my head, yelling: *Look what you've gone and done now! What did I tell you? Now you've gone and ruined everything!*

I guess it's a testimony to the strength of our friendship that Marty and I just resumed our usual schedule after that: rehearsals, gigs, beer, laughs. We never spoke of that night again. Just, la di dah, off we go!

Here's the thing I knew about Marty that I had never known about any other guy I'd been with: Marty Brown did not need me, not any more than I needed him. He was one of my best friends. Every one of my relationships to date had ended terribly. I did not want to run the risk of that happening with Marty. I needed him too much. Him and John. They were my biggest champions. That kind of chariot is rare, and I knew it.

Not long after that, I met a filmmaker called Henry and fell madly in love. It was a chance meeting. I was just at a party with a friend and, lo and behold, there he was; kind, clever, curious, older, handsome as fuck, and head over heels in love with me too.

We spent years together, many of them very happy. My friends, his friends, we made a family of it—filmmakers, actors, movie producers, music producers, art critics, photographers, entre-preneurs, cafe owners, musicians, poets, painters, Buddhists. And the adventures! In our beaten-up LandCruisers, EJ Holdens, and one orange vintage Monaro, we convoyed through deserts, camped on beaches, swam in oceans, dived from yachts, shared houses, struggled to pay our rent, then later, made our first big pay cheques, lent each other money, paid it back, dressed androgynously, then glamorously, wore wigs, attended each other's openings and launches, happenings and flash mobs, went to gigs upon gigs and all the things after gigs, danced until the sun came up, slow-cooked our meals, ate dinner at midnight and breakfast at lunch time. So many of the recipes I cook for dinner parties today were taught to me by these friends, in this precious pocket of time.

I was living at Compost by the time our second Red Raku album was being recorded, the one we called *Roda Leisis May*. I've no idea why we called it that, but it made sense on the night we named it. My day-to-day life was well established now. I was working at Bennetts Lane Jazz Club, and at an Indian goods shop called Ishka. I was in a great routine, and feeling steady and strong in myself. Me and my housemates—Ilka, Gil and Mem—shopped together at Preston Market at 7 am every Wednesday morning, got our coffee and our bomboloni from the same little shop. And every Sunday, we'd have a group dinner with everyone from the Compost community, everyone with a plate to share, rotating houses, and stories. This was just the living arrangement I had always longed for—the safety of being a part of a family-ish community, everyone contributing to a shared purpose, but with the full freedom to come and go as I pleased.

Once again, Marty and I were spending a lot of time together in the studio—still friends, just friends. I had a boyfriend, he had a girlfriend, nothing to see here.

One day, after reading *The Baron in the Trees* by Italo Calvino and then visiting my sister Anna—who was, by then, a mother of two with a third not far behind—I got that song feeling again, the one that appears in my chest like a little animal, and when I sat down at my piano, a most surprising thing came out: a happy song! I don't think I'd ever written a truly optimistic love song before. The chords were simple and repetitive, but it rolled itself out to me so easily, so intact—this story about a family who lived in a tree house in the middle of the 'burbs, who had two kids now, and the husband said he wanted a third. It was a song about a couple who were true partners; people who knew how to love each other. It's a song about a dad who was just as into kids as the mum was, and I guess that's what I'd always longed for: someone who could be a true partner not only to me and my dreams, but also to our kids and their dreams. This was a song about a man who didn't need saving—a man who just needed enjoying. A man who knew how to love.

On this side, things they work differently.
Me oh my, we're all that we hoped we'd be.
Because this time—we dared to believe.

I was pretty sure this was just the kind of song Henry would absolutely . . . *hate*. Too conventional. Too obvious. Too hopeful. I tucked it away for another time.

266

*

I loved Henry madly, would have done just about anything for him. He was not only my love, but also a mentor. In some secret part of me, I looked up to him so much I really did think he was God.

But still, when I was offered an exchange scholarship to the University of British Columbia, in Canada, I took it. Had to. Needed to. It was the final test, really, in working out whether I was actually recovered, was actually capable of taking care of myself.

Considering what happened last time I went overseas on my own, my parents must have been a little worried. But, as always, they tried very hard to show their confidence in me, and later, at the airport, although I told Mum not to, she of course slipped me an envelope with every holy medal from the shop inside, and a new rosary to boot. I was crying so much I couldn't stop laughing. Dad also slipped me an envelope— one of his legendary letters and a couple of hundred bucks, for luck, he said.

My father was a beautiful writer and had a most masterly way with words. His letters revealed a side of him, a playfulness and humour, that in the busyness of work and family life wasn't always on show. I sometimes forgot how well he knew me, and how dear I was to him, but his letter made these things clear. He began with a lovely list of what he saw to be my qualities, starting with my openness, which he called both convenient and inconvenient at the same time (he was rather honest, my dad). When I did go to Canada, there was one part of this letter I read to myself again and again, the one where he'd written:

> I expect you will meet with frustrating times as well as 'challenging' ones, but you have worked through such things before. And you will meet with depressing situations and things that are hard to cope with. Again, that's life, and those things will not hold you for too long. Disasters are never welcome, but you know my analogy to muscle-building, It is those tough times that we have faced and dealt with that have built up the strength of the Sandy Bows and, in the process, we have all the more to give to others. You see such a wonderful example in your mum.

It was an extraordinary year. I lived in a share house in downtown Vancouver, marvelled at the maple leaves in the fall, skied on the mountain-tops in winter, worked at the Museum of Anthropology, studied writing and Ethnomusicology, busked for my bus-fare on Vancouver Island, tried brand new songs at open mics all over town, took a train right across the country, went on a road trip to Mexico, volunteered at every writers' and music festival I could, wrote for the local student newspaper in exchange for gig tickets, hiked and camped in bear country, explored Japanese gardens and huge cedar-tree forests, was mentored by a senior radio producer at the CBC, then I myself made recorded radio documentaries, of a drag queen competition in Edmonton, and a pole-raising ceremony in the far Pacific north-west-coast island of Haida Gwaii. I even got to spend an hour interviewing Warren Ellis, the famous violinist from one of my favourite bands in the whole world, Dirty Three. I was *such a big fan* and so scared, I was shaking, and possibly chain-smoking (a minor lapse, I promise). But, most of all, I wrote songs about home. Every night, I slept with my guitar next to me in bed. I think that, really, this is the year I learned to play it properly (or as properly as a self-taught musician can). This is where I wrote so many of the songs that would later go on my first solo album, like 'Homage to my Dad and the ABC', 'Miss Unavailability' and 'Monday Comes'. I'd make tapes of them, and send them to Marty. John was studying full-time to become a music therapist now. We weren't sure what was going to happen next with Red Raku. I had the feeling that maybe these songs were meant for a side project. Like a solo album, or something? Maybe, when I got home, Marty and I could do a little recording together, if he had time?

I missed Henry something dreadful, and told him so, often. I took it rather personally that he hardly ever wrote back, or called. If I received two pieces of communication a month, it was a good month. He tried to reassure me. It wasn't personal, he said. It just wasn't his way. He loved me, he said. Don't doubt it.

But I did doubt it, terribly.

It is cruel to make comparisons but Marty Brown, on the other hand—now what a model of good communication he turned out to be. What a great friend he was! He wrote often, beautiful handwritten letters. (And some emails too. Bloody fancy!) In one letter I re-read a number of times, he said that he wanted to thank me for all I'd done for him, and then wrote

269

a list of all the reasons it was so good to be my friend, and how grateful he was to have me in his life. It was so beautiful! In it, he also said that, believe it or not, Triple J had played one of our songs on their Australian music show! It was a song from *Roda Leisis May* called 'Father's Daughter'. No way! And from what I could gather, Marty Brown's own career was now very much on its way. Our friendship groups—Henry's and John's and Ilka's and Defah's and Marty's—had all started merging, and new bands were springing up left, right and centre, many of them employing the increasingly popular drummer and recording engineer, Marty W. Brown. He sent me mixed tapes of all the different bands he was now recording, and playing in, and I sent him mixed tapes of new songs that may or may not have been about him, and the poet, and the cowboy, and the others. Through letters and tapes, we grew closer—I got to know and appreciate him in a new way. One night I fell asleep imagining what would happen if he ever came over to Canada to visit and we had to share a bed, how his feet would be hanging over the edge. Didn't he get cold feet at night? How was it he was so tall?

In my absence, Marty had joined a new band called Art of Fighting. Melbourne music lovers will know them now as the *legendary* Art of Fighting. Back then they were just . . . very fucking cool. And very fucking quiet. No one spoke much. With Ollie and Miles Browne, and bass player Peggy Frew, Marty Brown was in excellent company. Their album *Wires* was, we all agreed behind their backs, pretty much the best album we'd ever heard. Ever.

He had worked so hard for this moment of convergence, and we—his mates—could not have been happier for him. Marty and his band came back from a tour of Europe with stories of how artists were treated there: respectfully. At the very least, venues fed them and provided accommodation for the night, meaning there was a chance, at least, of breaking even. Just the tiniest bit of respect made everything so much easier. It looked like all those years of teaching himself to record songs and play drums—while also studying for a degree just in case—was going to work out. He was going to make it work.

(When I think back to this time, think back to some of the exceptional musicians we knew then and heard later had 'given up on music' I can't help but ache. For most of them, after years of living on the poverty line, attempting to create valuable art, art which contributes to how we understand our world, they have had to give up, because they can't pay their rent or support their families as artists in Australia. Yes, our population is relatively small, and it can be a challenge to find your audience, but I still can't understand why, in this day and age, we don't, as a country, better understand the contribution and early struggles of developing creative talent, and offer talented artists a basic living wage, even just for one year of their life? It should not take fame to get us to stand up and pay attention to the contribution artists make to our lives. In fact, I have always found fame to be a very *poor* measure of talent, or contribution. But, forgive me, I shall now step off my little box, and carry on with the story at hand.)

At the end of my studies in Vancouver, I was encouraged by one of my teachers to apply for a further scholarship, one

271

that would allow me to continue my studies in Canada. I was extremely happy there. I had proven to myself that I could take care of myself. More than that, I could go overseas and absolutely thrive. My fear of the breakdown returning left me that trip, never to return again. Yes, I still had to FAFL sometimes and, yes, I still had to FOF, but now, thanks to some excellent news, I was ready to return to Australia, head held high.

Defah rang and said, 'I have something to tell you.' What she told me next made me squeal: John and Defah were having a baby!

'Oh my God, you're such an adult!' I said to Defah.

'I know!' she said. 'Who even am I? Come home quick before I turn into a pumpkin!'

Upon my return to Melbourne, it became very clear very quickly that things were going to work out well for Marty and this music thing he'd bet his life on. Not only had his band, A.O.F., toured Australia and Europe, they were soon to head off to the United States! In this age of international travel, it's hard to explain what a big deal this was in our little arts community: that local musicians were being flown overseas to play gigs. Suffice to say, it was . . . a really big deal!

With recognition, of course, came groupies. Rumour had it (that is, Defah told me) that Marty Brown was now in the middle of what could only be described as a little bit of a purple patch with the ladies. All those years of being good old Steady Eddie, playing the tortoise not the hare, focusing on the quality of his output, hoping it would pay off and, now, would you look at him go!

Was he ever going to return my calls?

He did, he always did, but I loved teasing him about his rise to the big time, how he'd need to be sure to remember us little people when he won his first ARIA.

He laughed at that, and then bragged about how, in fact, funny I should mention it, Art of Fighting had, in fact, just been nominated for their first ARIA—Best Alternative Album, 2001.

No way!

Yes way!

I was gobsmacked! I mean, I loved the album, but since when did excellent bands get nominated for ARIAs? Wasn't it all commercial pop acts?

Yeah, he said. Pretty much. There was no chance they'd win— they were up against some big names—but a nomination was enough.

Through a big smile, I said, 'Oh my God! I hate you so much!' and he laughed and said, 'Your time will come, little Bowditch.'

I didn't believe him—not at all—but I did love making him laugh.

He mentioned he would be heading to New York in a couple of weeks. I told him I'd give him a lift to the airport, unless he already had a limousine booked?

*

It would be wrong to say Henry didn't try to make room for me in his life, because he did: he tried very hard. He tried so hard not to make it all about him that I got to thinking, is this always going to be about him? Try as both of us might to break whatever this dynamic was, we couldn't. We were at totally different stages of life, too, I guess. He was not just a boyfriend, he was also my hero, and that is a powerful love, but it's not an equal love. So, often, when he told me what he thought, gave me what he considered as the gift of his honesty, there was not—in my reading—enough love mixed in with the delivery to allow it to land correctly. I ended up feeling patronised and belittled. Somewhere along the line, I began to get his critique and Frank's voice mixed up. It was such a formative, pivotal time—he encouraged me to reach and keep reaching, to tell the brutal truth about what was working and what wasn't, both in our love life and in my art. But, one day, when we were riding our bicycles through a park together and he kept racing ahead, not waiting for me, I saw that this was how it would always be. I would always be asking for more—for things that I thought were small but that for him were so big. I pulled over, sat on a bench, and tried to work out what I was going to say. Ten minutes later, when he came back for me, looked at me, sat next to me, put his arm around me, we both knew it was curtains.

Turns out, Henry was just a human, like me.

I was honest with him then, told him I wanted more. Did he? He said he might one day, but not yet, no. I got it, and he got it, and we sat on that park bench together, crying in each other's arms at first, but then just sitting silently together with the body of what our love had been, an act of witnessing, a respectful bereavement for a death as significant as this.

Finally, a break-up that happened exactly as it was meant to.

Little did I know, the art of breaking up was not something I'd be needing in my future life.

❋

On the night Marty was due to fly to New York with Art of Fighting, the night I was due to give him a lift to the airport, I showed up a little early. Our plan had been to share a meal, play some new songs and say goodbye. Marty was already packed, his mates were over and he had pizza and a six-pack waiting.

I was still on a high from the arrival of John and Defah's healthy baby, a daughter, Ella. Defah was an absolute warrior that day, and she did it. Little Baby Ella, born at home, in a birthing pool. Defah had asked me to be one of her birth attendants, but in reality all I did was make tea for the professional midwives. But afterwards, Defah said, even though she didn't believe in God, would I be Ella's fairy godmother? And I cried. All right, I said, if you insist.

I'd drawn Marty a card; a little something to let him know that I—his old band mate, Clare Bowditch—was rather impressed by him. He would remember me, wouldn't he? He said 'Hmm, maybe . . .' and poked me in the ribs.

Just before we were due to leave for the airport, to get him on that plane to New York, Marty's housemate Dave turned on the TV, turned up the volume, and a minute later, told us all to shut up, shut up.

The date was 11 September 2001.

That's when we saw it on the news—a replay of footage of the first Twin Tower falling.

I couldn't work it out at first—I kept spiralling into disbelief. Was this a movie? I kept saying, 'Is this serious? Is this for real?'

Only a few moments later, live now on television, we watched footage of the second Twin Tower fall.

Marty's phone rang. Nobody would be flying to New York tonight.

We watched as the world changed, not sure if this marked the start of another world war.

The shock was terrible, and after hours in front of the television, Marty and I finally lay down next to each other on his bed, and tried to fall asleep.

How were people, were families, supposed to go on after something like this? The scale of it was beyond my capacity to comprehend, and the old shaking came back again.

Marty cuddled me, told me I should get some sleep.

I couldn't. What if Marty had gone a day earlier? What if he had been in one of those towers?

This was the night I was finally willing to admit to myself that, holy fuck, I loved him. I did. I loved Marty Brown. This was terrible—he was my friend. But I loved him.

Of course, this was not the night to declare that love, but I knew then that he was the person I wanted to be around, always. The thought I could have lost him without ever having the guts to tell him how I felt, or what he really meant to me, was almost unbearable.

*

In October 2001, indie band Art of Fighting surprised everyone, including the band themselves, by winning that ARIA for best Alternative Album of the Year. They were so sure they'd lose that they hadn't even bothered to show up to the ceremony. Instead, they were in Germany, playing a gig. It was a big victory for the little band that could. The world still felt very dark that month and this offered a little moment of light. Indie kids in pockets throughout the world united online in celebration.

Marty Brown had changed—or his clothes had, at least. These days, he dressed remarkably like Nick Cave, all black jeans and Rocco's boots, and seemed to walk with something of a strut. When he came home after the ARIA win, and we went to Brunswick Street for falafel, a young man in the ATM line asked him if he was Marty Brown, and he said, 'Why, yes, I am.'

The young boy from Ringwood, made good.

Too late, I thought. I have left my run too late.

That summer, after returning from yet another tour, Marty Brown finally found time in his busy schedule to come through on his promise to record my demos—a set of songs that would, one year later, go on to become my first solo album, *Autumn Bone*. Red Raku never broke up. In my mind, my solo album would just be one of my side projects; something to keep me busy while John settled into parenthood, and his new working life as a music therapist.

In the wood-panelled rumpus room of Marty's dad's house, way out in the semi-rural suburbs of Melbourne, I drank tea on the couch and watched in quiet admiration as Marty set up everything a girl like me could possibly need: one eighty-kilogram sound desk, one Tascam tape machine, two microphones, one guitar and a stool to sit on.

Once it was all set up, he said, 'Okay, you can sing now.'

We recorded all the songs I had. It took two days. I was nervous. John usually played guitar, and now I had to play it myself for the first time—but I had practised every day in Canada, and Marty was patient, encouraging. Take after take, he adjusted mics, gave direction, got everything just so.

The fact that I was singing songs about him, and my feelings for him, was not a thing we talked about, but with lyrics like 'Big man, you holy Tardis of silences, so wise you always know what not to say, somehow better that way' it would have been quite hard for him not to notice, surely?

I had no real way of knowing if he felt the same way, and it wasn't time yet to talk of love. First, business.

Marty asked me what I wanted to do with the demos once they were mixed and finished, and I said, 'Um . . .'

'Right,' he said. 'Here's what I think you should do.'

First, we would finish the demos. Then, he would help me write a grant application—the Arts Victoria one for recording. It awarded a handful of artists enough money to record a whole album. If we got the grant, we could buy ourselves a month off from our other jobs, rent a proper studio, and get this baby out into the world.

'Okay then!' I said, turning pink.

As if you'll get the grant, said Frank.

Guess what I said back? Fuck off, Frank.

It felt easier to say now that Marty was around.

It felt good, being a team.

*

The thing I remember most about these two days recording with Marty was how much we laughed.

On the kitchen bench at his father and stepmother's house there was a bowl of apples which, I discovered, but only after biting into one, were fake.

'Um, I think I just killed this fake apple. Sorry about that.'

Marty shook his head in faux disbelief and said, 'Why did you bite it?'

I said, 'I didn't know it was fake! I've never seen a fake apple before!'

He asked me what kind of fancy family I came from that there were no fake apples in the house, and I asked him how it was possible that his family were such bogans that they thought fake apples were an actual thing you should put on your actual kitchen bench. Who does that?! He asked me whether I was going to be equally dismissive of the 'actual' fake flowers—'as displayed here' (he fanned his hand out) 'in this high-quality vase on the bench?'

Sale of the Century eat your heart out!

He fed me, too: an old family recipe, he said. His ma's scrambled eggs, with chicken noodle soup flavouring, on white buttered toast.

Surprisingly delicious!

In the corridor leading to the makeshift studio, I spied photos of Marty as a little boy. I was reminded of the thought I had the first time I saw him—he looks like a cherub! A very tall cherub! His face had not changed since childhood. There were more photos of him holding his nieces, cradling them in his long arms like a total pro. He was so big, and they were so small. He looked confident. God, said my ovaries. He'd be a bloody great dad!

I was in such a cheeky mood, I said it aloud. I told him, 'My ovaries are flipping out, just looking at these photos.' I said, 'Dude, did you put these here on purpose to impress me?'

He laughed. 'No! I mean, yes! I mean . . . you know how much I love kids!' And then put on a cheesy smile.

And I said, 'That sounds like the kind of thing someone who wants to shag you would say, just so you shag them.'

Now it was his turn to turn pink.

Yes! I thought. Still in with a chance!

A week later, Marty called to say he'd finished the first mixes— would it be okay if he dropped them over tonight for a listen?

I said, 'Cool,' and he said, 'Oh, I'll bring dinner too.'

Wow. I mean, wow. Who even was this guy?

At 6 pm, Marty made his way through the Compost rear entrance, and knocked on the back door. He was carrying a CD, a bottle of champagne and a white paper bag, inside which was later revealed to be a big platter of fresh oysters and prawns.

Ilka and I laughed so much—you just didn't see meals like that at a place like Compost. Lentil soup, beetroot and carrot salad, yes . . . but oysters and champagne?

Ilka looked at me with a hooley-dooley-I-think-he-likes-you expression.

Holy crap, I thought. She's right. Oh my God. This is happening!

Naturally, as always on the cusp of everything good in my life, Frank cranked the fuck up.

What if this is a terrible mistake?

What if this ruins everything?

What if the only reason he is so nice is because he is already married and has children and . . .

Fuck off, Frank! I screamed in my head, but he was loud that night. Persistent.

I went quiet.

Later, in the backyard, under the grapevine, under the stars, I made the mistake of letting Frank speak for me. Out my mouth they tumbled, every little thing that could possibly go wrong, blurted out for no good reason, except that I was freaking the fuck out.

Safe to say, it spoiled the mood.

I mean, he hadn't even kissed me yet! And there I was, listing for him all the reasons why we couldn't, well . . . you should have heard me! I sounded as though I was trying to put him off proposing, or something!

You know how Marty responded?

In typical, Marty Brown fashion.

He heard me out, he said he got it, but then he said that it was probably time, now, to make a choice.

No, really—either we were going to go all in, or not at all.

I was shocked by his directness. I didn't know he had it in him, actually. And I saw clearly then that, when it came to love, Marty wasn't like other guys. He wasn't going to play it cool and string me along. He wasn't going to tell me he loved me, and then treat me like I didn't matter. He just put it all out on the table. Apparently, it had been clear to Marty for a long time that I was the one for him. Years, in fact. He said he had known it from the first day we met. It was the day John and I had our first jam together. He had walked into the house, heard my voice, followed it down the hallway, leaned on the wall listening, and just knew, before he'd even seen my face, that he was in love with me.

We were twenty-two years old then.

We were twenty-six now.

Would it have killed him to say something sooner? I thought.

Before I could say that aloud too, he kissed me, straight on the lips, gentle and sweet, and then just looked into my eyes, said goodnight, and left.

Marty says that when he walked out of the wooden Compost gates that night and drove away, he had already resigned himself to the fact that I was never going to have the courage to jump in. That was okay, he said, because at least he knew now what he wanted: someone like me.

I, in the meantime, was already inside, listening to our demos, thinking, shit, we sound awesome!

✻

Marty says he was surprised when I called the next day and asked what he was doing that night.

'Just . . . stuff,' he said.

'Do you want to go to the Punters Club with me and see a band?'

'Okay,' he said.

We drank until the early hours of the morning. After that, for kicks, he wheeled me around the streets of Fitzroy in a discarded shopping trolley.

'So strong!' I said.

'Why, Ms Bowditch, you flatter me.'

Back at his mate's place, still happy and drunk after everybody else had long gone to bed, we lay down together on the sticky share-house carpet, kissed again, and both proceeded to fall soundly, happily asleep.

In the morning, as I peeled myself off that carpet, I saw Marty's buddy ironing his shirt for work. When he walked past us, I thought I heard a small round of applause. Had I imagined it? Was I still drunk? No, apparently everyone had known this was coming. It was only me who had missed it.

The love story of Marty and Clare had finally begun.

✻

Around this time, I started a new job as a sort-of-secretary for Defah's aunty, Fabian, a high-level leadership expert (who you might recall for her kind words after my teenage performance in *The Boy Friend*). Look, I was not, shall we say, a *gifted* secretary, but I did try—all except for this one day when, for some reason, I noticed I was dozing off at my desk. *What is wrong with me?* I thought. When I looked at my calendar, I got quite a shock. Holy crap, was that the date? My period was really, *really* late.

When the pee stick showed up two stripes for 'yes', I peed myself all over again. Then I threw up. Then I smiled. Then I wept. Then I thought it over. Then I smiled again. Sure, this had come a little sooner than expected but, hey, I was mad about Marty—he was the kindest, most awesome man in the world, I knew that now for sure—and I had always wanted to be a mum. How hard could it be? I felt so excited, I threw up again.

That night, at a Dirty Three concert at the Forum Theatre in Melbourne, I still hadn't quite found the right moment to tell him. There'd been no chance. Later, I thought.

Violinist Warren Ellis then gave one of his world-famous song introductions, a violent ramble which ended with: 'And in summary, this song is called "Everything's Fucked".'

Marty decided I needed a little ribbing and said, 'How come you never come up with dramatic song titles like that, huh?'

I don't really know what came over me, but in a moment of cheekiness, I said, 'How about this for a song title: "I Am Having a Baby". Do you like that song title?'

I looked hard into his large, unblinking eyes, and it occurred to me for the first time that, oh no, this could actually go down . . . rather badly.

He said, 'Are you serious?'

I nodded. Then gulped.

And then, in a very high-pitched voice, he screamed. 'Oh my God! This is amazing! Are you serious? Oh my God!'

We must have looked like two happy drunk fools. We were laughing and screaming and hugging, and I was just so relieved he was as into this as I was. I mean, what were the chances? It was so early in our relationship that half our friends didn't even know we were a couple. And, yet, here we were about to become parents.

We left the gig there and then, hand in hand, stopping out the front to smile and kiss and hug, then walked up the hill towards our tram stop and into our new life—one in which there was no longer any question of how serious this would get. We were there. So much to talk about, but the conversation had now started! It was a relief, actually—now we could just get on with it, with the business of being a family.

We told ourselves a good story that night. One of the best ever, in fact.

We told ourselves, we could do this. We could.

Parenthood. How hard could it be?!

Ah. We were such kids.

Marty drove me to work the next morning. I was feeling very unwell, but it was still so early in our relationship I wasn't sure how much I was allowed to whinge yet. There was a bucket in my lap that I was nursing like a . . . child.

Oh my God—I was actually going to be a mother?

Marty was just in the middle of asking me if I'd like to talk about what we were going to do from here when I was overwhelmed by a rush of nausea.

I think I'm going to be sick, I told him. I was pretty sure it was the smell of his leather jacket making me nauseous, but I didn't tell him that. He'd been wearing that jacket for as long as I'd known him. I had rather liked it until then. Why had I only just noticed how funky the leather smelled? It smelled like, well, old leather. Urgh. I asked him to pull over, telling him I just needed a little break from the motion of the car.

I rolled down the window and gulped in fresh air. We sat in silence for a moment. 'Can I get you anything?' asked Marty. 'No, thank you,' I said. We were being so polite to each other; it was weird.

The nausea passed. I told him we could keep driving now. Sorry about that.

As he pulled back out onto the freeway, I glanced at his profile and saw that his eyes were wide and he was sitting up really straight. He looked . . . scared. But like he was pretending not to look scared. A kind of frozen casual look, except for his eyes, wide like saucers, which were doing that 'not blinking' thing again.

And suddenly I was scared, too. We'd only been dating for three months. This was insane!

I felt the panic rising in my stomach but from deep within came the encouraging voice of The Weekes, reminding me that all would be well, I just needed to FAFL—Face, Accept, Float and Let time pass. We were not the first young couple to find

286

ourselves unexpectedly pregnant. Marty loved me, and I loved him, and we were going to work this out.

When we arrived at the office I held my breath, kissed Marty briefly on the lips and put my bucket in the back seat. He said he'd pick me up around five, and maybe we could go to dinner at my favourite restaurant, the Moroccan Soup Bar on St Georges Road?

I was sorting applications for the next round of Up the Ladder in a Skirt, a corporate training program Fabian had established specifically to support women in leadership. As I looked through their résumés I was astonished by what these women had achieved, and equally stunned at the obstacles they had faced within organisations that didn't consider these women's health or their families' needs as worthy of consideration. To mention such things was seen as a weakness, I read. It struck me as insane that husbands were not allowed to take time off from their jobs to raise their children, yet there were no childcare or breastfeeding facilities at most of these workplaces, no flexible work policies. It was as though the whole world was pretending that working women did not have babies or, if they did, it was best for the company if they pretended they hadn't.

My nausea had passed now and I was feeling furious. Fabian told me she understood my fury, but she was also hopeful. We did not have to lead the way men before us had led, she said. She saw a new era dawning, in which society was able to appreciate different leaders had different strengths. Our corporate workforce currently favoured IQ over EQ, but there was a growing understanding that when corporations cared about their employees it had positive benefits not just for their culture, but also for their bottom line. I hoped she was right because, all of a sudden, I was looking down the barrel of needing to support a family and, to be honest, it all felt a bit hard. I still had absolutely no idea what that was going to look like.

I guess it was around this time I decided that I was going to learn everything I could about running a small business, because who had time to wait around for corporate culture to grow a heart? I wanted to make up my own rules—rules that were flexible and fair, and would make sense to our soon-to-be family.

In my early pregnancy, I'd often have flashes of boldness like this, and then, when the morning sickness returned, they'd just evaporate into impossibility. Yet with Fabian's encouragement (and her insistence that I be a guest at every one of her training courses as part of my own 'professional development'), I was able to keep returning there again and again, to this boldness. This story of possibility.

Marty arrived at 5 pm and we went straight to the Moroccan Soup Bar. Hana, the owner, found us a table quickly. After going through the menu, she asked if we had any food allergies or intolerances. When I said, 'No soft cheese,' she looked at me knowingly.

Marty and I and all our friends had been eating here since Hana opened the joint a couple of years back. It was a narrow space with terracotta-painted walls, jars of preserved lemons and a bookcase filled with pottery, and the food was, and is to this day, just brilliant. It was always full and always loud. Really loud. I'd never noticed how loud until that night.

The most famous dish—the chickpea bake—was also its most mysterious. Somewhere in the layers of yoghurt and butter and roasted almonds and pita bread there was another ingredient that none of us could quite work out.

When the dish was put on our table that night I took one whiff and knew immediately what at least one of those secret ingredients was—garlic. Motherfucking garlic. The scent made me feel so incredibly ill that all I could do was close my eyes and pray that I did not throw up. Was I really going to be denied the pleasure of this beautiful meal—one that had brought me so much joy? A rip had appeared in the fabric of life. I tried not to cry, but it was a fairly toothless attempt. Soon, big tears were dripping onto my plate.

Marty froze. 'Are you okay?'

'No,' I said.

'What do you need?'

I said, 'I need fresh air.'

Immediately Marty stood up, went to the counter, and explained to Hana that I was not feeling well and we would have to leave. He tried to pay for our meal but she wouldn't let him, just told him we should come back another day. 'Go,' she said, so we did.

The most awful feeling of fear and dread was rippling through me as Marty and I walked across the road to Edinburgh Gardens. It was dark outside, winter was coming. Marty linked his arm through my mine, and in stepped Frank with the thought: *Do you even know this guy?* I mean, yes, of course, I knew he was kind, and talented and that he loved me, but what the hell were we doing? And, also, that leather—I could not *stand* the smell of that leather jacket. I'd barely had time to grieve my break-up with Henry, and now I was having a baby with Marty?

As we walked, I started praying. Please, please, please, someone, something, give me a sign. I am absolutely terrified. Please let me know we're doing the right thing.

We walked onto the cricket pitch. All around us stood dozens of tall, glorious trees, blowing in the wind. For some reason, the first line of my song 'On This Side' started rolling through my mind:

We were living in a tree house,
In the middle of the 'burbs . . .

I gazed at the trees all around us. Which one would I be most likely to build my house in? I wondered. There were tall ones and small ones, but the tree I chose was somewhere in between. It was the one I considered to be the most majestic. Without thinking, I said to Marty, 'Of all the trees in this park, which one would you be most likely to build your house in?' It was a silly question, really. I don't know why I chose this as a test, but I did.

If Marty was aware it was a test, he didn't let on. He just looked at the trees, sizing them up, considering. Then he pointed. 'That one.'

Of all the trees in the park, he'd chosen the same tree I had. That was all I needed to know.

But if we were going to make this work, I knew then that I needed to start telling Marty the truth. I was going to have to run the risk of offending him. I could not be in a relationship where we were scared to tell each other hard and uncomfortable truths. And I was going to start right now.

'Marty,' I said as we headed back to the car, 'I need to tell you something.'

'Yes?' he said, his back stiffening.

'This is not easy to say aloud because I'm scared you'll take it the wrong way.'

'Go on,' he said, bravely bracing for the worst.

'It's about . . . your leather jacket. I don't mean to be rude, it's a very handsome jacket, but the smell of it while I'm pregnant is making me . . .' I shook my head.

I don't know what he thought I was going to say, but when he realised I was only asking him to take off his jacket, he looked terribly relieved. He took it off without hesitation and put it in the back seat. Then he opened the door for me. I got into the car, and realised I could still smell the jacket. Nausea. When he slid into the driver's seat I said, 'Marty?'

'Yes, Clarey?'

'The jacket. I'm sorry to be a pest, but I can still smell the jacket.'

'I understand,' he said. He got out of the car, opened the back door, grabbed the jacket and I heard the boot click shut. He returned to the driver's seat sans jacket.

At no point did he get angry at me for telling him what I wanted. He didn't then, and he doesn't now. When I am with him, my sensitivity does not feel like a liability—it just feels like the truth, sometimes inconvenient, but a truth that I'm allowed to speak without worrying that it will break us. Sure, he gets annoyed. But he does it with respect.

That night, when we got home, he escorted me to my bed, made sure I was comfortable, brought me a cup of mint tea and curled up next to me.

He was taking care of me.

I was taking care of our baby.

This was how a chain was made.

A week passed. We alternated between excitement and fear. My morning sickness had turned into full-blown all-day, all-night sickness. I was two months pregnant and feeling absolutely wretched. The only people we'd shared our happy news with were our best friends John and Defah. I was still trying to work out how I was going to tell my parents, but I couldn't think about that right at the moment because I was throwing up again. In the kitchen I could hear Marty's voice, talking to my housemate Gil. Marty and I were meant to be going to a comedy show; we'd bought the tickets ages ago. Gil's partner Meredith knocked on the bathroom door then walked in to check on me, asking if I was okay. I nodded and, figuring there was no point trying to hide it from her, croaked, 'I'm pregnant.'

'Oh, Clare,' said Mem, with so much sympathy that it frightened me.

'It's good news!' I blurted.

She just patted my back, repeating, 'Oh, Clare. Dear Clare.'

Apparently, I'd announced my pregnancy louder than I'd intended, because when I walked into the kitchen Gil and Marty were shaking hands, in very awkward silence.

I sat down at the table and put my head in my hands.

Mem said, 'Oh, Clare, Marty. What are you going to do?'

Marty and I looked at each other, then Marty said, 'We're going to make it work.'

Gil's face lit up then. 'Hey! My nephew Mark next door is moving to Malta, and his house is about to come up for rent.'

A flash of happiness cut through the grey cloud of nausea.

'You're kidding!' I said.

'I am not kidding!' Gil replied.

I looked at Marty. He was smiling at me and nodding.

One of the things I had been most worried about when I discovered I was pregnant was leaving the nest of Compost. It had been such a fortunate, stabilising home for me, such a wonderful place to live. Nothing made me happier than the thought of our kid being brought up in a neighbourhood like this.

Mem was excited by this prospect, too—she reminded me that this was one of the reasons they'd founded Compost all those decades ago: as a place where friends and family could live and raise children together, to share the load. However, by the time Mem and Gil and their friends had bought up all the houses, their kids were almost fully grown. Sure, it had been a twenty-year wait, but finally the first official Compost baby was on its way! How wonderful!

*

We moved in the following week. The house had three bedrooms and a study, a sunroom that looked out onto a dwarf
weeping willow tree in the backyard, a living room and a lovely
lemon-and-white kitchen. Even though the rent was very reasonable, we would still need to be incredibly crafty and frugal
with our money, as we'd be living on a combined taxable income
of around $20,000 a year. Our dear friend Jessie rented and
lived in the back shed, which helped in so many ways. I took
on extra work, teaching the musicians' self-management and
publicity course at Thornbury's Community House. In terms
of career, I was only ever one step further along the road from
my students, but I was more than happy to pass on what I
knew. During my pregnancy I would also complete Community
Singing Leadership Training with Fay White, and she would
teach me what I would go on over the next few decades to teach
thousands and thousands of doubters—that if you can speak,
you can sing. You really can! I started running workshops on
this very theme at CERES Community Environment Park in
East Brunswick (which Gil and Mem had helped found in the
1970s, turning it from a local tip into the community attrac-
tion it is now). I would also begin teaching a lunchtime choir at
Vic Health. Marty would take on extra hours in the accounting
room at his dad's business. As promised, we would do whatever
it took to make it work. Sadly, I decided I would retire, though,
from working on the door at Bennetts Lane Jazz Club. The
nights were late, and I was tired, and sitting on a stool grew
increasingly uncomfortable, as did riding my bicycle home on
cold winter nights. Also, sitting on a stool on the door of a jazz

bar when you're pregnant and can't drink isn't quite as much fun as . . . bed.

Years later, my old boss Meg at the club asked me why I never told her I was a singer. Too shy, I guess. Frank was always telling me that I wasn't a real singer—not like those guys. I also think, maybe, I was just taking my time. It felt like such a privilege, being paid to sit on a door and watch masters at work. Maybe I was just doing what I'd done from the beginning—watching, learning, mimicking, reading the room.

As we began to furnish our nest, Marty helped me to put up an enormous corkboard on a wall in the kitchen, so I could start pinning up any picture or object I could think of that might help my brain and heart catch up with the transformation we were going through. I had never heard of a vision board, and I'm loathe to call it that (because it felt so like an original idea at the time!), but I suppose that's what it was. On the board I pinned photographs of Marty and I from when we first met, and photos of us now. I pinned the first ultrasound of our baby, who we thought looked just like Marty in profile. Martin Junior, we called it. Then Marju, which was based on a *Simpsons* joke about Homer Junior (Hoju). Then Jessie started calling the bump Moodju. Then Moodjala. Then, eventually, we settled on just plain old Moodge. We pinned paintings of families we liked, drawings I'd doodled, and dreams and wishes and love hearts and angels and heroes. There were pictures of the Madonna and child, painted angels with baby angels, a Robert Mapplethorpe photograph of Patti Smith in her white shirt looking strong and confident. Sometimes it was hard to take in how much our lives had changed in only a few months.

These pictures on a pinboard was one of the ways I helped my brain play catch-up. Whenever doubt crept in, all I had to do was look at that board and remind myself where we had come from, and where we were headed and, all of a sudden, I felt brave again.

Although I was still worried about money. This was the year Marty and I had planned to record my first solo CD. We decided there was no reason we couldn't still do that; he could set up one of the spare bedrooms as a recording studio, and we could just work at it bit by bit until the baby came. We would have to save a little first—there were a few pieces of equipment we would need to hire along the way and, although he could record and mix, we would still need money for the mastering and production.

Around our fourth month of pregnancy, we found ourselves with something very special to pin up on the corkboard: a letter and cheque from the Victorian government. Marty and I have been awarded a 'Victoria Rocks' grant from Arts Victoria worth $7500! Seven thousand five hundred dollars! Marty and I jumped for joy in our kitchen and I squealed with happiness. I couldn't believe it! We were going to do this! Marty said he could believe it—he knew we'd get the grant. 'We're just too good to ignore,' he said. I loved his confidence; it was so foreign to me but I was learning, slowly, that there was power in holding things lightly, in assuming they were going to work out right. There was a peace to be found in that. Whatever happened, we would be okay. We were in this together.

*

You might be wondering about my mum and dad, and how they took the news of our unplanned pregnancy? You're probably aware that Catholics generally have certain expectations about the order of things: marriage *then* babies?

I told Marty that perhaps it would be best if I broke the news to my parents by myself. There was a chance they'd be a little shocked, I warned him. But he wouldn't hear of it. He said he wanted to be there, by my side. So, I called Dad and Mum and organised to bring Marty over for dinner the next night, then I lay awake all night trying to work out how I was going to deliver the bombshell.

The first problem was that they didn't really know Marty. They'd come to some of our Red Raku gigs and had been introduced, but as far as I knew they'd never had a conversation with him, and they certainly didn't know about our love story.

But it was okay, people, because I had a plan. I figured we'd arrive, I'd introduce Marty again, and we'd lead up to it slowly: the story of our friendship, how we'd started dating, then written each other letters when I was in Canada, how this had been a long time coming and we were serious about each other, and then, after dessert, when they'd had a glass of wine, I'd tell them we were having a baby.

On the way to Sandy the following evening, Marty and I stopped by a florist and I chose a huge bunch of white lilies, which I knew Mum would love. Back in the car again, I suddenly remembered my teacher Maryanne from Preshil telling us that in Renaissance times lilies signified purity and chastity, but they were also a traditional symbol of condolence in times of grief.

Oh goodness me—I'd picked the wrong flowers. Well, stuff it, there was nothing I could do now. And, in a way, perhaps this would be a small grieving for them; I mean, I wasn't married, you know? Let's just say I thought this would all come as a big shock.

By the time we arrived at my parents' house, I was so worked up I didn't quite know what to do with myself. When we got out of the car, I started pacing. Marty rubbed me on both my arms, said that it was all going to be all right. I led Marty around the side of the house, past Dad's latest fixer-upper— another Monaro—past the rowboat on a trailer that my Uncle Bruce had once built for my sister Lisa, up the back stairs and through the back door.

Mum had the log heater on and candles lit, and when she heard us coming in the back she ran to greet us. Before she could even kiss or hug me, I shoved the flowers into her outstretched arms and said, 'We're having a baby!'

Mum started laughing as though this was the funniest joke she'd heard all day.

Marty stood beside me, deadpan; neither of us were laughing.

I look at him apologetically and then repeated, 'Mum, we're having a baby.'

She had stopped laughing by now but she snorted a little in disbelief and said, 'Marty, it's nice to see you again—can I take your coat? Clarey, stop it now. It's not funny.'

I took a deep breath. 'Mum,' I said, 'I'm sorry, this must be a shock, but I am not joking. Marty and I really are having a baby.'

She stood unblinking and unmoving for several seconds, and then yelled in a high voice, 'Iaaaaaan!'

Dad came in quickly, moved straight in to shake Marty's hand and kiss me on the cheek.

Mum tapped him on the shoulder quite a few times and said, 'There is some news.'

Marty and I said together, 'We're having a baby.'

Dad looked at Mum, looked back at me, then without missing a beat his hand went straight back to Marty's hand for another handshake and he said, 'Welcome to the family, Matty.'

My father really was the very best of humanity, I tell you.

I did need to correct him though. 'Marty. It's Marty, Dad, not Matty.'

'Yes, of course!' he said. 'Marty. Marty. Now, this calls for a toast.' And he kind of scuttled back into the kitchen. I could hear clinking from the fridge, glasses being collected.

Mum was still in a bit of shock but saying, 'Right. Right-oh. Right. Shall we sit? Good then.'

We sat at the table and Mum blinked a few times and said, 'Good! This is good! Good!' and, 'I'm sorry, I'm a bit surprised but this is good!'

Dad came back with the beer, Mum—who rarely drank—said, 'Ian, get the wine,' and he did, rather quickly. He poured her a glass, she took a gulp, sniffed in a few times, gave a quick shake of the head, straightened her posture, took a big breath in, looked at Marty and said, 'Right, Marty, hello! Take a seat. Right, you're already sitting. Good. There you go. Now. Marty. Tell me about your family. Are you from a big family?'

The next few moments were . . . what is the word for this? Painful.

The lovely thing, though, was how hard everyone was working to make it less so. Marty, Dad, Mum, me—all of us talking, nodding, trying to get a flow going. Miraculously, the tension was broken when Mum hit the jackpot by asking, 'Marty, what is your middle name?'

Gee—what *was* his middle name? I had no idea. I didn't even know when his birthday was. (I'm terrible with that stuff. When I called to have the electricity connected in our new house, I could not, for the life of me, remember his actual birthday, so I just said the first date I could think of—I told them 11th of the 11th, 19 . . . 74. For the record, that is *not* his birthday. It created customer-verification problems for years to come.)

'My middle name is Walter,' said Marty.

'Hey!' said Mum, slapping the table.

Dad's eyebrows flew up and down. 'That's *my* middle name!' he said. 'And my father's first name, too,' he added.

Marty said, 'How strange, because Clare's middle name is Alison, which is my mother's middle name, and my grand-mother's first name!'

We had a match! It had been fated! More wine! (But not for me. I'd decided I was going to be a Perfect Mother, and never ever drink wine again. What a laugh!)

We all took a deep breath, relieved to have finally found some common ground over which to connect.

Mum said there was once a fine saint called Walter; she didn't know much about him, but she would find out and get back to Marty. She took a deep breath after that. 'Good,' she said. 'This is good.'

Marty told Mum that he'd actually been to Sandringham many times, as one of his old girlfriends lived here. Did Mum know Emma Smith?

'The Smiths?' said Mum. 'Oh, a *wonderful* family! Yes, yes! And Emma, such a sweetheart. Clearly it didn't work out, but all things considered that's probably for the best.' She was cracking jokes now. (Thank you, sweet Jesus, thank you.)

The last time he had been in the area was after Emma's Dad's fiftieth birthday, Marty went on, and Mum's eyes opened wider.

'Yes! Yes!' she said excitedly. 'Oh, Marty, yes, of course! Marty, you won't believe this, but I think I remember you! We sat next to each other at the dinner table that night. This is extraordinary. I remember thinking what a lovely young man you were, how intelligent and philosophical, a real thinker. Oh, *Marty*! Ian, do you remember? Marty, we prayed for you on the way home in the car! That you would find the truth you were looking for.'

Just to be clear, Mum prays for *everyone*. You could meet her at the supermarket checkout or at the back of one of my gigs and have a three-second conversation and she would *still* ask for your name and any special intentions and then include you in her prayers that night. Also, let's be honest: the chance that the young man Mum sat next to that night at the Smiths was actually Marty Brown, the father of her future grandchild, were very slim, but I wasn't going to be a doubting Thomas; I was just so happy this was going well. I glanced over at Dad, who winked at me. Marty was nodding, saying he thought he did remember, which surprised me a little, because surely that can't have happened? But the thing about Marty is, he always tells the truth. Even if it might crush your spirit a bit, Marty would always tell the truth. He values truth above all else. (He doesn't go about crushing people's spirits on purpose, of course, but if you ask a direct question and insist on an answer, he will give it to you straight.)

On the drive home that night I was greatly relieved. We'd told our parents, we would tell Marty's parents the next day, and after that we'd tell our friends. If I wasn't throwing up so much, I'd have called this one of the happiest and most exciting times of my life.

The next day Mum drove over with a photograph from Andrew Smith's fiftieth birthday celebration and, blow me down with a feather, there they were: a young Mum with a younger Marty Brown sitting next to each other, deep in conversation. How weird to think that Mum met Marty before I did! (Naturally, God got the credit.)

Defah called, sounding very, very tired. She asked if I could come over. When I arrived she was in the shower, standing there naked, the water running over her body. I asked what was wrong, and she said, 'Nothing's wrong, I'm just a bit scared.' What about?

'Clarey, you're not going to believe this, but John and I are pregnant again. We're gonna have another baby. I think I'm a month behind you.'

What are the chances! Ten years ago, as sixteen-year-olds in Defah's bedroom, we dreamed about this moment. We said that when we were grown-ups, we would move into houses around the corner from each other, marry best friends, have babies, and they would be best friends too. We dreamed it, but we did not plan it. We could not possibly have planned this, not even if we'd really tried. This was magic.

*

Just so you know, Marty did ask me to marry him. Kind of. On the back step of our new house the day we moved in, over a cup of tea, he said, 'Clare, about marriage: is that a thing you're interested in doing?'

'No!' I replied, a little too abruptly. 'Sorry, that came out wrong. What I mean is, I feel like we've got so much going on already. The thought of planning a wedding when we've only been together a few months is a bit overwhelming. Also, you might discover in about a year that you actually find me rather annoying and want out. How about you?'

Marty said that, to be clear, he was not planning on leaving me, ever. He knew that, if anything, a year from now he would be even more madly in love with me, and I need never worry, because he wasn't leaving unless I told him to. As for marriage, however, yes, he felt the same—that for now, we needed to concentrate on learning how to be outstanding citizens, how to make a living, and how to become people worthy of bringing a baby into the world. Marriage was something we could circle back around to later. The particulars of this conversation would become the source of some dispute in years to come when, three years after we became parents and he still had not proposed, my mother and sisters and I calculated that it couldn't be *too* far off Surely? On one memorable date night, when Marty rang Mum himself to ask if she could babysit, Mum was so sure *this was the night*, she snuck a bottle of champagne into our freezer, all ready for a toast when we came home. As I turned the key and walked in the door after the date, and caught a peek of Mum's expectant little face, all smile and high eyebrows, I quickly shook my head and gave her a thumbs down. Her joy muffled, she left quickly. I found the bottle of champagne exploded in the freezer the next morning. Really, I just should have told him what was on my mind. The pressure led to misunderstandings. But this is a story best left for later.

Over drinks recently, our friend Monique said something about my husband that pretty much sums him up, in a sentence: 'It's not that I want to steal your Marty *as such*, it's just that . . . how good would it be if all the men in the world had a little bit of Marty Brown DNA squished into them at birth?'

I said, true. I also said, 'Monique, keep your mitts to yourself.'

The truth is, Marty really is a gift of a man. He's kind, clever, handsome, even-tempered, enigmatic and, to top it all off, a true doer. Marty makes things happen—mainly because he rolls up his sleeves and gets the job done himself.

No, he's not perfect. Of course not. He snores, and doesn't stop tickling when you tell him to, and he does have quite a touch of facial blindness, and also, sometimes, when I've told him something that means a lot to me, and he's not 'reacting the right way', I do have to spell it out for him, say things like 'Marty? This is how empathy might sound, were you to try to emulate it—which would be a good idea about now . . .'

But, yes, he is the love of my life. Eighteen years, and going strong (that is, assuming he puts out the bins tonight like he promised).

12

Human being

I'm a human being
I'm a human being
I'm a human being
I have my fears also.

'HUMAN BEING'
(*Autumn Bone*, 2003)

To say that our friends were surprised when they heard our 'happy news' would be to put it delicately. Shocked would be more apt, although this might have had something to do with Marty's delivery—en masse at a party. I wasn't there—I was home with what had now developed into morning-noon-and-night sickness, but the story goes that in the middle of festivities, beer in hand, Marty stood up on a chair, shouted at the top of his lungs for silence from the crowd and then, into that silence, yelled the words, 'CLARE AND I ARE MOVING IN TOGETHER, AND ALSO WE ARE HAVING A BABY!' Cheers erupted until, above the din, one honest friend piped up with the question other people in the room would later confess to thinking: 'Um, which Clare? Do you mean Clare the singer? I didn't even know you were going out!' More cheering then, and laughter, and a good deal of backslapping for good old Marty Brown (The Quiet Achiever). In summary, I'd say that our friends and family were either delighted, or very good at pretending to be, and that was about as strong a start as we were hoping for.

No one needed to say it out loud, because Marty and I already knew—the statistical chances of us staying together through the intensity of a very quick courtship and transition into parenthood were, anecdotally speaking, rather slim. But Marty and I were never planning on become anecdotes. The fact it had taken years to get to this point made it quite obvious to both of us— this was no minor narrative. This was The Big Time. Although we adored each other, we both knew that it was going to take more than the first flush of limerence to build a life together. Fortunately, we were both up for the challenge.

For me, this meant observing with some diligence the kind of stories Frank told me about what was going to happen next for Marty and me. It was tempting, sometimes, especially in the fog of acute morning sickness, to fall into the trap of fear, of worry, about what would become of all of this. But I was getting better now at this practice of training Frank, and reminding myself of the truth, which was that we were bloody lucky to find each other, and I very much suspected this little pea of a baby would be the making of us. I reminded myself that Marty and I had already been close friends who worked together for almost five years, and we had never had a fight (although I'm sure we would, and we would get through them too). We knew how to make room for each other. We knew each other's weaknesses, and strengths. And, as fortune would have it, we both happened to be absolutely united in our idea of how we wanted our family and working lives to roll.

We were not, shall we say, the most traditional of couples, nor were we trying to be. As already discussed, marriage wasn't on the cards at this stage. Beyond the basics, neither of us cared very much about owning things, which left us relatively free to do exactly what we wanted with our lives. And what we both wanted more than anything was to make our living doing things that mattered, for as long as we could.

I still marvel at how much courage I was able to muster once I knew I was going to be a mother. I guess, in a way, it allowed me to override the voice of Frank much more easily than before. This wasn't just about me anymore—it was about Us; it was about our family. Marty felt the same way. We didn't say it out loud, but the thing both of us clearly wanted, above all else, was to be good (or even just good enough) parents to this itty-bitty baby, now growing in my belly.

In all these years of longing to become a mother, I must admit that I'd never given much thought to the idea of how the baby actually came out. I'd naively assumed that when it came time to give birth, I'd do it the same way my Oma had, and the same way Defah had—at home with an experienced and qualified team of midwives. I soon discovered, no, this was not to be. For reasons that really deserve their own essay, home birth in Australia is not only highly politicised and deeply stigmatised, it's also bloody expensive. Unlike in Holland or New Zealand, our health-care system does not support the option of a home birth. To give birth at home with qualified midwives would, at the time, have cost us about a quarter of our annual income. It just wasn't an option.

I thought hard about why I'd wanted to give birth at home and, in the end, I saw that at the core of it was my desire to do everything in my power to give this baby a good start in life. I was worried, you see, about my mental health: worried that giving birth in a hospital might remind me too much of Rowena's illness, of her death; that it might trigger panic, might lead to a spiral of intervention where, at the end, I was left traumatised and unable to bond with my baby—to tend to him or her the way she or he deserved. I wanted, more than anything, to give this child every chance of having a very strong, very well mother—a mother who she could count on and be proud of.

Fortunately, here in Australia, there was a second option available. Through the public heath-care system, we were offered the option of giving birth at a Family Birthing Centre. It wasn't home—it was in a hospital—but it didn't feel terribly 'hospital-like'. The lighting was gentle, the midwives were kind, they had time to give, and you could bring in things that reminded you of home. If felt to me that if I could give birth here, I might be in with a chance.

Although I tried my hardest to shut Frank out and not to worry about the way my body was changing, not to worry about the weight I was putting on, I must be honest and say that given my back-story, I didn't find being pregnant 'easy'. Mine was not one of those 'I've never felt so well in my life!' type pregnancies. I didn't like the waiting bit—I just wanted to meet this kid. I wanted to get on with the show! Sometimes when I couldn't sleep, Frank would show up, loud as ever with his terrible stories about how, if I got any fatter, my kid would be ashamed of me, and Marty would probably leave me, and my music career would be over before it had even begun.

I now knew better than to keep these stories to myself. I knew that even if my fears sounded stupid, it was always wiser to share them rather than let them circle, unchecked, in the zoo of my mind. So that's what I did—I spoke my fears, either in my diary, or to a therapist, or with friends who I knew could handle the truth. Speaking my fears always made them shrink.

Many of the fears I was carrying were about my career, and how the hell I was going to find the courage to do what I knew needed to be done in order to make a living making music. Frank, of course, yabbered quite often at me about how you can't be fat and successful as a female musician in Australia—for reasons never quite made explicit, it just wasn't done, I would have to lose the weight first and blah blah blah.

So when the local newspaper, *The Leader*, called to say they wanted to do a story on Marty and me winning the Arts Victoria grant, that they wanted to take some photos of us, I was not so much excited as terrified. Panicked. Of course, I was well aware that, in theory, being a musician would at some point mean having one's photo taken, but the thought of it actually happening, right now—the thought of people I didn't know recognising me, judging me—was well beyond my processing capacity. Although as a child I had desperately craved and jostled rather hard for attention, as an adult in my 'post-breakthrough' life, I really didn't want it. I was still scared, I suppose, that one day if, by some miracle, I did become a famous musician, people or the media would find out about Frank, and what had happened, and I would be called crazy, and I would be given no right of reply. Social media was still just a twinkle in the eye of the internet.

What also concerned me about the idea of 'potential fame' was that I liked being anonymous. I liked being able to slip in and out of cafe's and public transport and school yards without anyone recognising me. I didn't want to be watched. I wanted to be free to watch them. As a storyteller, this was one of my greatest strengths—the ability to listen and observe without being noticed. I hated the idea of losing that, even just a little bit.

This was one of Frank's favourite tricks—to make me aware of my fear, and then to call me an idiot for feeling afraid. Even though Frank told me I was a *dickhead* for getting so worked up over nothing, I decided that in the spirit of honestly, I would take these fears to my now music manager, Marty. So I did. I told him everything—my fears about it working out, and fears about it not working out; fears about what it would mean to be a woman, let alone a mother, in a tough workplace like the 'Australian rock'n'roll scene'; fears of playing to an empty room;

fears that the reason I didn't hear voices like mine on the radio was because I didn't have a place there, I didn't belong, and I'd never belong. I was also really scared of what I thought of as the 'fame machine', scared of being part of an industry that—so the stories seemed to indicate—told women like me how they should look and act and then judged them and dumped them when they didn't conform. I told him how I just wasn't made for this kind of career. I felt too shy and self-conscious to have photos taken of my face, front on. I didn't feel pretty enough, or thin enough, and I wasn't ready for that kind of pressure yet. One by one, we worked through these fears, starting with the one right in front of us. Marty said it didn't matter that I didn't want to show my face yet. Whatever. Might even work in your favour, he said. Might add to my mystique.

'Your "enigmahhh",' he said.

Huh! What a laugh. There was nothing mysterious or enigmatic about me or my body right about then—I had outgrown all my clothes and my belly stuck out like a basketball. Fat again—that's how I felt. He wasn't having any of that. He reminded me again and again that all I needed to do was keep writing songs, and singing songs, and playing guitar, and growing our baby. That was it. He'd take care of the other stuff for now. And this is how we muddled our way through—one small step at a time.

In the end, for the photo for *The Leader*, we worked out that even though I didn't want to be recognised, I was probably okay with them taking a profile shot. Now, of course, when it comes to the media, the truth is that it's their prerogative to use any photo they like, but I didn't know that then, and this conversation with Marty, this modicum of assumed control over my own face and where it appeared, did allow me to feel safe enough to get started. If you look at my early posters, you will see that they're all shots of me from the side, or photos that have been pixilated in some way. Nowadays, you could ask for a selfie of me at Fitzroy Pool in my red polka-dot bikinis and I doubt I'd blink an eyelid. But it took years for me to get over my fear of being seen. Years and years. I suppose I'm telling this story because I want to make the point—a career is a thing that's made up of one tiny step, one small act of courage after the other. It's only really when you look back later that it all makes sense.

But, underneath all those mind-tricks, what I also now knew was that it really was time to step up and try. I was going to be a mother soon; I really needed to give this everything I had.

And, so, I did.

The magazine covers on display at the newsagency with the headlines spruiking the wonders of a woman whose body 'bounced back quickly' after pregnancy, and the worry that my body would do no such thing, did fill me with dread. But they also filled me with fury and, it turns out, I'm not the kind of woman to let a good bout of fury go to waste. It was quite useful in the long run. In my career, in those incredibly challenging early years, my fury on behalf of the women I loved, on behalf of the world that I'd one day be handing to my children, and my desire to tell a different story, allowed me to remain clear about what I stood for, and why I was here, doing what I do. I was not here to play perfect. Perfect is not only impossible, it's also . . . bloody boring. Fuck that! I wasn't here for *that*. I was here to give it a *red hot crack*. Why not?

Frank's story—the one about how my body was wrong, and how it wasn't possible to be a good-enough mother and a woman of ambition, and how much shame I would bring to my family if anyone ever found out about me—remained loud. So loud I began to sense that perhaps this was not just my personal story, perhaps this was a collective story—one I'd picked up, somehow, from the world around me. I understood something new, then, about shame, and how it comes to settle inside us. Surely I wasn't the first woman to feel this way? I looked, then, for other women who had stood up to this feeling, and I found them everywhere. In books and newspapers; even in my own backyard.

Inside me, a song began to brew. This one was different. It was louder. My heart felt hot with excitement every time I thought about it. When the time was right, I grabbed some paper and a pen, I sat myself down on the floor in the front room—just me and that feeling and a guitar I called Ruby—and out came a song with lyrics so fully formed, all I had to do was to open my mouth:

I'm a human being
I'm a human being
I'm a human being
I have desires also.

As I sang those words loudly, and then louder, they grew to feel like one small line of defence against one of Frank's most

314

persistent stories—the one about how motherhood would be the end of me, and that, in order to be a good mother, I would have to cease to exist. My dreams would have to cease to exist. On behalf of the child who was coming, and the other women who felt what I was feeling, I just was not going to fall for it.

I called that rebellious little beast of a song 'Human Being'.

With Marty's help, it would go on to be my very first single; a song put in the world to ask the question, do you feel this way too?

Our child was due to be born in the first week of December, and was now thirteen days late. The obstetrician had already warned me that if I still hadn't gone into labour by day fourteen, I was going to need to be induced. This news made me very grumpy indeed. It was the middle of summer, I was hot and sticky, I wanted this baby born soon, but I didn't want to be induced. I wanted my baby to come in his or her own time (but quickly, please). I told Marty that I was going to try to get things moving on my own. This kid needed to be told, 'Buddy, the time is *now*!' I told Marty I was going out walking, and I wasn't coming home until I was in labour. He asked me to, please, don't overdo it. Don't walk too far. Look at me, I said, waddling in a circle. I doubt I'll make it around the block. If I get to Merri Creek, one kilometre down the road, I'm going to declare it a miracle. He packed me a water bottle, I packed myself some food, a mobile phone, and off I waddled, munching angrily on hand snacks all the way from Thornbury to Northcote, a trail of crumbs in my wake. Near Rucker's Hill, I heard a bell chiming, a church bell, and I decided that it was a sign. From who, or what, I was no surer then than I am today, but I followed that bell all the way to a Catholic church I'd never noticed before. I entered, put twenty cents in a slot that made an electric candle light up, said a short prayer ('For F's sake, gimme a hand here!') and then I just took a little break, sat on a pew munching crackers and crying in frustration until a kindly priest came over and asked me if I was all right. No, I barked, I was not all right, I was over this, I was *bloody over it* and, also, I was really, really scared. He clocked that. Then went on to ask rather helpfully whether I'd like a blessing, and in between chewing and tears I said, 'Oh, all right.' Mum and Dad would be bloody *rapt*.

Later that day, when the blessing and the walking had yielded little more than a small period-like pain that had eventuated into . . . well, nothing, I rang my big sister Anna for another bloody whinge. What the heck was I was supposed to do next? As advised by a neighbour, I'd already tried all the usual tricks; eating hot chillies, taking hot baths, and a near tedious amount of 'sexy time' (something about 'ripening the uterus'?). Nothing had worked. Anna asked me if there might be anything holding me back, like, something I needed to finish before the baby was born? I told her not really. Just an album. Well, one take from one song off the album. It was the song called 'Who Knows Who', but that couldn't be it, could it?

'Off you go!' she said. 'Get on with it.'

'What, now?'

'Yes,' she said. 'Now! Go!'

I hung up the phone and yelled down the hallway, 'Marty! Turn on the machines!'

The honeymoon was now well and truly over. I meant business.

The machines I was referring to were, of course, the tape machines in the front room, which we used to record my first solo album—an album I would later go on to call *Autumn Bone*. (No idea why. Made sense on the day.) Marty got to work setting up the studio—the same studio I'd had a mini-tantrum in only a week before because I kept running out of breath every second line. Day after day, we'd tried to get this take. No luck until now, when mysteriously I suddenly had more air available in my lungs. Maybe the baby had dropped? How would I know. Defah would know. Every time she saw me and felt my tummy she'd be like, 'Oh, there's a leg! There's an arm!' I didn't know what the hell she was talking about. It just felt like one big blob to me.

Standing in front of that microphone on that hot summer's day, swinging my body from side to side, all I knew was that it was my time to shine. And I did. With our baby kicking hard inside my belly, I sang my absolute heart out and, within the hour, we had it: the last take of my first solo album.

And, still, no bloody labour. I couldn't believe it! When Anna called back later that afternoon, I answered the phone breathlessly moaning, 'Someone, please, get this baby of out me!' She laughed, and told me there was only one thing left to do—I needed to go outside, and move around some pot plants. Why? She didn't know why—just that when she'd gone outside, moved a pot plant, given it a little bit of a twist and, whaddya know, her waters broke. Fine, I said. And outside I went to do the same. Maybe it was the pots, maybe it was me—all I know is that after moving every object I could get my hands on my waters did not break. Not even close. I was so grumpy by now, I reckon I could have lifted a car. And, still, the baby would not come out.

Although, something was different. My lips, actually. They felt swollen all of a sudden. Fluid retention? Who bloody cares.

On the way back inside, climbing up the back stoop, I suddenly noticed how very *filthy* our windows were, and I yelled, 'Marty? Do we have a ladder?'

We did have a ladder, but Marty said there was no way in hell he was going to let me climb it. And could I please stop yelling—it makes the neighbours fearful. I said, you don't understand; I need to clean the windows. He asked, what was I talking about? I said, look—and pointed to a window that he thought was clean enough, but I disagreed, firmly. I stomped inside and fetched vinegar, rags, newspapers and a bucket, and cleaned every single inch of every single window I could reach. As for the ones I couldn't reach, I told Marty I was not coming inside until they were *done*. Mum told me later that this is exactly what my Oma Annie used to do just before she gave birth—clean the windows. A question for science—did I get that urge because maybe this was a story I'd picked up as a child? Or was this my genetic coding at play? At the time, I couldn't have given less of a rat's arse. All I knew was that now the windows were proper and clean, I felt much, much better.

*

And, still, the child would NOT COME OUT!

Marty told me it might be a good idea to get some sleep as it had been a big day and I was probably a little bit tired? I said, I'm not tired but, all right, I'd take a rest. He lay down next to me, and read me a chapter of a book, as though I was two years old. I mumbled about how uncomfortable I felt, how I was never going to get to sleep, although I might just close my eyes for a moment and, when I next opened them, it was dawn, and Marty was snoring beside me with the book slightly crushed between us. I rolled out of bed, my back aching, crawled around on the carpet for a bit—I couldn't tell you why, I just felt like it—and then got dressed for another walk. I was barely twenty metres out the door when I felt the return of those pesky period pains again. Keep walking, Bowditch, I said. Keep walking.

A few steps later, the pain cranked up ten notches. I took a sharp breath inwards, and then just clung to a stranger's fence, panting. What the? Then, as quickly as it had come, the pain dissipated. I turned back in the direction of Compost, and began walking quicker now. When the pain returned, I paused, then clung to another fence. In between what I now suspected might in fact be contractions (can't be sure, keep walking!) I made my way, fence by fence, back home, through the gate, past the mulberry tree (where I again paused, clung to its bark, waited for the pain to pass). When I made it to our back step, I just sat down, took a breath, and yelled in my loudest voice, 'Maarrrty! Help!'

*

The big man had never roused himself from sleep so quickly—he was up and by my side in an instant, helping me up the steps into our home, asking me what he could do to help.

'Run a bath,' I said, and he did.

He helped me get undressed, get into the bath, and then he disappeared. Next, I heard the sound of jazz music, which I normally liked, but not today, sir.

'No jazz!' I cried, and off it went.

Then Marty, who was now fully awake, did as instructed by our birth-class attendant. He picked a flower and put it in a small vase on the corner of the bath, telling me in a soothing tone that it might be nice to have something pretty to concentrate on.

'Stop talking like that!' I yelled.

'Like what?' he said.

When my next contraction came, I knocked the flower to the floor and told him I didn't want to see anyone! No one! If anyone came to the door, he must make them go straight away, and then I heard this low noise coming from nowhere, like an animal growling, and realised with some surprise that the noise was coming from my own mouth.

*

Marty rang a midwife at the birthing centre who said, nup, she's ages away. Don't panic. Just stay at home as long as you can. It's probably not even real labour yet. Marty relayed this to me and all I said was, 'Grrr, grrr, grrr', which made me feel much better.

Next, Marty rang Defah, who we'd asked to be our support person. She was just a few streets away and got there in a flash. She herself was now almost eight months pregnant which, in my naivety, I hadn't quite factored in. I cried when I saw her, said, 'I am so sorry! I am so sorry!' and she said, 'I'm fine! It's all good! Give me a job to do.' She got me dressed, packed my bag, and agreed with Marty that it was probably time to go.

In the car, on the way down High Street, Northcote, we somehow got stuck behind a slow-moving farm tractor. Like some kind of cosmic joke, its wide tail appeared out of nowhere and proceeded to travel just in front of us, at seven kilometres an hour. When Marty said, 'Why is there a fucking farm tractor in Northcote?' I cracked up, but then I started moaning again, and swearing too, because the contractions were back now, and stronger than ever. The 'Grrr, grrr, grrr' sound started up again, but then the noise changed, beginning low but finishing high in a kind of ghosty, spooky guinea-pig of a sound that went 'GrrrrrIYIYIYIYIYIYIYIYIYI'.

Marty said, 'Keep it low, Clarey', just like the midwives had told him to. I was listening to him now. I did what he said. I heard that he was also scared, but he was trying. I wasn't alone. I asked him to please keep talking.

We arrived at the hospital and they examined me and told me I had ages to go, that I was only two centimetres dilated. My heart sank. I told Marty, don't call Mum and Dad yet. I don't want them to worry. We could be here for ages.

But things began to move very quickly after that. Before I even really knew what was happening, they transferred us over to the hospital ward. Said there was meconium in the water so I couldn't birth in the birthing suite after all.

Grrrrr, grrrrr, GRRRRRRR. By now, I didn't care where I was. I wasn't even aware of who was in the room. The pain in my back moved and I thought I might split in half, but Defah and Marty were working together, wearing rubber gloves, dipping cloth nappies in a bucket of hot water, flapping them in the air so they were just the right temperature of hot, and then slapping them on the small of my back, right where it hurt. I felt it then, the courage of this work, as I thought of the hundred billion women who had gone before me, as I thought of my grandmother, my mother, of my part in this line, and I felt the love of my sisters with me as Defah encouraged me to keep going, 'You will hold your baby in your arms before you know it.' The obstetrician said, 'Oh, wow, she's crowning!' and out came my baby's head, turning slowly clockwise as it prepared to edge its shoulders out of me, and into the world.

At this sight, Marty seemed to experience a brief moment of existential crisis. I heard him say, 'It's me! It's actually me', and I thought, *Oh, no! He's lost it!* But, later, I would see that he had a point.

On the count of three, I pushed—and out she came. A girl. We had a daughter, a healthy baby daughter. And her sweet face looked just like Marty's, like a tiny little cherub.

Using Marty's old camera, Defah took photos just after this moment, photos of our darling baby girl trying to elbow her way from my soft stomach, up towards her milk. Unfortunately, in the rush, no one remembered to put film in the camera, but if you could see this photo as Defah describes it, you would see Marty, a proud young father, with our love confirmed—a baby girl on my chest—and you would see me staring at her with a look on my face of absolute triumph. I am near hysterical with relief. The surgeon has just stitched me up, and I am so high on life that I couldn't care less.

I doubt I will ever know what it feels like to complete a marathon, but this was my equivalent. In this moment, when I looked at my body, all leaking and floppy and freshly stitched up, I felt nothing but absolute awe. This was the day I knew for sure what my body, my glorious piano accordion of a body, was truly capable of—it had made, and given birth to, an actual human being.

I had almost forgotten about my dream all those years ago, that one I had shortly after meeting Marty, when a baby girl came to me and told me her name was Asha, a word meaning hope and life. But Marty remembered. He was the one who said it first, 'Shall we call her Asha?'

And that is the day our old life ended, and our new life began.

*

Three months after Asha was born, feeding her early one morning with the radio on, I heard it for the first time, our song, 'Human Being', playing on Melbourne's most popular community radio station, Triple R FM.

All I could think to do was block Asha's ears and once again yell, this time in pure excitement, 'Marty! It's happening!'

I sat still as I listened to our new song on the radio, feeling the joy of progress, the joy of knowing that dreams do actually come true. Even though the song ended, and *might never be played again* (said Frank), it was out there now. My work in the world had begun.

Later in the day, humming the song to myself, a thought came to me: I used to wonder if there was a name for whatever it was that was wrong with my brain. Yes, actually, there is. And it's exactly the same name one could use to describe whatever it is that is right, and good, about my brain.

I'm a human being.

These storms make me ever more so.

Epilogue

Our brains are storytelling beasts, and that can work both against us, but also for us. Happiness, although fleeting, is real, and much closer than we think. It comes to us in moments, and seems to leave far too quickly, but there is always more good stuff to come. And if it's taking too long, well, we have the power to choose to retell our brains the story of that happiness any time we like. If I'm making that sound simple and easy—forgive me—it's neither of those things. It takes a good deal of dedication to develop the discipline to remember about this power. I still forget it all the time. I still need all the reminders I can get.

Twenty years on, Frank hasn't fucked off. He's still here, still banging away. For a long time I took this as a sign that I wasn't 'recovered enough'. I thought he was supposed to go away; his silence would be my signal that I was 'all good'. But as I've grown older, I've come to understand much more about Frank, and why he came and why he stays.

In the heady waters of a disrupted childhood, it was his voice that kept me company, his voice that gave me a story I could use—the one about how, if I was a good girl and stuck to the rules, I would one day be rid of all these bad feelings inside me. I would one day know the safety of what it felt like to fit in.

Even in Oxford, where he went too far in the wrong direction, the whole thing now makes much more sense. The voice of Frank was loud because I needed help. My breakdown was horrible, but it was also the moment that I became willing to stop lying—to be honest about what I was feeling, to be honest about what I really wanted to do with this life of mine.

We are quite polite to each other these days, Frank and I . . . I don't swear at him quite as much—a gentle 'No thanks, Frank, not today' generally seems to do the trick. But, in an emergency, Frank is the one I want on my team. He is the voice of my survival brain. He gets things happening, and quick. And he is also the one who forced me to learn how to accept life on life's terms.

We don't get to choose the circumstances into which we are born. We don't get to choose our genetics, the weather, not even what time the train is going to arrive. We don't get to control space, or time. Try as we might, the only person we get to choose to save is ourselves.

I know now that the nexus of my power lies in my higher brain's ability to choose which stories I'm going to listen to, which stories I'm going to believe, going to support, and going to act upon. Which stories I'm going to allow to be true.

Additional resources

One of the best things I can tell you about anxiety is this—that no matter how far up the garden path your anxiety has dragged you, recovery is absolutely and completely possible.

One of the most important tools I used in my recovery (besides FAFL and FOF) was the tool of telling the truth to someone who cared.

Telling your story to a psychologist or GP can seem (before you do it) like one of the most frightening things. It was for me, which is one of the reasons it took so long to find Ron, but I am so glad I found him.

I also want you to find that person who cares, which is why I asked my friend and colleague Dr Charlotte Keating to help me put together this letter, explaining where you can start.

My general advice is to just start here. Even if you can't quite articulate what you're feeling, or why you're struggling, and even if you think you're not worthy of asking for help, or that your problems are too complicated and no one could possibly understand you, I want you to ask for help anyway. It can't do any harm, and everything you need to know is further on in this section.

Talking to a professional one on one can help you see things you may not have considered and, with patience, might help to turn things around. Sometimes we have to try a few different therapists before we find the one who is right for us, so don't be afraid to keep trying until you find someone who can give you the time and care you deserve.

There's still a lot of stigma around mental ill-health. But what I know is that, since my breakdown, recovery is not only possible, so is living an amazing life; the one I had always hoped for.

Unlike when I was a child, there are now so many different forms of help out there. If you are a sensitive type, or someone who doesn't really like talking so much, you don't have to. Yes, there are talk therapists but there are also art therapists, music therapists, and even equine (horse) therapists. (Hey, don't knock it till you've tried it!)

If, from reading my story, you have even the slightest interest in having a chat with someone about how you're going, know that there are many humans out there who might just become your ticking clock in the storm, the bridge to your FAFL or FOF, the very thing that might give you permission to tell your Frank to fuck right off! The journey might be easier than you think and, in some moments, it might also be tougher but, I give you my word, it is well worth it.

If you are interested, here are some places to start. Some of the options won't cost you a thing:

General practitioner: A GP can potentially provide you with a referral to see a psychologist (or relevant health professional), along with a mental health care plan. The government currently gives you a certain number of psychological sessions with a Medicare rebate under the care plan.

Find a psychologist: A portal to find a psychologist near you. Australian psychological association:
https://www.psychology.org.au/Find-a-Psychologist

Headspace: If you are a young person (twelve to twenty-five years old) you can book an appointment, free of charge:
https://headspace.org.au/young-people/how-headspace-can-help/

eHeadspace: Online free support if you are a young person aged twelve to twenty-five years old:
https://headspace.org.au/eheadspace/

Lifeline: Crisis support and suicide prevention. Telephone counsellors who are available to help anonymously. Phone 13 11 14.

Further resources

Websites

Beyond blue—support in relation to anxiety or depression:
https://www.beyondblue.org.au/

The Butterfly Foundation—support for eating disorders:
https://thebutterflyfoundation.org.au/

Black Dog Institute—support for mental ill-health:
https://blackdoginstitute.org.au

Books

Self Help for Your Nerves by Dr Claire Weekes, Sydney: Angus & Robertson, 1962.

The Baron in the Trees by Italo Calvino (translated by Archibald Colquhoun), New York: Harcourt Brace Jovanovich, 1977.

Dark Nights of the Soul: A guide to finding your way through life's ordeals by Thomas Moore, New York: Gotham Books, 2004.

First, We Make the Beast Beautiful: A new journey through anxiety by Sarah Wilson, Sydney: Pan Macmillan, 2017.

Intimacy and Solitude by Stephanie Dowrick, Melbourne: William Heinemann, 1991.

Life Without Ed: How one woman declared independence from her eating disorder and how you can too by Jenni Schaefer with Thom Rutledge, New York: McGraw-Hill, 2004.

The Little Prince by Antoine de Saint-Exupéry, London: Egmont, ©1944, 2005.

The Little White Horse by Elizabeth Goudge, New York: Puffin Books, 2001.

Mental: Everything you never knew you needed to know about mental health by Dr Steve Ellen and Catherine Deveny, Melbourne: Black Inc. 2018.

A Path with Heart: A guide through the perils and promises of spiritual life by Dr Jack Kornfield, New York: Bantam Books, 1993.

The Prophet by Kahlil Gibran, New York: A.A. Knopf, 1923.

Radical Acceptance: Embracing your life with the heart of a Buddha by Tara Brach, New York: Bantam Books, 2003.

The Very Hungry Caterpillar by Eric Carle, New York: Collins Publishers, 1979.

When Things Fall Apart: Heart advice for difficult times by Pema Chodron, Boulder, Colorado: Shambhala, 2016.

The Woman Who Cracked the Anxiety Code: The extraordinary life of Claire Weekes by Judith Hoare, Melbourne: Scribe, 2019.

Fun stuff for you

Sometimes, we just need more fun stuff in our lives, which is why if you're ever in the mood to:

- bake my mother's world-famous Dutch Apple Tart
- learn how to make the very best cup of tea that ever existed
- listen to a full playlist of all the original songs mentioned in this book
- see childhood pictures of me, and Marty, and our children, and our pets
- download a comprehensive list of my dad's favourite camp-fire songs
- or the secret recipe for his famous Jam Pizza
- learn a very simple method to play fifty great songs on guitar
- or ukulele(!)
- or how to sing (especially for people who don't think they can sing)

then, I have just the place! It's my place: clarebowditch.com

Just go to the menu tab called 'Fun stuff'—it's all there waiting for you, with love.

CB xo

Acknowledgements

If you're still not sure whether or not you too have a Frank inside you, one way to find out for sure is to try writing a book. My friends warned me it would be hard, but I found it . . . *quite* hard. At a couple of points, I even wondered whether— twenty years from now—I might have cause to write a second book about the breakdown brought on by the writing of this first one! Fortunately, I made it out the other end of the tube in one piece, which is thanks only to the extraordinary love, skill and generosity of the following coterie of most excellent human beings.

My gutsy and brilliant publisher Kelly Fagan—how fortunate this book is to have found you, and how proud I am to have worked with you and the good people of Allen & Unwin on this baby of ours. Your love is patient and kind and fierce, and the good news is that we did it, and I will never be a first-time author again! Yay!

My editors Ali Lavau and Christa Munns—for your skill, grace and resilience in the face of the truly monumental task put before you. There are no words, except that I am so sorry, and thank you.

For the powerful publicity charm of both Louise Cornegé (Allen & Unwin) and Dina Kluska (Pitch Projects), you are an absolute dream team.

Pippa Masson and all the Curtis Brown team—your early, passionate and unwavering encouragement is the true reason this book found land.

Anna Robinson for capturing the photographs on both the front and the inside cover of this book, taken over three decades apart. You are absolutely brilliant.

Lisa White—thank you for the fabulous cover design.

Dr Charlotte Keating for your generous contribution to the closing letter.

This work was written over several years with thanks to the hospitality and fellowship of the following: Mossy Willow Farm, Varuna (The Writers' House), Jacky Winter Gardens. Thank you for giving these words a place to arrange themselves.

For your early, passionate and open-ended support of this little baby manuscript, and the wise counsel you offered about what to do with such a thing, very special thanks to the friends who have saved my life in one way or another: Defah Dattner, Libby and Madeleine Chow, Tom from the Catweazle Club, Cath who introduced me to Dr Claire Weekes, Jessie Neath, Anna Olijnyk, Jill French, Elisha Warren, Lynette Andrews, Aurora Kurth, Jessie Neave, Monique diMattina, Berry Liberman,

Kirsty Argyle, Adrian Holmes, Emily Lubitz, Danielle Caruana, to John Patrick Hedigan and all who loved him (you know who you are)—you have cared for me, and about me, and given me something worth passing on. Thank you.

For your early support, excellent writing, encouraging words and wise counsel: thank you dear Foong Ling Kong, Tara Moss, Zoe Dattner, Peggy Frew, Bernard Fanning, Danielle LaPorte, Kemi Nekvapil, Catherine Deveny, Liz Adams, my Compost Writers' Club, Sally Rippin, Rachel Power, Em Rusciano, Dr Susan Carland, Zoë Foster Blake, Joanna Murray-Smith, Joanne Woods, Carly Findlay, Joel Naoum, Holly Ringland, Sarah Wilson, Christos Tsiolkas, Heather Rose, Rhonda Hetzel, Paul Demspey, The Women of Letters, and Jamila Rizvi.

Jamila Rizvi—you have been the dear friend and cheerleader this book, and I, needed. At this book's messiest, most impossible moments, you showed up—baking treats, dropping off care packages, acting as a third editor, and telling me that this work mattered and I was going to finish it whether I wanted to or not. I could not have done this without your 100% all-hands-on-deck love and support—thank you.

To my curious therapists, all of whom remain unnamed or disguised in some way—I couldn't have got here without you. Thank you!

To the brilliant booksellers I've had the pleasure of spending time with over these many years while stalking your bookshelves and imaging that I might one day be brave enough to write a book myself—thank you for your patience, your excellent recommendations and the many hours of joy.

For allowing me to write in your quiet houses and empty offices: Berry and Danny, Lorena and Stephen, Jo and Bevan, Sue and John, and Christine Kenneally. To all in the north-side 'hood who kept us and our children fed, sheltered and entertained during the more gruelling portions of the writing of this book—thank you. With special mention of dear Cindee and Martin, who illustrate again and again exactly how it is that good neighbours become good friends.

For their extraordinarily generous and thoughtful words:

Annabel Crabb

Bernard Fanning

Clementine Ford

Peggy Frew

Missy Higgins

Dr Charlotte Keating

Danielle LaPorte

Professor Pat McGorry

Kate Miller-Heidke

Eddie Perfect

Jamila Rizvi

Leigh Sales

Kat Stewart

To our big-hearted audiences, both at live shows and during my years broadcasting on ABC Radio Melbourne—you have sustained me and my family all of these years, and we could never have got here without you. Thank you for showing up for Big Hearted Business, Sing Song Showtime, Tea with Jam and Clare, and all of our live shows. Honestly—thank you. A most especially special thanks to Greg, Lesley and dear Kerrie who always seem to be there right when we need them!

Thank you to Universal Music, Island Records and Mushroom Publishing for your patience as I've written this book (the album is nigh, I promise!).

To the dear musicians I've had the honour of performing and sharing friendships with over the decades—from my teenage years until today. You have meant, and continue to mean, the world to me. (How good is our job!)

To our second families from over the years—the Dattners, the Lubitzes, the Whites, the Freemans, the Andersons, the Andrews, the Sherlocks, the Warrens, and to everyone at the RCH who loved and cared for Rowena—thank you.

To the Francis family in Sandy who so generously invited us back into that gorgeous home with the warm tiled floors— thank you.

To Marty's dear family—with special thanks to Jenny Cacic for all the babysitting, Chris and Kellie for all the family roasts, and Sam Brown for 'getting it'.

To our nieces, nephews and precious god-children who inspired me to tell this story boldly—thank you.

And to my mother Marianna, my late father Ian, my brother James, and sisters Anna, Lisa and our darling Rowena—thank you for being the kind of family who, if I *had* been given a choice in the matter, I would have chosen, lickety-split. For your love, generosity and support in the writing of this book, and for all the years before that, I cannot thank you enough, but plan to show you every time I see you.

And, finally, to the ones who lived with me through the writing of this book—my beloved Marty, Asha, Elijah and Oscar. I wish every first-time writer had housemates like you guys. Your pep talks, back rubs, cups of tea, 'rocket-ships' and just good old-fashioned *love* have been the balm this lady needed. Thank you, sweethearts.